Lecture Notes in Computer Science   13578

More information about this series at https://link.springer.com/bookseries/558

Yuankai Huo · Bryan A. Millis · Yuyin Zhou ·
Xiangxue Wang · Adam P. Harrison ·
Ziyue Xu (Eds.)

Medical Optical Imaging and Virtual Microscopy Image Analysis

First International Workshop, MOVI 2022
Held in Conjunction with MICCAI 2022
Singapore, September 18, 2022
Proceedings

Editors
Yuankai Huo 🔟
Vanderbilt University
Nashville, TN, USA

Bryan A. Millis 🔟
Vanderbilt Biophotonics Center
Nashville, TN, USA

Yuyin Zhou 🔟
University of California, Santa Cruz
Santa Cruz, CA, USA

Xiangxue Wang 🔟
Nanjing University of Information Science
and Technology
Nanjing, China

Adam P. Harrison 🔟
Q Bio
San Carlos, CA, USA

Ziyue Xu 🔟
Nvidia Corporation
Santa Clara, CA, USA

ISSN 0302-9743   ISSN 1611-3349 (electronic)
Lecture Notes in Computer Science
ISBN 978-3-031-16960-1   ISBN 978-3-031-16961-8 (eBook)
https://doi.org/10.1007/978-3-031-16961-8

This Springer imprint is published by the registered company Springer Nature Switzerland AG
The registered company address is: Gewerbestrasse 11, 6330 Cham, Switzerland

Preface

The 1st International Workshop on Medical Optical Imaging and Virtual Microscopy Image Analysis (MOVI 2022) was held in Singapore, on September 18, 2022, in conjunction with the 25th International Conference on Medical Image Computing and Computer Assisted Intervention (MICCAI 2022).

The objective of the MOVI workshop is to promote novel scalable and resource-efficient medical image analysis algorithms for high-dimensional image data analysis, from optical imaging to virtual microscopy. Optical imaging and microscopy imaging are both ubiquitous and indispensable in biology, pathology, pharmacology, and education. Historically, optical microscopes had long magnifiers of light used to record intensities or resolve objects too small for the naked eye to see. Recently, however, medical optics and microscopy have been fundamentally transformed into multi-purpose sensing tools to capture the multi-modal high-dimensional functional information of an object. Moreover, the recent advances of digital imaging led to a paradigm shift of the imaging method from physical imaging to virtual imaging, which increases the convenience of accessing the slide sets and making the slides available to the medical image analysis and machine learning community. The current learning methods are not scalable to harness the exponentially growing high-dimensional pixel-resolution structural and functional optical and microscopy imaging data. The MOVI workshop provides a snapshot of the current progress in the field through extended discussions and gives researchers an opportunity to link the academic research with industry applications.

The MOVI 2022 workshop attracted high-quality and original submissions on novel scalable and resource-efficient medical image analysis and machine learning algorithms for high-dimensional image data analysis. MOVI 2022 received 25 full-paper submissions and 18 of them were accepted for presentation. All submissions underwent a double-blind peer review process, avoiding potential conflicts of interest. Each paper was rigorously reviewed by at least two reviewers. The reviewers were selected from our Program Committee, which was composed of 22 experts in the field. All accepted papers were presented by their authors during the workshop and are included in this Springer LNCS volume.

We appreciate our invited speakers for their insightful talks and visions. We thank all Program Committee members for their comprehensive reviews and constructive comments. We are grateful to all the authors and attendees for making a successful workshop.

September 2022

Yuankai Huo
Bryan A. Millis
Yuyin Zhou
Xiangxue Wang
Adam P. Harrison
Ziyue Xu

Organization

Program Committee Chairs and Workshop Organizers

Yuankai Huo	Vanderbilt University, USA
Adam P. Harrison	Q Bio, USA
Bryan A. Millis	Vanderbilt University, USA
Xiangxue Wang	Nanjing University of Information Science and Technology, China
Ziyue Xu	NVIDIA, USA
Yuyin Zhou	University of California, Santa Cruz, USA

Advisory Committee

Bennett A. Landman	Vanderbilt University, USA
Le Lu	Alibaba DAMO Academy, USA
Peter Louis	Rutgers University, USA
Anita Mahadevan-Jansen	Vanderbilt University, USA
Lena Maier-Hein	Heidelberg University, Germany
Jun Xu	Nanjing University of Information Science and Technology, China

Program Committee

Qinle Ba	Roche, USA
Gustav Bredell	ETH Zürich, Switzerland
Jinzheng Cai	Alibaba DAMO Academy, USA
Cheng Chen	The Chinese University of Hong Kong, China
Jieneng Chen	Johns Hopkins University, USA
Evan Cofer	Princeton University, USA
Riqiang Gao	Siemens Healthineers, USA
Yan Han	University of Texas at Austin, USA
Jin Tae Kwak	Korea University, South Korea
Jiayun Li	University of California, Los Angeles, USA
Siqi Liu	Paige, USA
Ling Luo	National Institutes of Health, USA
Martin Nørgaard	Stanford University, USA
Monjoy Saha	National Institutes of Health, USA
S. Shailja	University of California, Santa Barbara, USA

Contents

Cell Counting with Inverse Distance Kernel and Self-supervised Learning

Yue Guo[✉], David Borland, Carolyn McCormick, Jason Stein, Guorong Wu, and Ashok Krishnamurthy

University of North Carolina at Chapel Hill, Chapel Hill, NC, USA
yueguo@cs.unc.edu

Abstract. We present a solution to image-based cell counting with dot annotations for both 2D and 3D cases. Current approaches have two major limitations: 1) inability to provide precise locations when cells overlap; and 2) reliance on costly labeled data. To address these two issues, we first adopt the inverse distance kernel, which yields separable density maps for better localization. Second, we take advantage of unlabeled data by self-supervised learning with focal consistency loss, which we propose for our pixel-wise task. These two contributions complement each other. Together, our framework compares favorably against state-of-the-art methods, including methods using full annotations on 2D and 3D benchmarks, while significantly reducing the amount of labeled data needed for training. In addition, we provide a tool to expedite the labeling process for dot annotations. Finally, we make the source code and labeling tool publicly available.

Keywords: Cell counting · Self-supervised · Distance transform

1 Introduction

Our work focuses on cell counting from 2D images and 3D volumes, which is critical to a wide range of research in biology, medicine, and bioinformatics, among other fields. By casting this problem into an object detection or image segmentation problem, significant progress has been achieved with the help of recent successes in deep learning [3,9]. However, one drawback of these approaches is that they typically rely on full annotations of cells (whole-cell), the acquisition of which is a time-consuming and laborious process. To alleviate the burden of manual labeling, others propose using dot-annotations, which represent cells as a single pixel or voxel in the centroid of a cell, and attain competitive results [4,5,17]. Since dot annotations are too sparse for training, such methods typically construct a density map by "smoothing out" dot annotations via a Gaussian kernel and then train a deep model to learn a mapping between the inputs and the density maps. The final cell counting can be inferred via post-processing techniques (e.g., peak detection or connected component analysis) on the resulting density maps.

Y. Huo et al. (Eds.): MOVI 2022, LNCS 13578, pp. 1–10, 2022.
https://doi.org/10.1007/978-3-031-16961-8_1

Fig. 1. An example of 2 cells with dot annotations marked by red crosses (left). Due to cell overlapping, the resulting density map with Gaussian kernel (middle) becomes a blob, whereas the inverse distance kernel (right) remains separable. (Color figure online)

One remaining challenge is handling overlapping cells, as shown in Fig. 1, where the resulting density map becomes an inseparable blob, rendering post-processing techniques ineffective. An intuitive solution is to introduce a heuristic approach for finding the optimal width of the Gaussian kernel to avoid these blobs. However, it would be overwhelmingly difficult to design such an approach when there is a large number of cells. Inspired by recent success in crowd counting [11], we propose to replace the Gaussian kernel with the inverse distance kernel to address the overlapping issue. This distance transform uses the inverse distance of the nearest neighbor for each dot annotation to build the density maps and is able to separate overlapping cells effectively, as illustrated in Fig. 1.

Another challenge is that current deep learning-based methods are data-hungry, which is particularly problematic in the field of cell counting due to the lack of large-scale training datasets like ImageNet. Even with dot annotations, manual annotation of hundreds of cells still poses a significant challenge. On the other hand, recent progress in utilizing unlabeled data via self-supervised learning has been impressive [15,16,18]. One significant component of self-supervised learning is consistency regularization, which forces the model to yield similar outputs between the original and perturbed (e.g., adding noise) inputs for better generalization. We adopt the same idea for cell counting to reduce the reliance on manual annotations. However, we did not observe noticeable improvement during our initial implementation. Since these methods were designed for tasks like classification, with image-level labels, it is natural to apply perturbations on the same level. In contrast, our task involves pixel-level regression, with most of the image being noisy background. Applying perturbations on the whole image will mislead the model to learn image artifacts instead of the cells. Therefore, we propose a focal consistency loss, which will help the model "focus" on cells rather than the noisy background.

In addition, we notice a lack of cell labeling tools tailored for dot annotations. Current cell labeling tools are typically designed either for general labeling tasks, e.g., ImageJ, or specifically for segmentation with full annotations, e.g., Segmentor [2]. To address this issue, we developed modifications to Segmentor to directly support dot annotations. These include adjustable pre-processing to provide initial results for easy correction to reduce user workload, and visualizations to help track progress, which is especially useful for 3D volume labeling.

In summary, the contributions of this paper are four-fold:

1. A simple yet effective way to address the challenge of overlapping cells in image-based cell counting. Applying the inverse distance kernel instead of the Gaussian kernel on dot annotations enables separable density maps and outperforms state-of-the-art methods in a fully supervised setting.
2. A self-supervised approach with our novel focal consistency loss to exploit unlabeled data. It is effective when labeled data is scarce, even against methods with full annotations.
3. A labeling tool for dot annotations based on Segmentor [2], enabling a pipeline for image-based cell counting from labeling to modeling.
4. Source code and the interactive labeling tool are released to the community at https://github.com/mzlr/cell_counting_ssl, hoping to spur further investigation in this field.

2   Related Work

The relevant work related to this paper can be divided into two categories: image-based cell counting and self-supervised learning.

There has been significant progress in image-based cell counting, especially after the success of deep learning in various domains [5–7]. Since cell counting belongs to a broad topic of object counting, generic detection or segmentation based methods have been explored for 2D images [3] and 3D volumes [9]. Still, the reliance on time-consuming full (whole-cell) annotations hinders their impact. Alternatively, dot annotations have become increasingly popular for their simplicity. Notably, Xie et al. [17] applied the Gaussian kernel to dot annotations and used U-Net to learn a mapping between input images and resulting density maps. The final cell count is inferred by the integration of the density maps. Lu et al. [12] designed a Generic Matching Network to learn the exact mapping, which is capable of leveraging large object detection datasets for pre-training and adapting to target datasets. Guo et al. [4] later expanded the framework for 3D volumes and developed a unified network structure, SAU-Net, for various cell types, focusing on the universal nature of the method. However, these approaches rely on the Gaussian kernel to build the density maps and are subject to the issue of inseparable density maps for overlapping cells.

Self-supervised learning describes a class of algorithms that seek to learn from unlabeled data with auxiliary (pretext) tasks. It is a generic learning framework and can be applied in either unsupervised settings to learn useful representations for downstream tasks [8] or semi-supervised settings for a specific task [16]. This paper focuses on the latter for its simplicity. Given labeled data x and its labels y, and unlabeled data x', self-supervised learning generally has an objective function of the following form:

$$\underbrace{\mathcal{L}_l(f_\theta(x), y)}_{\text{primary task}} + \underbrace{w\mathcal{L}_u(f_\theta(x'))}_{\text{auxiliary (pretext) task}} , \tag{1}$$

where $\mathcal{L}_l$ is the supervised loss for primary tasks, e.g., Cross-Entropy (CE) loss for classification tasks or mean squared error (MSE) for regression tasks. $\mathcal{L}_u$ is the unsupervised loss for auxiliary tasks (e.g., consistency loss), w is a weight ratio between the two losses, and θ represents the parameters for model f. For example, Xie et al. [16] designed an auxiliary task by enforcing consistency constraints, i.e., the model is expected to generate consistent outputs given perturbations, and used advanced data augmentation methods as the perturbations. Sohn et al. [15] later extended this idea by considering a pair of weakly-augmented and strongly-augmented unlabeled samples. Ouali et al. [14] observed that injecting perturbations into deep layers of the network rather than the inputs is more effective for segmentation tasks and built an encoder-decoder network based on this observation. Despite numerous advances for self-supervised learning in multiple domains, its application to image-based cell counting has rarely been explored.

Inspired by recent crowd counting work [11], we propose using the inverse distance kernel to address the issue of inseparable density maps. Furthermore, we aim to take advantage of recent success in self-supervised learning for image-based cell counting and leverage unlabeled data to reduce the reliance on costly labeled data.

3 Method

Given dot annotations D, the resulting density map M traditionally can be seen as the sum of Gaussian kernels $\mathcal{N}$ with width σ centered on each individual dot annotation d: $M = \sum_{d \in D} \mathcal{N}(d, \sigma^2)$. With the corresponding image I and the resulting density map M, the goal is to train a model f with parameters θ for the mapping between the image and density map: $f_\theta(I) \to M$.

3.1 Inverse Distance Kernel

As shown in Fig. 1, Gaussian kernels suffer the problem of inseparable density maps. We propose to use the inverse distance kernel from [11]. Mathematically, we have

$$\forall i \in I, M_{dis}(i) = \frac{1}{L_2(i)^\gamma + C}, \tag{2}$$

where i denotes a pixel, and $L_2(i)$ is the Euclidean distance between pixel i and its nearest dot annotation, i.e., $\min_{d \in D} \|i - d\|_2$. Here, C is a constant to avoid dividing by zero, and γ is a decay factor to control the response rate between dot annotations and background. In practice, we set $C = 1$ and $\gamma = 0.02 L_2(i) + 0.75$, following [11].

3.2 Focal Consistency Loss

Following the general framework for self-supervised learning described above, our learning objective consists of two tasks: a primary task with a supervised

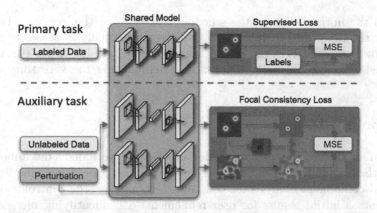

Fig. 2. Overview of the proposed method. α is the focal weight to "focus" on predicted cells instead of background noise, and MSE denotes mean square error.

loss on n labeled images I, $\frac{1}{n}\sum_I \|f_\theta(I) - M_{dis}\|_2^2$, and an auxiliary task with the consistency loss on n' unlabeled images I', $\frac{w}{n'}\sum_{I'} \|f_\theta(\delta(I')) - f_{\widehat{\theta}}(I')\|_2^2$. Here, we use the pixel-wise mean squared error (MSE) for both tasks. f_θ denotes the shared model with parameters θ, and $\widehat{\theta}$ is a fixed copy of the current θ, which is not updated via back propagation and can be viewed as containing pseudo-labels, as suggested in [16]. δ denotes the transform for perturbations. In practice we found that the vanilla framework did not generalize well to our task. Since our task is pixel-level, rather than an image-level task such as image classification for which the framework was originally proposed, adding perturbations to the whole image will inevitably learn the image artifacts in the background. Therefore, we propose a focal consistency loss, $\frac{w}{n'}\sum_{I'} \alpha\|f_\theta(\delta(I')) - f_{\widehat{\theta}}(I')\|_2^2$ with focal weight $\alpha = \sum_{d'\in D'} \mathcal{N}(d', \sigma^2)$, where D' is the set of the local maximums in the current predicted density maps $f_{\widehat{\theta}}(I')$, which are considered as predicted cells and can be inferred by a maximum filter. α ensures that we only calculate the consistency loss in the vicinity of the local maximum, i.e., focusing on cells and ignoring background. We also considered several commonly used perturbations, e.g., random contrast/sharpness/brightness/noise, etc., and found directly injecting noise into the last layer of the encoder yields the best performance, as suggested in [14]. Our final loss function is

$$\mathcal{L}_{\text{final}} = \frac{1}{n}\sum_I \|f_\theta(I) - M_{dis}\|_2^2 + \frac{w}{n'}\sum_{I'} \alpha\|f_{\theta_{\text{dec}}}(\delta(f_{\theta_{\text{enc}}}(I'))) - f_{\widehat{\theta}}(I')\|_2^2, \quad (3)$$

where $f_{\theta_{\text{enc}}}$ and $f_{\theta_{\text{dec}}}$ are the encoder and decoder of the network, respectively. The overview of the proposed method is shown in Fig. 2.

3.3   Implementation Details

This work uses SAU-Net [4] as the base model, favoring its versatile nature for both 2D and 3D. We use the Adam optimizer with a cosine decaying learning rate, and the initial value for the schedule is 0.001. For the weight w in Eq. 3 we follow the ramp-up schedule in [14], which exponentially increases from 0 to 1, avoiding noisy signals in the early stage of training. All the hyper-parameters are shared across 2D and 3D experiments, highlighting the versatility of our method.

4   Labeling Tool

To streamline the labeling process for dot annotations we added a dot annotation mode to the Segmentor 3D annotation tool [2]. We first apply Otsu's method and connected component analysis for cell detection, and use the centroids of each component as initial results for user refinement, e.g., identifying merged cells and making the appropriate corrections. In the 2D slice view, dot annotations in nearby z-axis slices are marked with separate visualizations to ease the effort of tracking completed regions. In an adjacent 3D view, volume rendering can be used to verify the placement of the dot annotations.

To quantify the decrease in labeling time for dot annotations vs. full (whole-cell) annotations, we asked four users to dot-annotate four 3D volumes with 156 cells in total and compared the time to the full annotation time previously reported in [2]. The average speed for dot annotation is $\sim$0.3 min per cell, whereas full annotations take $\sim$8 min per cell, a speedup of $\sim$27x. In addition to improved labeling efficiency, our experiments in the next section show that our dot-annotation method outperforms a state-of-the-art full-annotation method.

5   Experiments

We used two benchmarks to evaluate the proposed method, the 2D VGG dataset [10] and a 3D light-sheet dataset [9]. VGG is a synthetic dataset that contains 200 fluorescence microscopy cell images with an even split between training and test sets, and each image containing 174 ± 64 cells. The 3D dataset comprises light-sheet images of the mouse cortex with 16 training volumes and 5 test volumes. Each volume includes 861 ± 256 cells. This dataset contains full (whole-cell) annotations, and we convert them into dot annotations by using the centroids of the full annotations. Note that we only use a fraction of the training data to study reliance of the proposed method on labeled data; nonetheless, we always evaluate our method on the **whole** test set. Previous works [15,16] suggest self-supersized learning benefits from a large amount of unlabeled data. Following this, we use an additional 55 unlabeled samples for the 3D experiment on the light-sheet dataset, which are all the available unlabeled data from the original work. For the 2D experiment on the VGG dataset, we use 8 out of 100 training data for the supervised training and treat the remaining 92 of the unused training data as unlabeled data for self-supervised training.

We use two metrics to evaluate the proposed method: the mean absolute error (MAE) between the predicted and ground-truth cell counts, and the F_1 score for cell detection. We follow the post-processing techniques from [4,9], i.e., perform

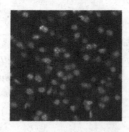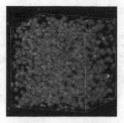

Fig. 3. Sample images of 2D VGG dataset (left) and 3D light sheet dataset with 2D (middle) and 3D (right) view. Dot annotations, typically in the centroids of cells, are marked with red cross overlays. (Color figure online)

Connected Component Analysis after thresholding and use the centroids of each component as cell locations. Depending on the type of annotations, a detection is valid when a predicted centroid lies within a full (whole-cell) annotation of a cell or a radius of a dot annotation, where the radius is an empirical radius of cells. MAE has an inherent deficiency since it is unable to distinguish correct cell counts. For a trivial case with only one cell, a method could miss that cell and yield a 0 F_1 score but pick up background noise as a cell and achieve a perfect MAE of 0. Without location information, it would be impossible to determine this error using MAE. Nonetheless, we still report MAE for a direct comparison with previous work.

5.1 Ablation Study

A 3D light-sheet dataset is used for our ablation study since its full annotations enable a comparison with more methods. This work focused on learning using limited data; therefore, only one volume is used for training. All the experiments are conducted with the same baseline SAU-Net, and the model is initialized from the same random weights, which could help us better attribute the source of improvement. Table 1 shows that using the inverse distance kernel already outperforms the baseline and SAU-Net with full annotations, and our proposed self-supervised learning further improves the performance.

Table 1. Ablation study

Method	MAE	$F_1(\%)$
Gaussian kernel (*baseline*)	57.8	93.55
Full annotations*	42.2	94.12
Inverse distance kernel	13.8	95.21
Inverse distance kernel + self-supervised learning (*proposed*)	**12.4**	**95.86**

*Implementation following [9] except replacing U-Net with SAU-Net for consistency.

Table 2. 2D VGG dataset

Method	MAE	$F_1(\%)$	N_{train}
Arteta et al. [1]	5.1	93.46	32
GMN [12]	3.6	90.18	32
SAU-Net [4]	**2.6**	94.51	64
Ours	5.6	**96.78**	8

Table 3. 3D light sheet dataset

Method	MAE	$F_1(\%)$	N_{train}
NuMorph [9] (*full-annot.*)	50.1	95.37	4
CUBIC [13] (*unsupervised*)	36.2	95.43	-
SAU-Net [4] (*dot-annot.*)	42.2	93.97	4
Ours (*dot-annot.*)	**12.4**	**95.86**	1

5.2 Comparison to State-of-the-Art

We compare our proposed method with other state-of-the-art approaches on the 2D VGG and 3D light-sheet datasets. To show that our method reduces the reliance on labeled data, we drastically limit the number of labeled data to **25% or less** of the amount used in other state-of-the-art approaches. Table 2 and 3 present the results. For both datasets, our method improves the performance in terms of F_1 score, even improving upon the full-annotation method, while substantially reducing the amount of labeled data needed for training. Our method does not outperform [4], the state-of-the-art Gaussian method, on the MAE metric for the VGG dataset. This is due to the fact that this synthetic dataset contains severe overlapping, as shown in Fig. 3, and the ground-truth is pre-defined; otherwise, it would be considerably challenging for human annotators. For those cases, the cell count can still be obtained by integration of the Gaussian density maps, although they are inseparable. On the other hand, our method attains better performance on the F_1 metric with location information. In our opinion, although widely used for cell counting, MAE provides a limited evaluation for cell counting methods. Since it ignores the location information of individual cells, we also calculate the F_1 score for a comprehensive review. Overall, by utilizing unlabeled data, our method outperforms most state-of-art methods in 2D and 3D cases with a quarter or less of labeled data.

6 Discussion

We introduce a framework for image-based cell counting using dot annotations, including a labeling tool and an improved model with a highly efficient training scheme. Compared to conventional Gaussian kernel methods, our model exploits the inverse distance kernel for separable density maps, enabling post-processing techniques for cell location in addition to cell counts. By leveraging unlabeled data, our self-supervised pipeline with a novel focal consistency loss allows a drastic reduction of labeled data and achieves state-of-the-art or very competitive performance on both 2D and 3D benchmarks, even compared to methods using full annotations. Finally, we add dot annotation specific features to an existing labeling tool to facilitate the annotation process. We notice that, in some works for image classification [15, 16], the advantage brought by self-supervised learning against fully supervised learning diminishes as the number of labeled data grows. In the future, we plan to investigate this matter for cell counting.

Acknowledgments. This work was supported in part by the National Science Foundation under grants OCI-1153775 and OAC-1649916. The authors would like to thank Carla Escobar and Tala Farah for their participation in the user study of our labeling tool.

References

1. Arteta, C., Lempitsky, V., Noble, J.A., Zisserman, A.: Detecting overlapping instances in microscopy images using extremal region trees. Med. Image Anal. **27**, 3–16 (2016)
2. Borland, D., et al.: Segmentor: a tool for manual refinement of 3D microscopy annotations. BMC Bioinform. **22**(1), 1–12 (2021)
3. Caicedo, J.C., et al.: Nucleus segmentation across imaging experiments: the 2018 data science bowl. Nat. Methods **16**(12), 1247–1253 (2019)
4. Guo, Y., Krupa, O., Stein, J., Wu, G., Krishnamurthy, A.: SAU-net: a unified network for cell counting in 2D and 3D microscopy images. IEEE/ACM Trans. Comput. Biol. Bioinform. (2021)
5. Guo, Y., Stein, J., Wu, G., Krishnamurthy, A.: SAU-net: a universal deep network for cell counting. In: Proceedings of the 10th ACM International Conference on Bioinformatics, Computational Biology and Health Informatics, pp. 299–306 (2019)
6. Guo, Y., et al.: Cross modality microscopy segmentation via adversarial adaptation. In: Rojas, I., Valenzuela, O., Rojas, F., Ortuño, F. (eds.) IWBBIO 2019. LNCS, vol. 11466, pp. 469–478. Springer, Cham (2019). https://doi.org/10.1007/978-3-030-17935-9_42
7. Guo, Y., Wrammert, J., Singh, K., Ashish, K., Bradford, K., Krishnamurthy, A.: Automatic analysis of neonatal video data to evaluate resuscitation performance. In: 2016 IEEE 6th International Conference on Computational Advances in Bio and Medical Sciences (ICCABS), pp. 1–6. IEEE (2016)
8. Kolesnikov, A., Zhai, X., Beyer, L.: Revisiting self-supervised visual representation learning. In: Proceedings of the IEEE/CVF Conference on Computer Vision and Pattern Recognition, pp. 1920–1929 (2019)
9. Krupa, O., et al.: Numorph: tools for cellular phenotyping in tissue cleared whole brain images. bioRxiv pp. 2020–09 (2021)
10. Lempitsky, V., Zisserman, A.: Learning to count objects in images. Adv. Neural. Inf. Process. Syst. **23**, 1324–1332 (2010)
11. Liang, D., Xu, W., Zhu, Y., Zhou, Y.: Focal inverse distance transform maps for crowd localization and counting in dense crowd. arXiv preprint arXiv:2102.07925 (2021)
12. Lu, E., Xie, W., Zisserman, A.: Class-agnostic counting. In: Jawahar, C.V., Li, H., Mori, G., Schindler, K. (eds.) ACCV 2018. LNCS, vol. 11363, pp. 669–684. Springer, Cham (2019). https://doi.org/10.1007/978-3-030-20893-6_42
13. Matsumoto, K., et al.: Advanced cubic tissue clearing for whole-organ cell profiling. Nat. Protoc. **14**(12), 3506–3537 (2019)
14. Ouali, Y., Hudelot, C., Tami, M.: Semi-supervised semantic segmentation with cross-consistency training. In: Proceedings of the IEEE/CVF Conference on Computer Vision and Pattern Recognition, pp. 12674–12684 (2020)
15. Sohn, K., et al.: Fixmatch: simplifying semi-supervised learning with consistency and confidence. arXiv preprint arXiv:2001.07685 (2020)
16. Xie, Q., Dai, Z., Hovy, E., Luong, M.T., Le, Q.V.: Unsupervised data augmentation for consistency training. arXiv preprint arXiv:1904.12848 (2019)

17. Xie, W., Noble, J.A., Zisserman, A.: Microscopy cell counting and detection with fully convolutional regression networks. Comput. Methods Biomech. Biomed. Eng. Imaging Vis. **6**(3), 283–292 (2018)
18. Zhai, X., Oliver, A., Kolesnikov, A., Beyer, L.: S4L: self-supervised semi-supervised learning. In: Proceedings of the IEEE/CVF International Conference on Computer Vision, pp. 1476–1485 (2019)

Predicting the Visual Attention of Pathologists Evaluating Whole Slide Images of Cancer

Souradeep Chakraborty[1(✉)], Rajarsi Gupta[2], Ke Ma[9], Darshana Govind[5], Pinaki Sarder[6], Won-Tak Choi[8], Waqas Mahmud[2], Eric Yee[7], Felicia Allard[7], Beatrice Knudsen[3], Gregory Zelinsky[1,4], Joel Saltz[2], and Dimitris Samaras[1]

[1] Department of Computer Science, Stony Brook University, Stony Brook, NY, USA
souchakrabor@cs.stonybrook.edu
[2] Department of Biomedical Informatics, Stony Brook University,
Stony Brook, NY, USA
[3] Department of Pathology, University of Utah School of Medicine,
Salt Lake City, UT, USA
[4] Department of Psychology, Stony Brook University, Stony Brook, NY, USA
[5] Department of Pathology and Anatomical Sciences, University at Buffalo,
Buffalo, NY, USA
[6] Department of Medicine, University of Florida at Gainesville, Gainesville, FL, USA
[7] Department of Pathology, University of Arkansas for Medical Sciences,
Little Rock, AR, USA
[8] Department of Pathology, University of California San Francisco,
San Francisco, CA, USA
[9] Snap Inc., Santa Monica, USA

Abstract. This work presents PathAttFormer, a deep learning model that predicts the visual attention of pathologists viewing whole slide images (WSIs) while evaluating cancer. This model has two main components: (1) a patch-wise attention prediction module using a Swin transformer backbone and (2) a self-attention based attention refinement module to compute pairwise-similarity between patches to predict spatially consistent attention heatmaps. We observed a high level of agreement between model predictions and actual viewing behavior, collected by capturing panning and zooming movements using a digital microscope interface. Visual attention was analyzed in the evaluation of prostate cancer and gastrointestinal neuroendocrine tumors (GI-NETs), which differ greatly in terms of diagnostic paradigms and the demands on attention. Prostate cancer involves examining WSIs stained with Hematoxylin and Eosin (H&E) to identify distinct growth patterns for Gleason grading. In contrast, GI-NETs require a multi-step approach of identifying tumor regions in H&E WSIs and grading by quantifying the number of Ki-67 positive tumor cells highlighted with immunohistochemistry (IHC) in a separate image. We collected attention data from pathologists viewing

Supplementary Information The online version contains supplementary material available at https://doi.org/10.1007/978-3-031-16961-8_2.

prostate cancer H&E WSIs from The Cancer Genome Atlas (TCGA) and 21 H&E WSIs of GI-NETs with corresponding Ki-67 IHC WSIs. This is the first work that utilizes the Swin transformer architecture to predict visual attention in histopathology images of GI-NETs, which is generalizable to predicting attention in the evaluation of multiple sequential images in real world diagnostic pathology and IHC applications.

Keywords: Visual attention · Digital microscopy · Cognitive pathology

1   Introduction

Attention tracking in digital histopathology images has been an evolving topic of research in medical imaging [5–7]. The development of techniques to analyze and predict the visual attention of pathologists during the examination of WSIs is critical for developing computer-assisted training and clinical decision support systems [4]. Interpretation of the attention behavior of pathologists has been considered in the early works of [8] that conducted eye tracking studies on grading tumor architecture in prostate cancer images and [9] capturing mouse movement as a reliable indicator of attention behavior. Other works [7,10] used eye tracking to explore the complexity of diagnostic decision-making of pathologists viewing WSIs. The attention behavior of pathologists has also been collected using a web-based digital microscope and analyzed to reveal distinct scanning and drilling diagnostic search patterns [10]. Recently, the work in [4] presented ProstAttNet, a fine-tuned ResNet34 model [14], for analyzing and predicting visual attention heatmaps of WSIs from prostate cancer.

Here we propose PathAttFormer, a deep learning model based on Swin transformer [13] that is able to predict visual attention for multiple cancer types. The Swin transformer model more efficiently leverages the global contextual information across cells and nuclei regions within sub-patches of a WSI patch compared to other conventional models. This paper demonstrates the application of PathAttFormer to predict the viewing behavior of pathologists in the task of evaluating and grading Gastrointestinal Neuroendocrine tumors (GI-NETs). GI-NETs require pathologists to examine H&E WSIs and corresponding salient regions in additional tissue sections stained with Ki-67 immunohistochemistry (IHC) to grade tumors by quantifying brown colored Ki-67 positive tumor cells. In contrast, pathologists assign Gleason grades to prostate cancer based on the primary and secondary patterns of tumor growth viewed in H&E images only. Given that pathologists routinely examine multiple tissue sections, stained with H&E and other IHC biomarkers, to evaluate numerous types of cancers, this work represents a generalizable methodology that can be broadly useful in digital pathology. We depict the slide examination processes for the Prostate cancer and GI-NETs WSIs in Fig. 1.

To the best of our knowledge, we are the first to analyze attention data on GI-NET WSIs and to present a generalizable methodology to predict visual attention for multiple cancer types. Our study also represents a strong proof of concept for collecting WSI navigation data to study visual attention in pathologists evaluating cancer without the need for specialized eye-tracking equipment. While [4] only analyzed the one-stage examination process in prostate cancer, we also study attention in a two-stage examination with different sequential tasks (tumor detection and nuclei counting) for the more complex GI-NETs, where we show (Fig. 4, Table 2) that attended WSI regions at stage 1 influence attention at the next stage. Lastly, our work is important because our framework can be used to characterize and predict pathologist visual attention across cancer types involving multiple stages of examination in real world digital pathology workflows. In clinical terms, our work can be used to develop clinical applications for training residents and fellows and for reducing observer variability among pathologists via clinical decision support.

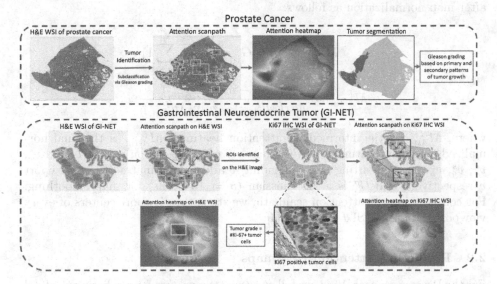

Fig. 1. Demonstration of visual attention heatmap generation by analyzing the viewing behavior of pathologists in Prostate cancer (top) and GI-NET (bottom). The yellow boxes indicate the viewport boxes and the scanpath is constructed by joining the viewport centers. Greater attention is indicated by hotter (redder) color. (Color figure online)

2 Methods

2.1 Data Collection and Processing

For Prostate cancer, we used the same dataset of 22 H&E WSIs as in [4]. Among the 22 WSIs, attention data for 5 was collected from 13 pathologists and attention data for the remaining 17 was collected from a Genitourinary (GU) specialist. The GU specialist also annotated the Gleason grades on all the 22 WSIs.

Following the procedure described in [4], we used QuIP caMicroscope [11], a web-based toolset for digital pathology, data management and visualization to record the attention data of pathologists as they viewed GI-NET WSIs [2,12]. We collected the attention data from 21 resection H&E WSIs and the corresponding 21 Ki-67 IHC WSIs. Two pathologists participated in the GI-NET attention data collection. They viewed the H&E and the Ki-67 IHC WSIs sequentially and graded the tumors. The average viewing time per slide per pathologist was 37.67 s for the H&E WSIs and 131.98 s for the Ki-67 IHC WSIs.

We process attention data in terms of attention heatmap and attention scanpath as shown in Fig. 4. The aggregate spatial distribution of the pathologist's attention is captured using the attention heatmap and the temporal information is recorded in the attention scanpath. Following [4], a value of 1 is assigned at all image pixels within a viewport and the values are summed up over all viewports to construct the attention heatmap. The final attention heatmap is obtained after map normalization as follows:

$$M'^I_{Attn.}(x,y) = G^\sigma * \sum_{v=1}^{V}(\sum_{v_x^s}^{v_x^e}\sum_{v_y^s}^{v_y^e}1)$$

$$M^I_{Attn.} = \frac{M'^I_{Attn.} - min(M'^I_{Attn.})}{max(M'^I_{Attn.}) - min(M'^I_{Attn.})}$$

(1)

where, $M'^I_{Attn.}$ is the intermediate attention heatmap, $M^I_{Attn.}$ is the final normalized attention heatmap, V is the number of viewports on a WSI I, and v_x^s, v_x^e, v_y^s, v_y^e are the starting and the ending x and y coordinates of the viewport v respectively, and G^σ is a 2D gaussian ($\sigma = 16$ pixels) for map smoothing. For constructing the attention scanpath, we stack the viewport centers of every viewport, v in the WSI I following [4].

2.2 Predicting Attention Heatmaps

For the Prostate cancer WSIs, we follow a two-step process for predicting the final attention heatmap. In the first step, we produce the patch-wise attention labels and assemble the patch-wise predictions to construct the attention heatmap on the WSI. In the next step, we refine the patch-wise attention predictions using a self-attention based visual attention refinement module that considers pairwise similarities between the patches to update the patch-wise attention labels. For the GI-NET WSIs, we first predict the attention heatmap on the H&E WSI similar to Prostate cancer. Next, we cascade the attention prediction modules for the H&E and Ki-67 IHC WSIs by using the patch-wise attention predictions on the H&E WSI (from Stage 1) and the Ki-67 positive nuclei detection map (discretized patch-wise similar to the H&E attention heatmap) on the Ki-67 IHC WSI as inputs (each input encoded to a 20-dimensional feature vector) to the model for predicting attention on Ki-67 IHC WSIs. We depict our attention prediction model, PathAttFormer for the two cancer types in Fig. 2 and Fig. 3.

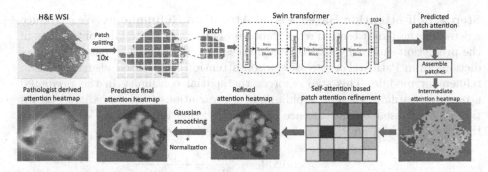

Fig. 2. Our model, PathAttFormer, for predicting visual attention in Prostate grading.

Step 1: Patch-Wise Attention Prediction. Similar to [4], we formulate attention prediction as a classification task where the aim is to classify a WSI patch into one of the N attention bins. $N = 5$ in our study, which best reconstructs the attention heatmaps. $N < 5$ leads to inaccurate reconstruction of the attention heatmap and $N > 5$ provides us minimal improvement in the reconstructed attention heatmap while reducing the accuracy of patch classification performance. During training, we discretize the average pixel intensity of every heatmap patch into an attention bin and at inference we assign the average pixel intensity of a predicted bin to the image patch to construct the intermediate patch-wise heatmap. Our model comprises of a Swin Transformer (a Swin-Base model using patch size $p = 4$, window size $w = 7$, operating on 224×224 images) [13] pre-trained on the ImageNet 1K dataset as the backbone feature extractor, followed by a fully connected layer $fc(1024, 5)$ as the classifier.

Training Details: During training PathAttFormer on the Prostate cancer WSIs, we froze the swin transformer and updated the last fully-connected layer only. We used 500×500 image patches (resized to 224×224 for training) extracted from 15 WSIs at 10× magnification (the most frequent magnification used by pathologists per our analysis) for training while using 2 WSIs for validation. We performed data augmentation [16] by introducing color jitter and random horizontal and vertical image flips during training. We used the weighted Cross-Entropy loss between the predicted and the pathologist-derived attention bins. The class weight for a bin was inversely proportional to the number of training instances for the class. We only processed patches with tissue area >30% of the total patch area, which provided us with 11K H&E patches for training.

For the GI-NET WSIs, we trained separate models for the H&E and the Ki-67 IHC WSIs corresponding to patches extracted at 4X and 40X magnification (image sizes 1250×1250 and 125×125 respectively). These correspond to the most frequent magnification levels for the two slide types per our analysis. We used 9K H&E patches and 267K Ki-67 patches for training following a similar training method as Prostate WSIs. We used the AdamW optimizer [15] with an initial learning rate of 0.01. Training converged within 16 epochs with a training time of approximately 8 h on a Nvidia Titan-Xp GPU for both cancer types.

Step 2: Self-attention Based Visual Attention Refinement. We introduce a dense method for attention refinement that eliminates spatial discontinuities in the prediction caused by patch-based processing. We refine the patch-wise predictions from PathAttFormer using a self-attention (SA) based visual attention refinement module. This step enforces the spatial continuity in the predicted attention heatmap, thereby avoiding abrupt variations in the predicted attention labels caused by the absence of the contextual information. We compute the contribution of an image patch q to an image patch p as:

$$w_{q:d_{p,q}\leq d^t}(p) = \frac{\exp(-\frac{||F_p-F_q||^2}{2\hat{\alpha_1}^2} - \frac{||l_p-l_q||^2}{2\hat{\alpha_2}^2})}{\sum_{r:d_{p,r}\leq d^t}\exp(-\frac{||F_p-F_r||^2}{2\hat{\alpha_1}^2} - \frac{||l_p-l_r||^2}{2\hat{\alpha_2}^2})} \tag{2}$$

where F_p denotes the 1024-dim. feature vector encoded by the Swin Transformer and l_p denotes the location of the patch p, $d_{p,r}$ is the euclidean distance between the patch p and r, and d^t is the threshold distance. The Gaussian kernel parameters are selected as: $\hat{\alpha_1}, \hat{\alpha_2} = \arg\min_{\alpha_1,\alpha_2}||L_{refined}^{Val} - L_{GT}^{Val}||^2$, where $L_{refined}^{Val}$ and L_{GT}^{Val} denote the refined and the ground truth patch labels. We used grid search on our validation set [17] to find the optimal kernel parameters $\hat{\alpha_1} = 1.6$, $\hat{\alpha_2} = 1$ and threshold distance factor $d_t = 0.3 \times I_{Dg}$ (I_{Dg} = image diagonal length), respectively. Next, we update the label of the patch p based on the weights $w_q(p)$ obtained in Eq. 2 as: $L_{refined}^{I}{}'(p) = \sum \sum_q w_q(p)L_{coarse}(q)$, where $L_{refined}^{I}{}'$ is the

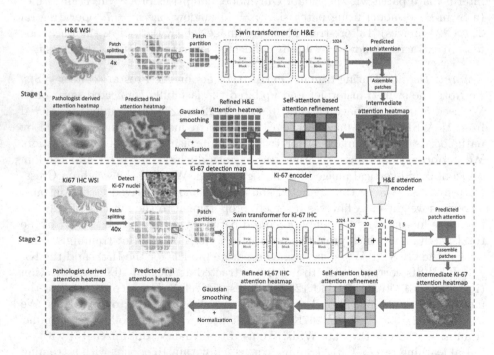

Fig. 3. Cascaded PathAttFormers for predicting visual attention in GI-NET.

refined patch label and L_{coarse} is the patch label predicted using PathAttFormer. Finally we construct the attention map $M_{refined}^{I}{}'$ by assembling $L_{refined}^{I}{}'$. The map $M_{refined}^{I}{}'$ is further smoothed and normalized.

In order to reduce the compute time for GI-NET WSIs, which involved a higher number of patches per WSI at 40× magnification, we computed the attention weights for alternate pixels in the image and applied bilinear interpolation to the intermediate refined attention heatmap, $M_{refined}^{I}{}'$ for computing the final attention heatmap, $M_{refined}$. This step reduced compute time 16 times although model complexity remained $O(N^2)$. Average number of patches per slide for prostate and GI-NET test sets were 834 (10×) and 16.8K (40×) respectively.

3   Results

3.1   Qualitative Evaluation

Figure 4(a), row 1 shows the visual scanpath of a pathologist with the magnification at each viewport center and the attention heatmap computed from the viewport boxes for a test H&E WSI instance. We see that the pathologist mostly viewed the WSI at 10× magnification. We also compare the attention data with the tumor annotation we obtained from the GU specialist. The attention heatmap correlates well with the tumor locations in the ground truth tumor annotation.

We compare the attention heatmaps predicted by our model with 4 baseline models: (1) ResNet34 [14] and (2) Vision Transformer (ViT) [22], as the backbone feature extractor, (3) ProstAttNet [4], (4) DA-MIL [3], in Fig. 4(a). The multiple instance learning model (DA-MIL) [3] was trained on the WSIs with the primary Gleason grades as the bag labels. We also compare the predictions obtained using the proposed self-attention (SA) based attention refinement module to the predictions using Dense Conditional Random Fields [17] (CRF) as an alternative method to refine the attention heatmap. PathAttFormer produces more accurate attention heatmap compared to the baselines. Moreover, the SA module improves the overall spatial consistency in the predicted attention heatmaps compared to the patch-wise predictions from the baseline models.

In Fig. 4(b), we show the attention scanpaths with the magnification at each viewport center and the computed attention heatmaps for a H&E and Ki-67 IHC WSI instance from our GI-NET dataset. While the pathologist viewed all image regions in the H&E WSI to detect the tumor regions, as seen in the H&E scanpath, their attention on the Ki-67 IHC WSI was mostly confined within the tumor regions detected on the H&E WSI. Also, the regions examined on the Ki-67 IHC WSI are well correlated with the Ki-67 positive nuclei detection map obtained using [1]. We also compare the attention data with the tumor segmentation (on the H&E WSI) obtained from [1]. The attention heatmap correlates well with the tumor locations in the tumor segmentation map. We also compare the attention heatmaps predicted by PathAttFormer to the other models in row 3 in Fig. 4(b) for the same test Ki-67 IHC WSI instance. We observe that

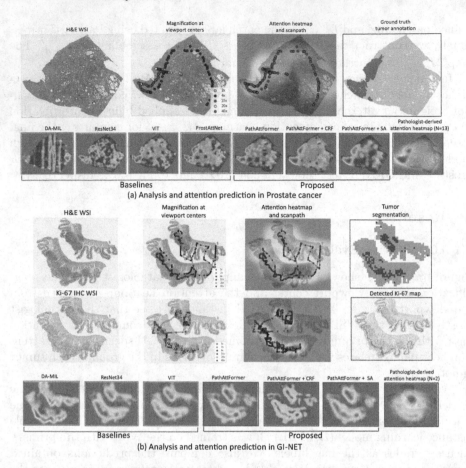

Fig. 4. Visualization of observed attention data on a test WSI of (a) Prostate cancer, and (b) GI-NET. We also compare the predicted attention heatmaps to the pathologist-derived attention heatmap (row 2 in (a) and row 3 in (b)). PathAttFormer+SA best predicts the attention data. More results in the supplementary.

PathAttFormer produces more accurate attention heatmaps compared to the baselines using ResNet34 and ViT as the backbone feature extractors, as well as the DA-MIL method. Also, the predicted attention heatmap correlates well with the corresponding tumor segmentation map.

3.2   Quantitative Evaluation

We quantitatively evaluate the model performance using four metrics: weighted F1-score of attention intensity classification, Cross Correlation (CC), Normalized Scanpath Saliency (NSS), and Information Gain (IG) [18]. A higher weighted F1-score indicates a better class-balanced classification performance. A high CC value indicates a higher correlation between the map intensities. NSS measures the average normalized attention intensity at the viewport centers and IG measures the average information gain of the predicted attention heatmap over a center prior map at viewport centers [18,19]. To ensure that the distributions of the predicted and pathologist-derived attention heatmaps are similar, we perform histogram matching [20] of the two maps as a pre-processing step [4,21]. In Tables 1 and 2, we report the 4-fold cross-validation scores CC_{Attn}, NSS_{Attn} and IG_{Attn} between the predicted and the pathologist-derived attention heatmaps and the corresponding weighted F1-score. We also show the CC_{Seg} score between the predicted attention heatmap and the ground truth tumor segmentation map.

For Prostate WSIs (Table 1), PathAttFormer with attention refinement (SA) best predicts the attention heatmap in terms of the CC and IG metrics compared to pathologist-derived attention data, while the PathAttFormer model has the best NSS score. PathAttFormer + SA also best predicts the tumor segmentation in terms of CC. The proposed model improves performance by first using a Swin Transformer backbone instead of a convolutional model (e.g. ResNet34) for predicting attention on a WSI patch, followed by refining patch-wise predictions using an attention refinement module. PathAttFormer also outperforms ProstAttNet [4] on our test set. For GI-NET Ki-67 WSIs (Table 2), our PathAttFormer + SA model best predicts the attention heatmap in terms of all metrics compared to the pathologist-derived attention data, while the PathAttFormer model with the H&E and Ki-67 detection map as inputs best predicts the ground truth tumor segmentation in terms of the CC metric.

Table 1. Comparison of the 4-fold cross validation performance on the baseline models (blue) and the PathAttFormer models (red) for five test H&E WSIs of prostate cancer.

Model	Weighted-F1	CC_{Attn}	NSS_{Attn}	IG_{Attn}	CC_{Seg}
ResNet34 [14]	0.327 ± 0.01	0.710 ± 0.03	0.382 ± 0.01	0.978 ± 0.04	0.675 ± 0.07
ViT [22]	0.321 ± 0.01	0.706 ± 0.03	0.441 ± 0.02	0.241 ± 0.01	0.682 ± 0.07
ProstAttNet [4]	0.329 ± 0.01	0.712 ± 0.02	0.408 ± 0.01	1.046 ± 0.04	0.678 ± 0.07
DA-MIL [3]	-	0.504 ± 0.03	0.275 ± 0.03	0.042 ± 0.02	0.303 ± 0.08
PathAttFormer	0.348 ± 0.01	0.737 ± 0.02	$\mathbf{0.584 \pm 0.02}$	1.032 ± 0.04	0.681 ± 0.07
PathAttFormer+CRF	0.348 ± 0.01	0.743 ± 0.02	0.526 ± 0.02	0.702 ± 0.04	0.684 ± 0.07
PathAttFormer+SA	$\mathbf{0.348 \pm 0.01}$	$\mathbf{0.751 \pm 0.02}$	0.580 ± 0.02	$\mathbf{1.087 \pm 0.04}$	$\mathbf{0.689 \pm 0.07}$

Table 2. Comparison of the 4-fold cross validation performance on the baseline models (blue) and the PathAttFormer models (red) for five Ki-67 IHC WSIs of GI-NET.

Model	Weighted-F1	CC_{Attn}	NSS_{Attn}	IG_{Attn}	CC_{Seg}
ResNet34 [14]	0.273 ± 0.01	0.728 ± 0.05	0.514 ± 0.01	0.718 ± 0.03	0.820 ± 0.05
ViT [22]	0.270 ± 0.01	0.726 ± 0.06	0.526 ± 0.02	0.764 ± 0.03	0.809 ± 0.05
DA-MIL [3]	-	0.521 ± 0.07	0.383 ± 0.03	0.104 ± 0.02	0.692 ± 0.06
PathAttFormer	0.291 ± 0.01	0.732 ± 0.05	0.566 ± 0.02	0.758 ± 0.03	0.819 ± 0.04
PathAttFormer (w/ H&E attn.)	0.291 ± 0.01	0.741 ± 0.06	0.568 ± 0.02	0.763 ± 0.03	0.827 ± 0.04
PathAttFormer (w/ H&E attn.+Ki-67)	0.291 ± 0.01	0.744 ± 0.06	0.562 ± 0.02	0.771 ± 0.04	$\mathbf{0.835 \pm 0.04}$
PathAttFormer+CRF (w/ H&E attn.+Ki-67)	0.291 ± 0.01	0.758 ± 0.06	0.565 ± 0.02	0.479 ± 0.03	0.826 ± 0.04
PathAttFormer+SA (w/ H&E attn.+Ki-67)	$\mathbf{0.291 \pm 0.01}$	$\mathbf{0.762 \pm 0.06}$	$\mathbf{0.573 \pm 0.02}$	$\mathbf{0.802 \pm 0.04}$	0.834 ± 0.04

4   Conclusion

We have shown how pathologists allocate attention while viewing prostate cancer and GI-NET WSIs for tumor grading and presented a generalizable deep learning model that predicts visual attention on WSIs. Our work forms the foundation for research on tracking and analysing the attention behavior of pathologists viewing multiple stained images in sequence in order to grade the tumor type. In the future, we will collect attention data in a larger study with more WSIs in order to improve our attention prediction model. Additionally, we aim at predicting the attention scanpaths of pathologists that can reveal insights about the spatio-temporal dynamics of viewing behavior.

References

1. Govind, D., et al.: Improving the accuracy of gastrointestinal neuroendocrine tumor grading with deep learning. Sci. Rep. **10**(1), 1–12 (2020)
2. Matsukuma, K., Olson, K.A., Gui, D., Gandour-Edwards, R., Li, Y., Beckett, L.: Synaptophysin-Ki-67 double stain: a novel technique that improves interobserver agreement in the grading of well-differentiated gastrointestinal neuroendocrine tumors. Mod. Pathol. **30**(4), 620–629 (2017)
3. Hashimoto, N., et al.: Multi-scale domain-adversarial multiple-instance CNN for cancer subtype classification with unannotated histopathological images. In: Proceedings of the IEEE/CVF Conference on Computer Vision and Pattern Recognition, pp. 3852–3861 (2020)
4. Chakraborty, S., et al.: Visual attention analysis of pathologists examining whole slide images of Prostate cancer. In: 2022 IEEE 19th International Symposium on Biomedical Imaging (ISBI), pp. 1–5. IEEE, March 2022
5. Brunyé, T.T., Drew, T., Kerr, K.F., Shucard, H., Weaver, D.L., Elmore, J.G.: Eye tracking reveals expertise-related differences in the time-course of medical image inspection and diagnosis. J. Med. Imaging **7**(5), 051203 (2020)
6. Sudin, E., et al.: Eye tracking in digital pathology: identifying expert and novice patterns in visual search behaviour. In: Medical Imaging 2021: Digital Pathology, vol. 11603, p. 116030Z. International Society for Optics and Photonics, February 2021
7. Brunyé, T.T., Mercan, E., Weaver, D.L., Elmore, J.G.: Accuracy is in the eyes of the pathologist: the visual interpretive process and diagnostic accuracy with digital whole slide images. J. Biomed. Inform. **66**, 171–179 (2017)
8. Bombari, D., Mora, B., Schaefer, S.C., Mast, F.W., Lehr, H.A.: What was I thinking? Eye-tracking experiments underscore the bias that architecture exerts on nuclear grading in prostate cancer. PLoS ONE **7**(5), e38023 (2012)
9. Raghunath, V., et al.: Mouse cursor movement and eye tracking data as an indicator of pathologists' attention when viewing digital whole slide images. J. Pathol. Inform. **3**, 43 (2012)
10. Mercan, E., Shapiro, L.G., Brunyé, T.T., Weaver, D.L., Elmore, J.G.: Characterizing diagnostic search patterns in digital breast pathology: scanners and drillers. J. Digit. Imaging **31**(1), 32–41 (2018)
11. Saltz, J., et al.: A containerized software system for generation, management, and exploration of features from whole slide tissue images. Can. Res. **77**(21), e79–e82 (2017)

12. Govind, D., et al.: Improving the accuracy of gastrointestinal neuroendocrine tumor grading with deep learning. Sci. Rep. **10**(1), 1–12 (2020)
13. Liu, Z., et al.: Swin transformer: hierarchical vision transformer using shifted windows. In: Proceedings of the IEEE/CVF International Conference on Computer Vision, pp. 10012–10022 (2021)
14. He, K., Zhang, X., Ren, S., Sun, J.: Deep residual learning for image recognition. In: Proceedings of the IEEE Conference on Computer Vision and Pattern Recognition, pp. 770–778 (2016)
15. Loshchilov, I., Hutter, F.: Decoupled weight decay regularization. arXiv preprint arXiv:1711.05101 (2017)
16. Tellez, D., et al.: Whole-slide mitosis detection in H&E breast histology using PHH3 as a reference to train distilled stain-invariant convolutional networks. IEEE Trans. Med. Imaging **37**(9), 2126–2136 (2018)
17. Krähenbühl, P., Koltun, V.: Efficient inference in fully connected CRFS with gaussian edge potentials. In: Advances in Neural Information Processing Systems, vol. 24 (2011)
18. Bylinskii, Z., Judd, T., Oliva, A., Torralba, A., Durand, F.: What do different evaluation metrics tell us about saliency models? IEEE Trans. Pattern Anal. Mach. Intell. **41**(3), 740–757 (2018)
19. Kümmerer, M., Theis, L., Bethge, M.: Deep gaze I: boosting saliency prediction with feature maps trained on imagenet. arXiv preprint arXiv:1411.1045 (2014)
20. Gonzales, R.C., Fittes, B.A.: Gray-level transformations for interactive image enhancement. Mech. Mach. Theory **12**(1), 111–122 (1977)
21. Peacock, C.E., Hayes, T.R., Henderson, J.M.: Center bias does not account for the advantage of meaning over salience in attentional guidance during scene viewing. Front. Psychol. **11**, 1877 (2020)
22. Dosovitskiy, A., et al.: An image is worth 16x16 words: transformers for image recognition at scale. arXiv preprint arXiv:2010.11929 (2020)

Edge-Based Self-supervision
for Semi-supervised Few-Shot Microscopy
Image Cell Segmentation

Youssef Dawoud[1(✉)], Katharina Ernst[2], Gustavo Carneiro[3],
and Vasileios Belagiannis[4]

[1] Universität Ulm, Ulm, Germany
youssef.dawoud@uni-ulm.de
[2] Ulm University Medical Center, Ulm, Germany
katharina.ernst@uni-ulm.de
[3] The University of Adelaide, Adelaide, Australia
gustavo.carneiro@adelaide.edu.au
[4] Otto von Guericke University Magdeburg, Magdeburg, Germany
vasileios.belagiannis@ovgu.de

Abstract. Deep neural networks currently deliver promising results for
microscopy image cell segmentation, but they require large-scale labelled
databases, which is a costly and time-consuming process. In this work,
we relax the labelling requirement by combining self-supervised with
semi-supervised learning. We propose the prediction of edge-based maps
for self-supervising the training of the unlabelled images, which is combined with the supervised training of a small number of labelled images
for learning the segmentation task. In our experiments, we evaluate on
a few-shot microscopy image cell segmentation benchmark and show
that only a small number of annotated images, e.g. 10% of the original training set, is enough for our approach to reach similar performance
as with the fully annotated databases on 1- to 10-shots. Our code and
trained models is made publicly available https://github.com/Yussef93/
EdgeSSFewShotMicroscopy.

Keywords: Cell segmentation · Few-shot microscopy ·
Semi-supervised learning

1 Introduction

The analysis of microscopy images is usually focused on cell detection, counting, and segmentation. For instance, the analysis of changes in cell number and
morphology induced by bacterial protein toxins contributes to assessing their
activity [7], where these toxins are the causative agents of severe diseases like

Supplementary Information The online version contains supplementary material
available at https://doi.org/10.1007/978-3-031-16961-8_3.

diphtheria, anthrax or whooping cough. Moreover, the cell number and morphology is used to assess residual activity of inactivated toxins in vaccines or to investigate inhibitors of toxins in order to develop novel therapeutic strategies [7,15]. Data-driven approaches, such as deep neural networks [3,13], represent a key contribution towards reliably automating the tasks of cell detection, counting and segmentation [21]. However, one major drawback associated with deep neural networks is their dependence on large-scale labelled data sets for learning a fully-supervised model. This requires exhaustive manual labelling for every new microscopy data set on a pixel-level basis.

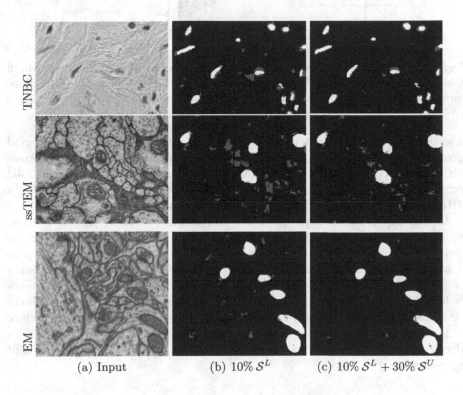

(a) Input   (b) 10% $\mathcal{S}^L$ (c) 10% $\mathcal{S}^L + 30\% \mathcal{S}^U$

Fig. 1. Visual Result. We visually compare the joint training of our proposed edge-detection proxy task using labelled images plus 30% of unlabelled images (i.e. $10\% \mathcal{S}^L + 30\% \mathcal{S}^U$) to a supervised model trained on the labelled images only (i.e. $10\% \mathcal{S}^L$). The red color corresponds to false positive, the green color to false negative, the black color to true negative, and the white color to true positive. Best viewed in color. (Color figure online)

Self-supervised and semi-supervised learning approaches target addressing the problem of limited available labels in different ways. In self-supervised approaches, the supervision stems from the data itself by learning proxy tasks such as rotation prediction [9] or using contrastive learning [1]. Semi-supervised approaches work with a small portion of labelled data, while there are label-free

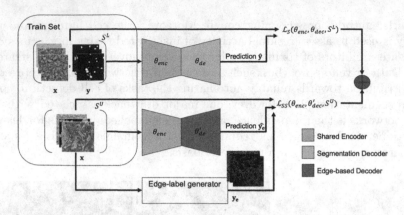

Fig. 2. An overview of our learning algorithm. We perform joint training with both labelled set $\mathcal{S}^L$ and unlabelled images $\mathcal{S}^U$, where we utilize a Canny edge filter [6] to generate edge-based supervision using the unlabeled images in $\mathcal{S}^U$.

objective functions for the unlabelled part, e.g. entropy minimization [10] and consistency enforcing [2,11], similar to self-supervision. In medical image analysis, JigSaw [17] and rotation proxy tasks are typical for self-supervision in 3D computed tomography (CT) scans [19]. Furthermore, brain segmentation from MRI images can be accomplished with a limited number of labelled data [4].

In this paper, we relax the extensive labelling requirement for cell segmentation. Motivated by self-supervision, we leverage unlabelled images of different microscopy databases to extract edge-based image features, which we propose as a new proxy task for training the deep neural network. Next to training for predicting image edges, we also assume a small number of labelled images for learning the segmentation task, as in semi-supervised learning. We evaluate our approach on the few-shot microscopy image cell segmentation benchmark by Dawoud *et al.* [5]. To the best of our knowledge, this is the first work on edge-based self-supervision for semi-supervised microscopy cell image few-shot segmentation.

2   Method

2.1   Problem Definition

We consider the collection of data sets $\mathcal{S} = \{\mathcal{S}_1, \mathcal{S}_2, \ldots, \mathcal{S}_{|\mathcal{S}|}\}$. Each data set $\mathcal{S}_m = \{\mathcal{S}_m^L, \mathcal{S}_m^U\}$ consists of the labelled subset of microscopy images $\mathcal{S}_m^L$ and the unlabelled image subset $\mathcal{S}_m^U$ respectively. Moreover, each dataset consists of different microscopy image type and cell segmentation task. The labelled subset is defined as $\mathcal{S}_m^L = \{(\mathbf{x}, \mathbf{y})_k\}_{k=1}^{|\mathcal{S}_m^L|}$, where $(\mathbf{x}, \mathbf{y})_k$ is a pair of the microscopy image $\mathbf{x}$ and pixel-level binary annotation $\mathbf{y}$. Moreover, the unlabelled subset $\mathcal{S}_m^U = \{(\mathbf{x})_k\}_{k=1}^{|\mathcal{S}_m^U|}$ contains a significant larger number of images such that $|\mathcal{S}_m^U| >> |\mathcal{S}_m^L|$.

Our objective is to learn a generic segmentation model $\hat{\mathbf{y}} = f(\mathbf{x}; \theta)$, represented by a deep neural network with parameters θ, by leveraging all information of $\mathcal{S}$. Afterwards, we aim to segment cells on the target data set $\mathcal{T}$ with the generic model. However, the microscopy images in $\mathcal{T}$ differ from $\mathcal{S}$ and thus we should adapt the segmentation model. This is a common situation in actual microscopy problems. For this reason, we assume access to a small annotated image set in the target set $\tilde{\mathcal{T}} \subset \mathcal{T}$, e.g. 5 images, which we can use for fine-tuning our model. Under this definition, we target a semi-supervised few-shot microscopy image cell segmentation problem with a self-supervised learning algorithm. Next, we present our approach to a generic segmentation model with edge-based self-supervision and a small number of annotated images.

2.2 Learning Algorithm

Edge extraction is a well-suited task for microscopy images given the shape and form of the cells. We propose an edge-based objective function for the unlabelled subset $\mathcal{S}_m^U$. To that end, we employ the Canny-edge detector [6] to create an edge map for each unlabelled microscopy image. The updated subset $\mathcal{S}_m^U = \{(\mathbf{x}, \mathbf{y}_e)_k\}_{k=1}^{|\mathcal{S}_m^U|}$ now contains a binary edge map $\mathbf{y}_e$ for each microscopy image $\mathbf{x}$, which acts as a proxy task to learn the model parameters. In practice, we observed that it is not meaningful to completely rely on the same model for cell segmentation and edge prediction. For this reason, we decompose the segmentation model $f(\cdot)$ into the encoder and decoder parts, which are parametrized by θ_{en} and θ_{de}, where $\theta = \{\theta_{en}, \theta_{de}\}$. Then, we design a second encoder-decoder model for edge prediction that shares the same encoder with the cell segmentation model. To train the edge prediction deep neural network, i.e. $\theta' = \{\theta_{en}, \theta'_{de}\}$, we define the self-supervised objective as following:

$$\mathcal{L}_{SS}(\theta_{en}, \theta'_{de}, \mathcal{S}^U) = -\frac{1}{|\mathcal{S}^U|} \sum_{\mathcal{S}_m^U \in \mathcal{S}^U} \sum_{(\mathbf{x}, \mathbf{y}_e) \in \mathcal{S}_m^U} \sum_{\omega \in \Omega} [\mathbf{w}(\omega)\mathbf{y}_e(\omega) \log(\hat{\mathbf{y}}_e(\omega)) + (1 - \mathbf{y}_e(\omega)) \log(1 - \hat{\mathbf{y}}_e(\omega))], \tag{1}$$

where $\mathcal{S}^U = \{\mathcal{S}_1^U, \mathcal{S}_2^U, \ldots, \mathcal{S}_{|\mathcal{S}^U|}^U\}$ corresponds to all unlabelled subsets, $\omega \in \Omega$ denotes the spatial pixel position in the image lattice Ω and $\hat{\mathbf{y}}_e(\omega)$ represents the output of edge prediction model at the pixel location (ω). The proposed objective is a pixel-wise binary-cross entropy scaled by foreground weighting factor $\mathbf{w}(\omega)$, which equals to the ratio of background to foreground classes in $\mathbf{y}_e$. Note that it is important to use the weighting factor because of the imbalanced foreground to background ratio in the data sets.

Apart from the unlabelled data, we also use the labelled microscopy images of each data set, which we group as $\mathcal{S}^L = \{\mathcal{S}_1^L, \mathcal{S}_2^L, \ldots, \mathcal{S}_{|\mathcal{S}^L|}^L\}$. Similarly to Eq. 1, we define the objective as the weighted binary cross entropy, given by:

$$\mathcal{L}_S(\theta_{en}, \theta_{de}, \mathcal{S}^L) = -\frac{1}{|\mathcal{S}^L|} \sum_{\mathcal{S}_m^L \in \mathcal{S}^L} \sum_{(\mathbf{x}, \mathbf{y}) \in \mathcal{S}_m^L} \sum_{\omega \in \Omega} [\mathbf{w}(\omega)\mathbf{y}(\omega) \log(\hat{\mathbf{y}}(\omega)) + (1 - \mathbf{y}(\omega)) \log(1 - \hat{\mathbf{y}}(\omega))], \tag{2}$$

where $\hat{\mathbf{y}}(\omega)$ is the output of the segmentation model at the pixel location ω, while the weighing scheme is identical to Eq. 1. Finally, the parameters of segmentation and edge prediction models are jointly learned based on Eq. 2 and Eq. 1. Our complete objective is described by:

$$\arg\min_{\theta_{en},\theta_{de},\theta'_{en}} [\mathcal{L}_{SS}(\theta_{en},\theta'_{de},\mathcal{S}^U) + \mathcal{L}_S(\theta_{en},\theta_{de},\mathcal{S}^L)], \qquad (3)$$

where the minimization is accomplished with backpropagation and mini-batch stochastic gradient descent for the parameter update. Our learning algorithm is illustrated in Fig. 2.

We only keep the segmentation model after completing the joint learning. The last step of our approach is to fine-tune the segmentation model with the few annotated images i.e. K-shots from the target data set $\tilde{\mathcal{T}}$. This optimization is described as:

$$\theta^* = \arg\min_{\theta_{enc},\theta_{de}} [\mathcal{L}_S(\theta_{enc},\theta_{de},\tilde{\mathcal{T}})]. \qquad (4)$$

Finally, the fine-tuned model with the updated parameters θ^* is evaluated on the target test set $\hat{\mathcal{T}} = \mathcal{T} \setminus \tilde{\mathcal{T}}$.

Implementation. We rely on the encoder-decoder model of the fully convolutional regression network (FCRN) from [20]. Additionally, we implement the loss functions for each mini-batch. We train with two Adam optimizers to update each decoder separately and apply the same model modifications and hyperparameters, as in [5].

3   Experiments

We perform our evaluation based on the protocol from [5]. In particular, we use the B5 and B39 data sets from the Broad Bioimage Benchmark Collection (BBBC) [12]. The former contains 1200 fluorescent synthetic stain cells images, while the latter contains 200 fluorescent synthetic stain cells. Second, we have ssTEM [8] and EM [14] data sets which contains 165 and 20 electron microscopy images respectively of mitochondria cells. At last, the TNBC data set consists of 50 histology images of breast biopsy [16].

We split each data set to 10% labelled and use the rest as unlabelled, similar to semi-supervision protocol in [18]. We study the effect of jointly learning the edge prediction and cell segmentation tasks on the overall segmentation performance after fine-tuning on the K-shots and testing on the test set of the target data set. To this end, we first train a fully-supervised model on 10% of $\mathcal{S}^L$, then we incrementally add 30%, 60%, and 100% from $\mathcal{S}^U$. We train for 50 epochs with batch size of 64 and Adam optimizer with 0.001 learning rate. We also compare our approach against entropy [10] and consistency regularization [11]. Furthermore, we compare our approach of edge-detection as self-supervised task against the self-supervised contrastive learning (SimCLR) [1] and rotation prediction [9]. We adapt SimCLR and rotation prediction approaches to the microscopy image domain by pre-training the encoder on all the images in $\mathcal{S}^U$. For SimCLR, we pre-train the encoder using the contrastive loss for 200 epochs with a batch size of 1024, an Adam optimizer with 0.003 learning rate and cosine annealing scheduler. As for rotation prediction we pre-train the encoder to classify the rotation degree i.e. images which are rotated with either $0°$, $90°$, $180°$, or $270°$. Moreover, we train for 50 epochs with a batch size of 64 and an SGD optimizer with 0.1 learning rate. Afterwards, a decoder is trained on top of the pre-trained encoders from SimCLR and rotation on the cell segmentation task using $\mathcal{S}^L$. Finally, all the pre-trained models are fine-tuned on $\tilde{\mathcal{T}}$ and tested on $\hat{\mathcal{T}}$. The mean intersection over union (IoU) is computed over 10 random selections of 1-, 3-, 5-, 7-, 10-shots.

3.1 Results and Discussion

Table 1. Mean intersection over union (IoU) results for each target dataset using our edge-based learning (*Ours*), consistency [11] and entropy [10] semi-supervised approaches. Also, we show results of SimCLR [1], rotation [9], and supervised learning [5].

Target: TNBC						
Setting	Method	1-shot	3-shot	5-shot	7-shot	10-shot
100% $\mathcal{S}^L$	Supervised	31.4 ± 8.2	42.4 ± 2.4	44.7 ± 2.4	45.9 ± 2.4	48.5 ± 1.3
100% $\mathcal{S}^U$	SimCLR	35.8 ± 3.7	40.2 ± 2.9	42.3 ± 1.9	42.6 ± 2.4	45.9 ± 1.7
	Rotation	37.0 ± 3.0	41.4 ± 2.7	43.9 ± 1.8	44.4 ± 2.6	48.3 ± 1.5
10% $\mathcal{S}^L$	Supervised	34.9 ± 2.9	39.3 ± 2.8	41.0 ± 2.0	40.9 ± 2.5	44.0 ± 1.8
+30% $\mathcal{S}^U$	Entropy	37.1 ± 3.9	41.4 ± 2.4	44.8 ± 1.9	45.6 ± 2.2	49.0 ± 1.6
	Consistency	37.2 ± 6.5	42.0 ± 2.1	45.5 ± 1.8	46.4 ± 2.5	49.1 ± 1.7
	Ours	38.6 ± 4.8	43.5 ± 2.6	46.7 ± 2.3	47.1 ± 2.5	49.5 ± 1.2
+60% $\mathcal{S}^U$	Entropy	37.2 ± 6.5	42.0 ± 2.1	45.5 ± 1.8	46.4 ± 2.5	49.1 ± 1.7
	Consistency	28.3 ± 5.0	39.6 ± 2.6	42.8 ± 2.1	43.9 ± 3.0	47.6 ± 2.0
	Ours	37.8 ± 6.8	43.3 ± 2.4	46.9 ± 1.7	47.1 ± 2.4	50.3 ± 1.3
+100% $\mathcal{S}^U$	Entropy	39.2 ± 5.4	42.7 ± 1.7	45.0 ± 1.7	45.9 ± 2.4	48.7 ± 1.3
	Consistency	36.9 ± 6.3	41.9 ± 2.2	44.5 ± 1.6	45.7 ± 2.8	48.2 ± 1.7
	Ours	37.9 ± 8.5	43.1 ± 2.0	46.1 ± 1.7	46.4 ± 2.1	49.1 ± 1.2

(*continued*)

Table 1. (*continued*)

Target: EM

Setting	Method	1-shot	3-shot	5-shot	7-shot	10-shot
100% $\mathcal{S}^L$	Supervised	48.6±3.0	55.6±2.3	58.7±1.6	60.9±1.6	63.7±2.3
100% $\mathcal{S}^U$	SimCLR	44.0±3.3	57.8±3.3	64.1±3.5	46.3±1.8	51.0±1.3
	Rotation	40.5±2.1	54.8±2.4	60.6±2.8	62.6±1.7	64.7±3.1
10% $\mathcal{S}^L$	Supervised	31.5±1.3	44.9±2.1	50.2±2.0	65.0±2.6	66.0±2.7
+30% $\mathcal{S}^U$	Entropy	42.3±2.4	57.1±3.0	60.9±3.0	63.3±2.0	65.6±3.1
	Consistency	33.8±1.1	52.6±2.6	58.9±2.7	62.3±1.7	64.4±2.8
	Ours	47.8±2.3	59.9±2.0	63.0±1.8	65.0±2.6	66.7±2.4
+60% $\mathcal{S}^U$	Entropy	45.1±2.6	58.3±3.3	61.3±2.7	64.5±3.3	66.2±3.3
	Consistency	38.5±1.6	54.9±3.1	61.3±2.4	63.3±2.9	66.3±2.8
	Ours	44.5±2.5	59.3±2.3	63.0±1.6	64.6±2.8	66.0±2.7
+100% $\mathcal{S}^U$	Entropy	43.8±2.2	57.2±2.6	61.3±2.8	64.8±2.5	66.3±2.7
	Consistency	44.5±1.7	58.0±3.6	61.9±2.7	65.2±2.6	66.3±3.3
	Ours	43.5±2.5	59.2±2.0	62.7±2.3	66.0±3.4	68.0±1.8

Target: ssTEM

Setting	Method	1-shot	3-shot	5-shot	7-shot	10-shot
100% $\mathcal{S}^L$	Supervised	44.3±3.2	58.7±9.9	60.8±2.0	62.1±2.4	63.7±2.3
100% $\mathcal{S}^U$	SimCLR	30.3±1.3	49.5±7.1	51.7±1.9	55.1±1.8	55.2±2.4
	Rotation	32.3±1.8	52.3±2.5	57.4±2.2	59.9±1.8	60.5±1.8
10% $\mathcal{S}^L$	Supervised	25.7±1.1	45.5±6.5	48.5±1.5	52.1±1.4	52.5±1.9
+30% $\mathcal{S}^U$	Entropy	42.6±3.5	57.3±2.8	61.5±2.4	63.6±2.3	64.0±2.7
	Consistency	32.0±2.1	52.7±2.7	57.8±2.6	59.7±2.4	60.5±2.1
	Ours	46.3±2.8	61.7±9.5	63.5±2.3	65.2±2.5	66.6±2.3
+60% $\mathcal{S}^U$	Entropy	43.3±3.4	58.0±3.3	63.0±2.9	64.6±2.2	65.7±3.1
	Consistency	34.2±2.6	54.5±2.8	59.9±2.6	61.4±2.5	62.2±3.1
	Ours	46.5±3.0	61.3±8.6	63.2±1.9	64.9±2.0	66.5±1.5
+100% $\mathcal{S}^U$	Entropy	46.5±2.8	57.6±2.6	63.0±2.6	64.1±2.9	66.0±2.6
	Consistency	43.8±3.4	58.2±2.9	63.1±2.4	64.5±2.9	66.0±2.5
	Ours	42.1±2.7	58.6±9.4	61.0±2.0	63.1±2.4	64.7±2.0

In Fig. 3a, b, c, d and e, we show the mean IoU of our approach for different percentage of unlabelled and labelled data averaged over all data sets for 1 to 10-shots. We compare our results with entropy [10] and consistency regularization [11]. Additionally, in Fig. 3e we compare the best result of our edge-detection task with the results from [5], which is a supervised model trained using 100% $\mathcal{S}^L$. Also, we compare to a supervised model train using 10% $\mathcal{S}^L$ as well as SimCLR [1] and rotation [9]. Moreover, we present mean IoU results in Table 1 for each

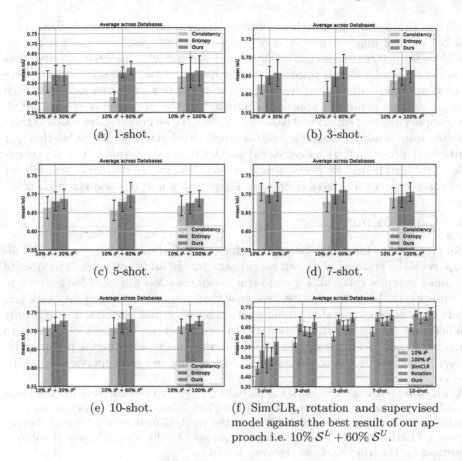

(a) 1-shot.

(b) 3-shot.

(c) 5-shot.

(d) 7-shot.

(e) 10-shot.

(f) SimCLR, rotation and supervised model against the best result of our approach i.e. $10\% \, \mathcal{S}^L + 60\% \, \mathcal{S}^U$.

Fig. 3. Mean intersection over union (IoU) comparison using all data sets. We show results of training on $10\% \, \mathcal{S}^L$ and $\{30\%, 60\%, 100\%\} \, \mathcal{S}^U$ with consistency, entropy and our edge-detection task (Ours). Results are reported for 1 to 10-shot learning. Moreover, we compare the best result of our approach i.e. $10\% \, \mathcal{S}^L + 60\% \, \mathcal{S}^U$ to SimCLR, rotation and fully-supervised models.

target dataset individually. Our visual results are illustrated in Fig. 1. Additional visual and numerical results could be viewed in supplementary material.

First, it is clear from Fig. 3a, b, c, d and e that training with our approach outperforms entropy and consistency regularization when fine-tuned to the target using few annotated samples. Second, we notice that the overall performance of our approach is further boosted by using 60% of $\mathcal{S}^U$ across all K-shot learning experiments. Nevertheless, the use of 100% $\mathcal{S}^U$ slightly drops the segmentation performance. We attribute this drop as an over-regularization case, where adding more unlabelled data for learning the proxy task negatively impacts the model's performance on the cell segmentation task. Next, it is clear from Fig. 3f that training a fully-supervised model only on 10% $\mathcal{S}^L$ results in poor performance relative to all other approaches. Furthermore, we notice that by utilizing 60% of $\mathcal{S}^U$ for learning our proposed edge-detection task jointly with 10% $\mathcal{S}^L$, we achieve far better results than a fully-supervised model. Finally, we observe that relying on SimCLR and rotation as self-supervised tasks lags behind our proposed approach. In Table 1, we observe mostly better performance across each target dataset using our approach compared to the proposed semi-supervised, self-supervised and supervised baselines. Although, we notice at few cases slightly better results using consistency and entropy regularization. We argue that our proposed proxy task is more related to the microscopy image cell segmentation problem, hence, we demonstrate an overall better performance suitable for microscopy image datasets of different image types and cell segmentation task.

4   Conclusion

We proposed to form edge-based maps for unlabelled microscopy images to self-supervise the training of a deep neural network. In addition, a small number of training samples containing ground-truth segmentation was used for learning to segment cells. In our evaluations, we show that training with our proxy task and only 10% of the annotated training sets achieves equal performance to a fully supervised approach, which dramatically reduces time and cost of experts to annotate cells in microscopy images. Moreover, we reach a better performance than the related works on semi-supervised learning and self-supervised learning.

Acknowledgments. This work was partially funded by Deutsche Forschungsgemeinschaft (DFG), Research Training Group GRK 2203: Micro- and nano-scale sensor technologies for the lung (PULMOSENS), and the Australian Research Council through grant FT190100525. G.C. acknowledges the support by the Alexander von Humboldt-Stiftung for the renewed research stay sponsorship.

References

1. Chen, T., Kornblith, S., Norouzi, M., Hinton, G.: A simple framework for contrastive learning of visual representations. In: International Conference on Machine Learning, pp. 1597–1607. PMLR (2020)
2. Cheplygina, V., de Bruijne, M., Pluim, J.P.: Not-so-supervised: a survey of semi-supervised, multi-instance, and transfer learning in medical image analysis. Med. Image Anal. **54**, 280–296 (2019)
3. Ciresan, D., Giusti, A., Gambardella, L., Schmidhuber, J.: Deep neural networks segment neuronal membranes in electron microscopy images. Adv. Neural. Inf. Process. Syst. **25**, 2843–2851 (2012)
4. Cui, W., et al.: Semi-supervised brain lesion segmentation with an adapted mean teacher model. In: Chung, A.C.S., Gee, J.C., Yushkevich, P.A., Bao, S. (eds.) IPMI 2019. LNCS, vol. 11492, pp. 554–565. Springer, Cham (2019). https://doi.org/10.1007/978-3-030-20351-1_43
5. Dawoud, Y., Hornauer, J., Carneiro, G., Belagiannis, V.: Few-shot microscopy image cell segmentation. In: Dong, Y., Ifrim, G., Mladenić, D., Saunders, C., Van Hoecke, S. (eds.) ECML PKDD 2020. LNCS (LNAI), vol. 12461, pp. 139–154. Springer, Cham (2021). https://doi.org/10.1007/978-3-030-67670-4_9

6. Ding, L., Goshtasby, A.: On the canny edge detector. Pattern Recogn. **34**(3), 721–725 (2001)
7. Ernst, K., et al.: Pharmacological cyclophilin inhibitors prevent intoxication of mammalian cells with bordetella pertussis toxin. Toxins **10**(5), 181 (2018)
8. Gerhard, S., Funke, J., Martel, J., Cardona, A., Fetter, R.: Segmented anisotropic ssTEM dataset of neural tissue. figshare (2013)
9. Gidaris, S., Singh, P., Komodakis, N.: Unsupervised representation learning by predicting image rotations. arXiv preprint arXiv:1803.07728 (2018)
10. Grandvalet, Y., Bengio, Y., et al.: Semi-supervised learning by entropy minimization. In: CAP, pp. 281–296 (2005)
11. Lee, H., Jeong, W.-K.: Scribble2Label: scribble-supervised cell segmentation via self-generating pseudo-labels with consistency. In: Martel, A.L., et al. (eds.) MICCAI 2020. LNCS, vol. 12261, pp. 14–23. Springer, Cham (2020). https://doi.org/10.1007/978-3-030-59710-8_2
12. Lehmussola, A., Ruusuvuori, P., Selinummi, J., Huttunen, H., Yli-Harja, O.: Computational framework for simulating fluorescence microscope images with cell populations. IEEE Trans. Med. Imaging **26**(7), 1010–1016 (2007)
13. Long, J., Shelhamer, E., Darrell, T.: Fully convolutional networks for semantic segmentation. In: Proceedings of the IEEE Conference on Computer Vision and Pattern Recognition, pp. 3431–3440 (2015)
14. Lucchi, A., Li, Y., Fua, P.: Learning for structured prediction using approximate subgradient descent with working sets. In: Proceedings of the IEEE Conference on Computer Vision and Pattern Recognition, pp. 1987–1994 (2013)
15. Markey, K., Asokanathan, C., Feavers, I.: Assays for determining pertussis toxin activity in acellular pertussis vaccines. Toxins **11**(7), 417 (2019)
16. Naylor, P., Laé, M., Reyal, F., Walter, T.: Segmentation of nuclei in histopathology images by deep regression of the distance map. IEEE Trans. Med. Imaging **38**(2), 448–459 (2018)
17. Noroozi, M., Favaro, P.: Unsupervised learning of visual representations by solving jigsaw puzzles. In: Leibe, B., Matas, J., Sebe, N., Welling, M. (eds.) ECCV 2016. LNCS, vol. 9910, pp. 69–84. Springer, Cham (2016). https://doi.org/10.1007/978-3-319-46466-4_5
18. Sohn, K., Zhang, Z., Li, C.L., Zhang, H., Lee, C.Y., Pfister, T.: A simple semi-supervised learning framework for object detection (2020)
19. Taleb, A., et al.: 3D self-supervised methods for medical imaging (2020)
20. Xie, W., Noble, J.A., Zisserman, A.: Microscopy cell counting and detection with fully convolutional regression networks. Comput. Methods Biomech. Biomed. Eng. Imaging Vis. **6**(3), 283–292 (2018)
21. Xing, F., Yang, L.: Robust nucleus/cell detection and segmentation in digital pathology and microscopy images: a comprehensive review. IEEE Rev. Biomed. Eng. **9**, 234–263 (2016)

Joint Denoising and Super-Resolution for Fluorescence Microscopy Using Weakly-Supervised Deep Learning

Colin S. C. Tsang[✉], Tony C. W. Mok, and Albert C. S. Chung

Department of Computer Science and Engineering, The Hong Kong University of Science and Technology, Kowloon, Hong Kong
{sctsangab,cwmokab,achung}@cse.ust.hk

Abstract. Recent studies have shown that joint denoising and super-resolution (JDSR) approach is capable of producing high-quality medical images. The training process requires noise-free ground truth or multiple noisy captures. However, these extra training datasets are often unavailable in fluorescence microscopy. This paper presents a new weakly-supervised method, in which different from other approaches, the JDSR model is trained with a single noisy capture alone. We further introduce a novel training framework to approximate the supervised JDSR approach. In this paper, we present both theoretical explanation and experimental analysis for our method validation. The proposed method can achieve an approximation accuracy of 98.11% compared to the supervised approach. The source code is available at https://github.com/colinsctsang/weakly_supervised_JDSR.

Keywords: Super-resolution · Denoising · Weakly-supervised

1 Introduction

Fluorescence microscope is an essential tool in biology and chemistry. It can visualize the biochemical processes on a molecular scale. Fluorescence microscopy images usually suffer from high noises. The noise source is typically a combination of Poisson noise from photon counting, thermal noise of the sensor, and background auto-fluorescence [2]. On the other hand, the diffraction limit limited the resolution of the image [2]. Some researchers use imaging techniques such as Structure Illumination Microscopy (SIM) [7] to obtain noise-free and high-resolution (HR) fluorescence microscopy images. Another approach is to use image processing techniques to generate a high-quality image from multiple captures [29]. However, these techniques generally require a long acquisition time and high illumination doses. It could damage or even kill cells under study because of the photo-toxicity increase in the sample [3].

Supplementary Information The online version contains supplementary material available at https://doi.org/10.1007/978-3-031-16961-8_4.

Studies have shown that the joint denoising and super-resolution (JDSR) approach outperforms the sequential application of denoiser and super-resolution model (SDSR) [18, 26, 29]. Nevertheless, the noise-free ground truth images or the multiple noisy captures are often unavailable in many fluorescence microscopy applications. Thus, it is desired to develop a weakly-supervised deep learning model to perform JDSR without these additional data. The main contributions of this work are listed as follows. We

- present, to the best of our knowledge, the first weakly-supervised JDSR model trained with a single noisy capture alone. It can generate high-quality fluorescence microscopy images with a lower risk of damaging the samples.
- provide a novel blind-spots training framework with both theoretical and experimental analyses.
- demonstrate that our approach is an accurate approximation (98.11% approximation accuracy) to other approaches that require extra training data.

2 Related Work

2.1 Supervised Deep Learning-Based Super-Resolution

Recent deep learning-based methods have shown outstanding super-resolution performances for natural [23] and medical images [15, 16, 21, 25]. However, most of these methods assume that the low-resolution (LR) input images are noise-free. Studies have shown that if the input images are noisy, it will significantly reduce the robustness of most super-resolution methods [4, 20]. Hence, it motivates the development of the JDSR approach instead of SDSR approach for fluorescence microscopy images.

2.2 Unsupervised Deep Learning-Based Denoising

Most deep learning-based denoising methods require noise-free training targets [1, 5, 24, 28] or multiple noisy captures [14]. Since acquiring these training targets for fluorescence microscopy is difficult or sometimes impossible, we aim to use an unsupervised approach for denoising. Xu et al. [27] presented a Deformed2Self model for dynamic medical image denoising. It requires multiple captures for training. Krull et al. [10] proposed an unsupervised deep learning model using blind-spots training for natural images, which is followed by some extensions in recent years [6, 9, 11, 13, 17]. Another unsupervised approach would be Neighbor2Neighbor [8]. This method uses downsampling to generate two sub-images to learn denoising in coarse space. It contradicts our JDSR task as we are seeking HR images.

2.3 Joint Denoising and Super-Resolution

Despite having promising results, the JDSR approach is relatively unexplored due to the absence of a suitable dataset. Xing et al. [26] presented a supervised model for joint demosaicing, denoising, and super-resolution for natural images.

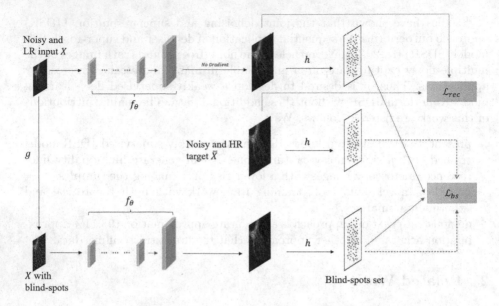

Fig. 1. The overall scheme of our proposed blind-spots training framework for JDSR.

For optical coherence tomography (OCT) images, Qiu *et al.* [18] proposed a weakly-supervised method trained with multiple noisy captures. For fluorescence microscopy images, Zhou *et al.* [29] employed the supervised approach to train a JDSR model with noise-free ground truth obtained by SIM. As we mentioned in Sect. 1, multiple captures or SIM images are often unavailable in practice. As a result, there is a strong need to develop a weakly-supervised method to perform JDSR with only a single noisy capture.

3 Methods

3.1 Joint Denoising and Super-Resolution with Multiple Noisy Captures

In this section, we revisit the idea of the N2NSR-OCT [18] model for JDSR on OCT images. Suppose we have a noise-free HR image $\bar{S}$ and two noisy HR observations, $\bar{X}$ and $\bar{Y}$. Let X and Y be the corresponding noisy LR image generated by some unknown downsampling method. Our goal is to recover $\bar{S}$ from X. We first consider the supervised training with training data $(X, \bar{S})$. We aim to optimize

$$\underset{\theta}{\text{argmin}} \, \| f_\theta(X), \bar{S} \|_2^2, \tag{1}$$

where f_θ is a JDSR model parameterized by θ. The training data is $(X, \bar{Y})$ when we are training the model with multiple noisy captures. The goal of training is to minimize

$$\underset{\theta}{\text{argmin}} \, \| f_\theta(X), \bar{Y} \|_2^2. \tag{2}$$

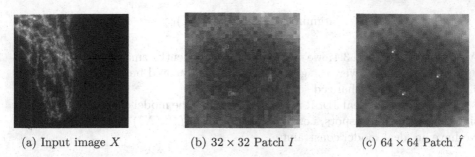

(a) Input image X (b) 32×32 Patch I (c) 64×64 Patch $\hat{I}$

Fig. 2. An illustration of our proposed blind-spots implementation with $N = 32$, $m = 3$, and $s = 2$. (a): a 32×32 patch I is randomly selected in the input image X. (b): $g(I)$. The blind-spots set consists of m pixels indicated in red color. We randomly select a neighboring pixel to replace each blind-spot. (c): The 64×64 patch $\hat{I}$ after upscaled by a factor of $s = 2$. The corresponding blind-spots set is indicated by four different colors. The function $h(\hat{I})$ output this blind-spots set while ignoring the rest of the image.

The ground truth image for $\bar{X}$ and $\bar{Y}$ is both $\bar{S}$ theoretically. In practice, there could be motion or lighting variation causing differences between multiple observations, especially when capturing living cells in fluorescence microscopy. Let $\varepsilon = \mathbb{E}_{\bar{X}|\bar{S}}(\bar{X}) - \mathbb{E}_{\bar{Y}|\bar{S}}(\bar{Y})$ denotes the gap between the underlying noise-free HR ground truth image of $\bar{X}$ and $\bar{Y}$. If ε is sufficiently small, then the N2NSR-OCT training in Eq. 2 is an accurate approximation for the supervised training in Eq. 1. Section 2.1 of [18] and Section 3.2 of [8] provide a comprehensive discussion of this approximation strategy with multiple noisy captures.

3.2 Joint Denoising and Super-Resolution with a Single Noisy Capture

Since repeat exposures are harmful to the cells under study, multiple captures are often unavailable in fluorescence microscopy. In this section, we present a novel blind-spots training framework to perform JDSR with a single noisy capture. Inspired by [8,10,14,27], we begin the derivation by approximating the N2NSR-OCT [18] training mentioned in Sect. 3.1.

Assume that we only have the noisy HR target $\bar{X}$ and the corresponding noisy LR image X. We propose a novel blind-spots implementation strategy specifically designed for the JDSR task. The procedure can be described by two functions: g and h. The function $g(I)$ selects some pixels in I to be blind-spots and modify them. The function $h(I)$ output the blind-spots while ignoring the rest of the image. The detailed implementation will be discussed in Sect. 3.3.

The key idea is that the training data $(y(X), \bar{X})$ is as good as the training data $(X, \bar{Y})$ in N2NSR-OCT, and hence a good approximation to the training data $(X, \bar{S})$ in supervised training. A straightforward way to train our JDSR model f_θ would be minimizing the difference of the altered pixels

$$\underset{\theta}{\text{argmin}} \ \|h(f_\theta(g(X))), h(\bar{X})\|_2^2. \tag{3}$$

As discussed in Sect. 3.1, we need ε to be sufficiently small to have a good approximation. However, the ground truth in Eq. 3 could be a relatively large ε since the function g changed some of the pixels.

We consider an ideal JDSR model f_θ^* such that the model can recover the true signal from the blind-spots, i.e., $f_\theta^*(X) = \bar{S}$ and $h(f_\theta^*(g(X)) = h(\bar{S})$. Therefore, we have an ideal model constraint

$$h(f_\theta^*(g(X))) - h(f_\theta^*(X)) = h(\bar{S}) - h(\bar{S}) = 0. \tag{4}$$

Since an ideal JDSR model should satisfy the constraint in Eq. 4, we proposed the following optimization problem to train our network

$$\underset{\theta}{\text{argmin}} \ \|h(f_\theta(g(X))), h(\bar{X})\|_2^2 + \alpha\|h(f_\theta(g(X))), h(f_\theta(X))\|_2^2 = 0, \tag{5}$$

where α is some positive constant. This constraint can be considered as an ideal model correction term such that the model output with original noisy LR image should be close to the model output with blind-spots. Figure 1 shows the overall scheme of our proposed blind-spots training framework for JDSR.

3.3 Blind-Spots Implementation

In this section, we discuss the implementation detail of our novel blind-spots training framework for JDSR. For the input image X, we randomly select an image patch $I \in \mathbb{R}^{N \times N}$. Our blind-spots set $\{I_p | p = 1, ..., m\}$ contains m pixels randomly selected in I by stratified sampling. For each I_p in the blind-spots set, we randomly select a surrounding pixel from a 3×3 square window to replace it. This modified image patch would be the output of the function $g(I)$ mentioned in Sect. 3.2.

Assume that we have an upscale factor s, then we have s^2 corresponding blind-spot pixels for each I_p in the HR output. The blind-spots set for HR output image patch $f_\theta(I) = \hat{I}$ is given by $\left\{\hat{I}_{p,q} | p = 1, ..., m, q = 1, ..., s^2\right\}$. This set of blind-spots pixels would be the output of the function $h(\hat{I})$ mentioned in Sect. 3.2. Figure 2 illustrated an example of $N = 32$, $m = 3$, and $s = 2$.

We use the loss function that we derived in Sect. 3.2 to train our JDSR model f_θ. We have

$$\mathcal{L} = \mathcal{L}_{bs} + \mathcal{L}_{rec}$$
$$= \|h(f_\theta(g(X))), h(\bar{X})\|_2^2 + \alpha\|h(f_\theta(g(X))), h(f_\theta(X))\|_2^2 + \beta\|f_\theta(X), \bar{X}\|_2^2, \tag{6}$$

where α and β are some control parameters, $\mathcal{L}_{bs}$ is the blind-spots loss presented in Eq. 5, and $\mathcal{L}_{rec}$ is the standard reconstruction loss for super-resolution. Note that $\mathcal{L}_{bs}$ is calculated on the blind-spots only while $\mathcal{L}_{rec}$ is calculated on all the pixels.

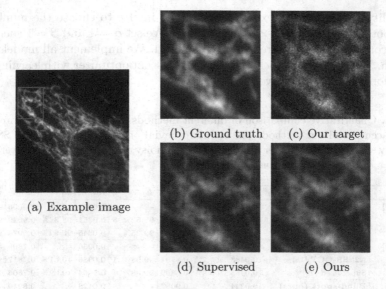

(a) Example image   (b) Ground truth   (c) Our target   (d) Supervised   (e) Ours

Fig. 3. Visualization results of U-Net with scale $s = 2$ and noise level $\eta = 1$. (a) is the example image and (b)–(e) are the zoom-in area of the red box. The supervised result (d) is trained by the noise-free ground truth image (b). Our result (e) is trained by the noisy target (c). Our method can give an accurate approximation to the supervised method without any access to (b). (Color figure online)

4   Experiments

Dataset. We evaluate our method with a publicly available dataset [29], which consists of 360 sets of fluorescence microscopy images. We randomly choose 240 sets as our training data and 120 sets as our testing data. There are 400 raw images of the same scene with resolution of 512×512 pixels in each set. For each set, we generate a single capture $\bar{X}$ by randomly selecting η raw images and taking the average. For the N2NSR-OCT method [18], we randomly select extra η images from the remaining raw images to generate another capture $\bar{Y}$. The noise-free ground truth image $\bar{S}$ is used only for evaluation purposes, which is generated by averaging all 400 raw images (i.e., $\eta = 400$).

Training Details. We follow the works presented in [10, 18] to choose a modified version of U-Net [19] with depth of 2 as our model architecture. An extra upscale layer is added at the end to perform super-resolution. We also test our method with LapSRN [12]. All models are re-trained with 100 epochs and scale $s = 2$ on GPU: NVIDIA GeForce RTX 3080 Ti with 12 GB memory and CPU: Intel Core i7-7700. For every training batches, we randomly select 30 patches from the training dataset with size of 128×128 pixels as our noisy HR training target. The noisy LR input patches are generated by bicubic downsampling. We augment the training data by randomly rotating it by $90°$, $180°$, $270°$ with equal probability. We follow the experimental result in [10] to choose the number of blind-spots to be N for a $N \times N$ input patch. We set $\alpha = 1$ and $\beta = 1$ such that all loss components are approximately balanced. We implement all models with PyTorch. We employ the stochastic gradient descent optimizer with learning rate 10^{-5}, momentum 0.9, and weight decay 10^{-5}.

Table 1. Quantitative comparison of different methods. Φ_1 and Φ_2 show the approximation accuracy of our method. The standard deviation for both RMSE and SSIM is negligibly small. The parameter η is the number of noisy observations used in averaging. A smaller η means a higher noise level.

Model f_θ	Method	η	RMSE	Φ_1	SSIM	Φ_2	η	RMSE	Φ_1	SSIM	Φ_2
U-Net [19]	**Blind-spots (ours)**		0.0282	-	0.9173	-		0.0357	-	0.9006	-
	N2NSR-OCT [18]	16	0.0273	96.81%	0.9217	99.52%	8	0.0351	98.32%	0.9049	99.52%
	Supervised [29]		0.0264	93.62%	0.9242	99.25%		0.0346	96.92%	0.9074	99.25%
U-Net [19]	**Blind-spots (ours)**		0.0482	-	0.8754	-		0.0966	-	0.7809	-
	N2NSR-OCT [18]	4	0.0483	100.2%	0.8791	99.58%	1	0.0986	102.1%	0.7817	99.90%
	Supervised [29]		0.0485	100.6%	0.8809	99.38%		0.1004	103.9%	0.7805	100.1%
LapSRN [12]	**Blind-spots (ours)**		0.0344	-	0.9087	-		0.0428	-	0.8910	-
	N2NSR-OCT [18]	16	0.0331	96.22%	0.9084	100.0%	8	0.0399	93.22%	0.8914	99.96%
	Supervised [29]		0.0329	95.64%	0.9096	99.90%		0.0402	93.93%	0.8924	99.84%
LapSRN [12]	**Blind-spots (ours)**		0.0563	-	0.8624	-		0.1069	-	0.7543	-
	N2NSR-OCT [18]	4	0.0518	92.01%	0.8650	99.70%	1	0.1005	94.01%	0.7656	98.52%
	Supervised [29]		0.0527	93.61%	0.8655	99.64%		0.1021	95.51%	0.7641	98.72%

Measurement. We use the standard assessment metrics root mean square error (RMSE) and structural similarity index (SSIM) [22] to measure the performances. As discussed in Sect. 3.2, we claim that our approach is a good approximation to the other two approaches while we do not need extra training data. We calculate the approximation accuracy Φ_1 and Φ_2 of our blind-spots method to other methods by the following formulas:

$$\Phi_1 = \frac{RMSE_{method}}{RMSE_{blind-spots}} \times 100\%, \text{ and } \Phi_2 = \frac{SSIM_{blind-spots}}{SSIM_{method}} \times 100\%. \quad (7)$$

Quantitative and Qualitative Analysis. We compare our novel blind-spots method for JDSR with two other approaches: *N2NSR-OCT* [18] and *Supervised* [29]. The N2NSR-OCT method and the supervised method are trained with the multiple captures and the ground truth images, respectively. In practice, it can be risky to obtain these extra training data because many cells are intolerant to multiple exposures. Our method reduces this risk by training with a single noisy capture while maintaining comparable performance.

We illustrate a visual comparison of our method and the supervised method in Fig. 3. The supervised method has a clean ground truth image as a training target. Although our training target is noisy, our method can still generate a result similar to the supervised method. The supplementary presents more figures for illustration.

Table 1 shows the approximation accuracy of our method compared to the N2NSR-OCT and the supervised method. The result demonstrates that our blind-spots method is a robust approximation to both methods. On average, our method achieves an approximation accuracy of 98.10% to the N2NSR-OCT method and 98.11% to the supervised method. As such, we can accomplish a similar performance even though we have no access to the multiple captures and the noise-free ground truth. On top of that, our method even outperforms other methods (i.e., $\Phi_i \geq 100\%$) for the U-Net model in some high noise levels. The N2NSR-OCT approach and the supervised approach do not have any specified component for denoising. At the same time, our blind-spots framework can provide a denoising effect. Thus, our framework is more consistent than other approaches in high noise levels. Lastly, results show that our proposed framework is compatible with different model architectures f_θ. In principle, any super-resolution model can apply our framework to fit a weakly-supervised JDSR task.

Ablation Study. Here, we conduct ablation studies on our proposed framework. Table 2 lists the results. Firstly, our method outperforms the SDSR approach, where the blind-spots denoiser [10] and the super-resolution model are applied sequentially. The performance drop in RMSE/SSIM is +127.4%/-9.052% in average. It demonstrates the necessity of a joint model instead of two separate models. Secondly, we test the performance of the control parameter α in Eq. 5. When we remove the ideal model correction term, i.e., $\alpha = 0$, a drop in performance can be observed. The performance drop in RMSE/SSIM is +63.60%/-5.313% in average. As α increases, the ideal model correction term improves the result. When α is too large, it dominates the loss, dropping the performance again.

Table 2. Ablation on SDSR vs JDSR and different weights. RMSE/SSIM results are evaluated on U-Net with different noise level η. The leading zeros are omitted for better readability.

	SDSR	JDSR	$\alpha = 0$	$\alpha = 1$	$\alpha = 8$	$\alpha = 20$
$\eta = 16$	.1024/.8176	.0282/.9173	.0707/.8553	.0282/.9173	.0283/.9171	.0416/.8938
$\eta = 8$	.0971/.8066	.0357/.9006	.0673/.8427	.0357/.9006	.0360/.9004	.0428/.8791
$\eta = 4$	.0903/.7914	.0482/.8754	.0646/.8251	.0482/.8754	.0485/.8751	.0481/.8578
$\eta = 1$	.0845/.7395	.0966/.7809	.0778/.7628	.0966/.7809	.0968/.7805	.0837/.7799

5   Conclusion

In summary, we have presented a novel blind-spots training framework for the JDSR task. It is the first weakly-supervised JDSR model trained with a single noisy capture. It will allow researchers to access high-quality fluorescence microscopy images without risking the sample cells under SIM or multiple exposures. We have demonstrated that our method is a robust approximation to the supervised approach across different noise levels. Our proposed method can be easily applied to different super-resolution models. We believe that our method's simplicity and general applicability will lead to widespread use in fluorescence microscopy, where multiple captures or noise-free data are often impossible to obtain.

References

1. Anwar, S., Barnes, N.: Real image denoising with feature attention. In: Proceedings of the IEEE Conference on Computer Vision and Pattern Recognition, pp. 3155–3164 (2019)
2. Belthangady, C., Royer, L.A.: Applications, promises, and pitfalls of deep learning for fluorescence image reconstruction. Nat. Methods 16(12), 1215–1225 (2019)
3. Chakrova, N., Canton, A.S., Danelon, C., Stallinga, S., Rieger, B.: Adaptive illumination reduces photo-bleaching in structured illumination microscopy. Biomed. Opt. Express 7(10), 4263–4274 (2016)
4. Choi, J.H., Zhang, H., Kim, J.H., Hsieh, C.J., Lee, J.S.: Evaluating robustness of deep image super-resolution against adversarial attacks. In: Proceedings of the IEEE International Conference on Computer Vision, pp. 303–311 (2019)
5. El Helou, M., Süsstrunk, S.: Blind universal Bayesian image denoising with gaussian noise level learning. IEEE Trans. Image Process. 29, 4885–4897 (2020)
6. Goncharova, A.S., Honigmann, A., Jug, F., Krull, A.: Improving blind spot denoising for microscopy. In: Bartoli, A., Fusiello, A. (eds.) ECCV 2020. LNCS, vol. 12535, pp. 380–393. Springer, Cham (2020). https://doi.org/10.1007/978-3-030-66415-2_25
7. Gustafsson, M.G.: Surpassing the lateral resolution limit by a factor of two using structured illumination microscopy. J. Microsc. 198(2), 82–87 (2000)
8. Huang, T., Li, S., Jia, X., Lu, H., Liu, J.: Neighbor2Neighbor: self-supervised denoising from single noisy images. In: Proceedings of the IEEE Conference on Computer Vision and Pattern Recognition, pp. 14781–14790 (2021)
9. Khademi, W., Rao, S., Minnerath, C., Hagen, G., Ventura, J.: Self-supervised poisson-gaussian denoising. In: Proceedings of the IEEE/CVF Winter Conference on Applications of Computer Vision, pp. 2131–2139 (2021)
10. Krull, A., Buchholz, T., Jug, F.: Noise2Void: learning denoising from single noisy images. In: Proceedings of the IEEE Conference on Computer Vision and Pattern Recognition, pp. 2129–2137 (2019)
11. Krull, A., Vičar, T., Prakash, M., Lalit, M., Jug, F.: Probabilistic Noise2Void: unsupervised content-aware denoising. Front. Comput. Sci. 2, 5 (2020)
12. Lai, W.S., Huang, J.B., Ahuja, N., Yang, M.H.: Deep laplacian pyramid networks for fast and accurate super-resolution. In: Proceedings of the IEEE Conference on Computer Vision and Pattern Recognition, pp. 624–632 (2017)
13. Laine, S., Karras, T., Lehtinen, J., Aila, T.: High-quality self-supervised deep image denoising. In: Advances in Neural Information Processing Systems, vol. 32 (2019)
14. Lehtinen, J., et al.: Noise2Noise: learning image restoration without clean data. In: International Conference on Machine Learning, pp. 2965–2974 (2018)
15. Li, Y., Sixou, B., Peyrin, F.: A review of the deep learning methods for medical images super resolution problems. IRBM 42, 120–133 (2021)

16. Peng, C., Zhou, S.K., Chellappa, R.: DA-VSR: domain adaptable volumetric super-resolution for medical images. In: de Bruijne, M., et al. (eds.) MICCAI 2021. LNCS, vol. 12906, pp. 75–85. Springer, Cham (2021). https://doi.org/10.1007/978-3-030-87231-1_8

17. Prakash, M., Lalit, M., Tomancak, P., Krul, A., Jug, F.: Fully unsupervised probabilistic Noise2Void. In: IEEE 17th International Symposium on Biomedical Imaging, pp. 154–158 (2020)

18. Qiu, B., et al.: N2NSR-OCT: Simultaneous denoising and super-resolution in optical coherence tomography images using semisupervised deep learning. J. Biophotonics **14**(1), e202000282 (2021)

19. Ronneberger, O., Fischer, P., Brox, T.: U-Net: convolutional networks for biomedical image segmentation. In: Navab, N., Hornegger, J., Wells, W.M., Frangi, A.F. (eds.) MICCAI 2015. LNCS, vol. 9351, pp. 234–241. Springer, Cham (2015). https://doi.org/10.1007/978-3-319-24574-4_28

20. Shocher, A., Cohen, N., Irani, M.: "zero-shot" super-resolution using deep internal learning. In: Proceedings of the IEEE Conference on Computer Vision and Pattern Recognition, pp. 3118–3126 (2018)

21. Sui, Y., Afacan, O., Gholipour, A., Warfield, S.K.: MRI super-resolution through generative degradation learning. In: de Bruijne, M., et al. (eds.) MICCAI 2021. LNCS, vol. 12906, pp. 430–440. Springer, Cham (2021). https://doi.org/10.1007/978-3-030-87231-1_42

22. Wang, Z., Bovik, A.C., Sheikh, H.R., Simoncelli, E.P.: Image quality assessment: from error visibility to structural similarity. IEEE Trans. Image Process. **14**(4), 600–612 (2004)

23. Wang, Z., Chen, J., Hoi, S.: Deep learning for image super-resolution: a survey. IEEE Trans. Pattern Anal. Mach. Intell. **43**, 3365–3387 (2020)

24. Weigert, M., et al.: Content-aware image restoration: pushing the limits of fluorescence microscopy. Nat. Methods **15**(12), 1090–1097 (2018)

25. Wu, Q., et al.: IREM: high-resolution magnetic resonance image reconstruction via implicit neural representation. In: de Bruijne, M., et al. (eds.) MICCAI 2021. LNCS, vol. 12906, pp. 65–74. Springer, Cham (2021). https://doi.org/10.1007/978-3-030-87231-1_7

26. Xing, W., Egiazarian, K.: End-to-end learning for joint image demosaicing, denoising and super-resolution. In: Proceedings of the IEEE Conference on Computer Vision and Pattern Recognition, pp. 3507–3516 (2021)

27. Xu, J., Adalsteinsson, E.: Deformed2Self: self-supervised denoising for dynamic medical imaging. In: de Bruijne, M., et al. (eds.) MICCAI 2021. LNCS, vol. 12902, pp. 25–35. Springer, Cham (2021). https://doi.org/10.1007/978-3-030-87196-3_3

28. Zhang, K., Zuo, W., Chen, Y., Meng, D., Zhang, L.: Beyond a gaussian denoiser: residual learning of deep CNN for image denoising. IEEE Trans. Image Process. **26**(7), 3142–3155 (2017)

29. Zhou, R., El Helou, M., Sage, D., Laroche, T., Seitz, A., Süsstrunk, S.: W2S: microscopy data with joint denoising and super-resolution for widefield to SIM mapping. In: Bartoli, A., Fusiello, A. (eds.) ECCV 2020. LNCS, vol. 12535, pp. 474–491. Springer, Cham (2020). https://doi.org/10.1007/978-3-030-66415-2_31

MxIF Q-score: Biology-Informed Quality Assurance for Multiplexed Immunofluorescence Imaging

Shunxing Bao[1(✉)], Jia Li[3], Can Cui[2], Yucheng Tang[1], Ruining Deng[2],
Lucas W. Remedios[2], Ho Hin Lee[2], Sophie Chiron[4],
Nathan Heath Patterson[14,15], Ken S. Lau[4,10,13], Lori A. Coburn[5,6,8,9],
Keith T. Wilson[5,6,7,8,9], Joseph T. Roland[10], Bennett A. Landman[1,2,11,12],
Qi Liu[3,4], and Yuankai Huo[1,2]

[1] Department of Electrical and Computer Engineering, Vanderbilt University,
Nashville, TN, USA
shunxing.bao@vanderbilt.edu
[2] Department of Computer Science, Vanderbilt University, Nashville, TN, USA
[3] Department of Biostatistics, Vanderbilt University Medical Center,
Nashville, TN, USA
[4] Center for Quantitative Sciences, Vanderbilt University Medical Center,
Nashville, TN, USA
[5] Division of Gastroenterology, Hepatology, and Nutrition, Department of Medicine,
Vanderbilt University Medical Center, Nashville, TN, USA
[6] Vanderbilt Center for Mucosal Inflammation and Cancer, Nashville, TN, USA
[7] Program in Cancer Biology, Vanderbilt University School of Medicine,
Nashville, TN, USA
[8] Department of Pathology, Microbiology, and Immunology,
Vanderbilt University Medical Center, Nashville, TN, USA
[9] Veterans Affairs Tennessee Valley Healthcare System, Nashville, TN, USA
[10] Epithelial Biology Center, Vanderbilt University Medical Center,
Nashville, TN, USA
[11] Department of Biomedical Engineering, Vanderbilt University, Nashville, TN, USA
[12] Department of Radiology, Vanderbilt University Medical Center,
Nashville, TN, USA
[13] Department of Cell and Developmental Biology, Vanderbilt University School
of Medicine, Nashville, TN, USA
[14] Department of Biochemistry, Vanderbilt University, Nashville, TN, USA
[15] Mass Spectrometry Research Center, Vanderbilt University, Nashville, TN, USA

Abstract. Medical image processing and analysis on whole slide imaging (WSI) are notoriously difficult due to its giga-pixel high-resolution nature. Multiplex immunofluorescence (MxIF), a spatial single-cell level iterative imaging technique that collects dozens of WSIs on the same histological tissue, makes the data analysis an order of magnitude more complicated. The rigor of downstream single-cell analyses (e.g., cell type annotation) depends on the quality of the image processing (e.g., multi-WSI alignment and cell segmentation). Unfortunately, the high-resolutional and high-dimensional nature of MxIF data prevent the researchers from performing comprehensive data curations manually, thus leads to misleading biological findings. In this paper, we propose a learning based MxIF quality score (MxIF Q-score) that integrates automatic image segmentation and single-cell clustering methods to conduct biology-informed MxIF image data curation. To the best of our knowledge, this is the first study to provide an automatic quality assurance score of MxIF image alignment and segmentation from an automatic and biological knowledge-informed standpoint. The proposed method was validated on 245 MxIF image regions of interest (ROIs) from 49 WSIs and achieved 0.99 recall and 0.86 precision when compared with manual visual check on spatial alignment validation. We present extensive experimental results to show the efficacy of the Q-score system. We conclude that a biological knowledge driven scoring framework is a promising direction of assessing the complicated MxIF data.

Keywords: MxIF · Data curation · scRNA-seq · Quality assurance

1 Introduction

Crohn's disease (CD), leads to chronic, relapsing and remitting bowel inflammation [3], with high prevalence [5]. To study such disease, we acquired formalin-fixed paraffin-embedded tissues from the terminal ileum (TI) and ascending colon (AC), followed by Multiplexed Immunofluorescence (MxIF) and imaging [2]. The MxIF provides a unique opportunity to understand cell composition, functional state, cell to cell mapping, cell distribution, and protein expression profiles as a function of the spatial and molecular information about the inflammation associated with CD.

MxIF performs iterative staining and imaging using dozens of protein markers on a whole slide tissue section to investigate spatial and single-cell level

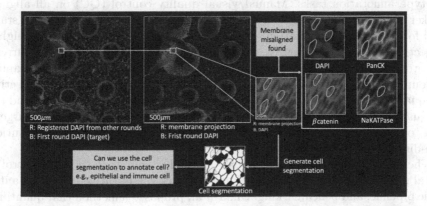

Fig. 1. Here, we present an extreme case that in micron level (500 μm), we can see two DAPI images co-register not well. The membrane projection are generated used β-catenin, panck, nakatpase images. After zooming in, we can observe a bow severe of the mis-alignment, which lead bias for a sample cell segmentation. Ideally, each marker images are supposed to be co-registered together. The yellow contour are manually annotated on the PanCK. (Color figure online)

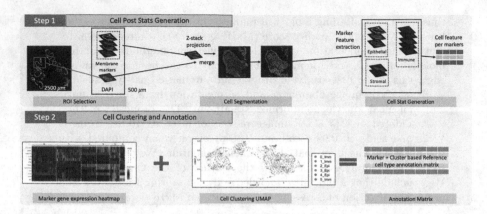

Fig. 2. The workflow of creating a reference data. Briefly, we do cell segmentation on a reference patch, and create a reference cell type matrix using marker gene expression and total number of target clusters (epithelial, stromal, immune). The reference matrix is then utilized by in-coming testing MxIF data for identifying cell type with an automated single cell annotation pipeline.

cellular types and function. Our MxIF acquisition pipeline starts with staining cell nuclei using DAPI for each round. All DAPI images were computationally co-registered, allowing each rounds of fluorescent images to be overlaid. The registered structural markers are projected and merged together to supply complimentary cellular structure information for the further cell segmentation tasks. However, the unprecedented information obtained via MxIF is accompanied by challenges for imaging due to the image alignment or registration, segmentation, and stains quality. These variabilities may introduce biases to downstream cell type annotation tasks. Manual/visual quality control (QC) on all aligned marker images and cell segmentation has been regarded as the *de facto* standard for MxIF dataset curation. However, such curation procedures are highly subjective and resource-intensive at the cellular level. Figure 1 shows the current QC process on a MxIF sample with selective structural markers. The manual contours were placed on β-catenin. Unfortunately, there is no existing objective and quantitative metrics to evaluate (1) the quality of spatial alignment, and (2) the quality of segmentation, beyond visual inspection. Thus, there is an urgent need to have automatic and quantitative metrics for the QC on high-resolution high-dimentionality MxIF data.

There are a few related research works focused on solving the quality control of digital pathology images in terms of image quality, quantitative metrics of automatic pipeline, and benchmarking. Dima et al. proposed a method that quantifies cell edge character and estimates how accurately a fluorescence microscopy images of cells segmentation algorithm would perform [6]. Yu et al. provided a measurement to detect or avoid cell cross-contamination for cell line annotation [17]. Feng et al. developed a method to assess quality of synthetic fluorescence microscopy images with quality metrics to assess fluorescence microscopy images synthesized by different methods [7]. Janowczyk et al. proposed HistoQC, to identify image artifacts and compute quantitative metrics describing visual attributes of WSIs to the Nephrotic Syndrome Study Network digital pathology repository [8]. Kose et al. introduced a quality assurance to assess the lesional area by using reflectance confocal microscopy images and coregistered dermoscopy images together [9]. However, none of the above works were trying to provide image processing quality control starting from the usefulness of the fluorescence images, specifically, the cell type annotation for the MxIF images.

In this paper, we propose a scoring framework, MxIF Q-score that integrates an automatic image segmentation pipeline and a single-cell clustering method to conduct MxIF image processing quality guidance. The contribution of this paper is three-fold:

1. An biological knowledge-informed metrics, MxIF Q-score, is proposed for an objective and automatic QC on high-resolution and high-dimensionality MxIF data.
2. Comprehensive experiments on different MxIF Q-score thresholds have been conducted that demonstrate the usefulness analysis of the MxIF Q-score framework.
3. To our knowledge, MxIF Q-score is the first quantitative and objective metrics to meet the emergent needs of curating MxIF data.

2   Methods

In the current workflow, we typically need to visually inspect cellular level overlays of dozens of markers. Such a quality check is accurate but unscalable. The proposed MxIF Q-score S_q aims to alleviate the currently resource-intensive QC process via biological knowledge informed single cell clustering.

2.1   Q-score for Spatial Alignment

The first step of Q-score is to inspect the quality of spatial alignment score $S_{spatial}$. We hypothesize that a coarse nuclei segmentation on DAPI channels can be served as reference standard because well aligned DAPI image should generate consistent nuclei segmentation overlay. Herein, we aim to use a Q-score spatial alignment $S_{spatial}$ to filter out stain samples with misalignment issues. We setup the Ilastik to automatically perform nuclei segmentation for each DAPI images. Then we compare each segmentation output to the first round DAPI segmentation mask using Dice similarity coefficient (DSC). If group-wise DSC is smaller than selective DSC threshold T_{DSC}, then $S_{spatial}$ is set as true.

2.2   Making Reference Data for Q-score Cell Clustering

Broadly, we can use MxIF marker images to classify the WSI into epithelial, stromal, and immune compartments. A more detailed cell type can be defined as fibroblasts, proliferating, stem goblet, endocrine, leukocyte, myeloid, monocytic and lymphocytic cell. For MxIF cell type annotation analysis, once the cell segmentation task is completed, a common practice is to extract cell image intensity features across all marker images, apply clustering method and run cell type annotation processing [4,14]. In this work, we hypothesize that if the quality of stains is acceptable, we could use nuclei segmentation to generate adequate features to classify cells into two broad groups: epithelial and stromal/immune. Thus, we first drive a cell type annotation for using a reference data, and then employ the reference data to drive the grading mechanism. If the stain is problematic, the cell clustering would fail to map to the reference data without any cell type being assigned, which is the key design criteria for Q-score on cell clustering. The full workflow to make a reference data is illustrated in Fig. 2.

Construct the Reference MxIF ROI. We found an epithelial region (500 μm), ran z-stack max projection on β–catenin, NaKATPase, PanCK, and Vimentin in the same ROI [12,13], and merged the stacked membrane images with the DAPI channel. We utilized the Ilastik random forest pixel classification model (the model was trained interactively by a domain expert using eight α-Actinin patches (at 50 μm) with partial manually traced labels)) to process the merged image and generate the membrane and nuclei segmentation masks [16]. Next, we overlayed the nuclei segmentation masks of ten markers (epithelial group: BetaCatenin, NaKATPase, PanCK; stromal group: Vimentin and SMA; immune group: CD3D, CD4, CD8, CD68 and CD11B) to build up nuclei-based mean intensity features.

Reference ROI Cell Clustering and Annotation. We modeled cell states as neighborhoods on a K-nearest neighbor (KNN) graph-based approach for clustering using $resolution = 0.3$, where cells are embedded in a graph structure, and then partitioned into highly connected communities. Then, we engaged scMRMA pipeline to map clusters to a collection of average marker gene expression features to determine cell types [10]. Let cell type t be a collection of N marker genes $(t_1, t_2, ...t_N)$. Then the average expression of gene t_i in the cluster c is defined as $v_{t_i,c}$. For a given cluster cell type t at cluster c, scMRMA calculates an cell type activity score $AS_{t,c}$ by 1 each cluster's cell type by

$$AS_{t,c} = \frac{\sum_N^{i=1} v_{t_i,c} * w_{t_i}}{N^r}, w_{t_i} = 1 + \sqrt{\frac{max(f) - f_{t_i}}{max(f) - min(f)}} \tag{1}$$

where r is a constant factor to adjust the score for the total number of markers in each cell type, w_{t_i} is the weights of marker t_i,

$$w_{t_i} = 1 + \sqrt{\frac{max(f) - f_{t_i}}{max(f) - min(f)}} \tag{2}$$

where f_{t_i} is the frequency of a marker t_i.

To train the reference annotation model, we empirically integrated nine makers (β-catenin as mentioned above) and yielded reference data into six such groups, three epithelium groups and three immune groups. One of the immune groups was empirically assigned as a stromal group due to lack of stromal signal in the reference ROI. The whole reference matrix is then applied log-normalization for further cell annotation. Finally, a seventh group would be marked as 'unassigned' by low expression other than six cell groups.

2.3   Q-score for Cell Clustering

For a given MxIF ROIs, we retrieve post stats from any cell or nuclei segmentation approaches and process marker feature matrix with same KNN clustering method. To annotate cell type, we applied a canonical automatic scRNA-seq annotation tool, singleR [1], to assign the cell type. A p-value is computed for cell/nuclei on each group, the cell/nuclei would fall on a specific group if $p - value < 0.05$. Otherwise the cell/nuclei would be marked as unassigned. The overall Q-score grading workflow for cell clustering $S_{cluster}$ is demonstrated in Fig. 3, which is biologically informed with multiple thresholds mainly based on (1) the popularity of local unassigned cells threshold T_L, (2) local unassigned cells threshold T_G and (3) cell types conflicts between epithelial cells and immune/stromal cells threshold T_C. The workflow contains a local *warning* number, which will be added by any of above three threshold conditions. By the end of workflow, if the *warning* is larger than the warning threshold T_w, then $S_{cluster}$ will be set as True. In summary, the overall binary Q-score S_Q is modeled as Eq. 3.

$$S_Q = S_{spatial}(T_{DSC}) \bigcap S_{cluster}(T_L, T_G, T_C, T_w) \qquad (3)$$

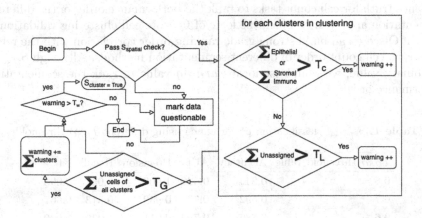

Fig. 3. The Q-score grading workflow for cell clustering is biological informed with multiple thresholds at local cluster level and global cluster level, basing on (1) the popularity of unassigned cells and (2) cell types conflicts between epithelial cells and immune/stromal cells.

3   Data and Experimental Setting

49 sample biopsies have been collected from 20 CD patients and 5 healthy controls across three batches of imaging, where 24 tissues are from the terminal ileum and 25 tissues are from the ascending colon (paired samples from each patient). The sites and disease spectrum that is employed in this study is so far the most representative MxIF study for gastrointestinal tract. The 49 slides have scores that range from normal, quiescent, mild, moderate, and severe, which are all from CD patients. The selective MxIF markers for MxIF Q-score were stained in the following order - DAPI(every round if following markers are included), CD45, CD11B, β-atenin, HLA-A, CD4, PanCK, CD3D, CD8, NaKATPase, CD68, Vimentin, ERBB2, and SMA with group-wise linear normalization. We computed the tissue masks that covered the tissue pixels that contained all markers across all staining rounds to ensure effective learning. Then, for experiment design purposes, and to ensure the generalizability of cell clustering, for each sample, we visually selected five ROIs with size of 500 μm that with obvious view of a group of epithelial, immune, and stromal cell groups when overlaying relevant markers images into different color channels. In summary, there are in total of 245 ROIs available to be graded by MxIF Q-score.

To validate Q-score spatial alignment $S_{spatial}$, we used the same segmentation model as defined in Sect. 2.2. We processed all rounds of DAPI images without merging any structural marker images. The goal is to get coarse nuclei segmentation to verify DAPI images overlapping, the effectiveness of cell separation is not considered. The manual alignment check of the registration is served as the ground truth.

To validate Q-score cell clustering $S_{cluster}$, due to lack of the cell membrane true labels, we take a step back, rather than validating the accuracy of individual segmentation pipelines, we aim to provide nuclei manual labels to serve as the reference truth for cell count tasks to rank the performance order of the different segmentation approaches. Then, the logic of Q-score cell clustering validation is to see if Q-score can build strong grade ranking order correlation with the reference truth cell count order of different segmentation methods. Although $S_{cluster}$ is a binary value, we would use local *warning* value to rank the segmentation performance order.

Table 1. $S_{spatial}$ classification performance using different T_{DSC} threshold

T_{DSC} threshold value	Accuracy	AUC	Precision	Recall	F1
0.8	0.245	0.526	1.000	0.051	0.098
0.7	0.592	0.706	0.952	0.513	0.667
0.6	0.886	0.794	0.911	0.949	0.930
0.5	0.861	0.675	0.858	0.990	0.919
0.4	0.820	0.567	0.818	0.995	0.898

For each 500 μm ROI patch, we reviewed DAPI image and searched easy nuclei annotation on epithelial region at the scale of 25 μm. Two researchers manually annotated the nuclei on separate sets of ROIs. If cell count was same, we used the DSC metric to rank the segmentation pipeline. We used the C-index score to verify the ranking competence matching performance [15]. Two nuclei segmentation pipelines were chosen to generate cell features, again, one was the model as described in section [15]. Another Ilastik based segmentation pipeline was chosen with more sophisticated morphological post-processing steps to reconstruct membrane lines and identify the cell separation [11]. We only used nuclei masks for the cell count and cell feature selection.

4 Results

Q-score spatial alignment classification results based on batch-based, group-based DSC value as shown in Table 1. When T_{DSC} is 0.5, the recall is 0.99 with precision 0.858. Figure 4 shows cellular level selective markers alignment using different Q-score threshold. The lowest batch based mean DSC threshold yields higher accuracy and F1 score across all 245 testing ROIs. We empirically set T_w equals from 1 (single cluster fail pass threshold) to 1/3 of total number of clusters. Then we separately tuned T_L, T_G, T_C and using three threshold together from setting threshold value from 0.05 to 0.2 with step of 0.01. All testing cases showed high C-Index = 1, which means the $S_{cluster}$'s *warning* levels can predict consistent ranking order match segmentation cell count rank. If we set T_{DSC} as 0.5, then there were 32 false positive samples that passed Q-Score $S_{spatial}$.

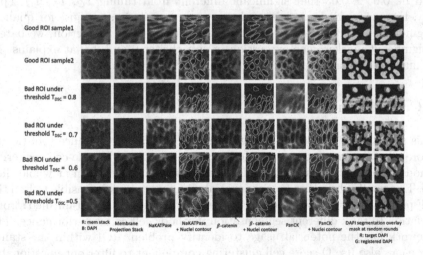

Fig. 4. The qualitative Q-score spatial alignment results that filtering good and bad ROI using different thresholds. The yellow contours are manual labeled nuclei boundary are overlayed that aims to assist to identify the cell boundary alignment qualify across three membrane markers. (Color figure online)

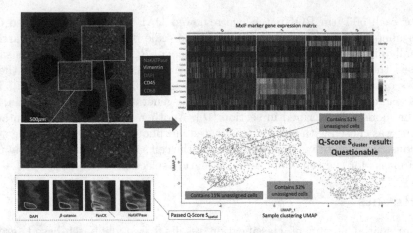

Fig. 5. A qualitative of cell clustering type result of a sample that Q-score $S_{spatial}$, but the Q-score $S_{cluster}$ marked the sample as questionable. The cell type annotation use the reference data, the marker gene expression matrix is shown as qualitative guidance for the potential issue of the ROI, either due to segmentation or stains, which needs to be further validated.

For Q-Score $S_{cluster}$, if ratio value is set as 0.05 to 0.2 and tuned T_C, T_L, T_G individually, the $S_{cluster}$ could filter those questionable registration samples guided by visual check, with average miss classification rate $(mean \pm SD)$: $T_C(0.19 \pm 0.14)$, $T_L(0.21 \pm 0.08)$, $T_G(0.58 \pm 0.23)$, respectively. If we assign the same ratio to T_C, T_L, T_G simultaneously, the average miss classification rate would be 0.05 ± 0.03 that significant different from tuning T_C, T_L, T_G separately. Figure 5 shows sample's marker gene expression matrix just for qualitative guidance about the accuracy of scoring. From visual inspection, we barely see significant marker gene expression in sub cluster 0 and 2 that explains the high number of unassigned cells.

5   Conclusion

In this paper, we propose a learning-based MxIF quality assurance tool (MxIF Q-score) that integrates automatic image segmentation and single-cell clustering methods to conduct biology-informed MxIF image data curation at whole slide scale. The results show that Q-score spatial alignment check is feasible to find the MxIF potential shift issues, and the Q-score cell clustering QC established strong correlation to rank different segmentation methods cell count performance. The framework has the potential usage to identify problem ROI within the stains, and we can also use Q-score cell clustering component to filter out questionable cells for further downstream analysis. Our next step is to provide a reference Q-score range and train a data driven learning model to train and test the scoring threshold and extract reference dataset in automatic manner.

Acknowledgements. This research was supported by the Leona M. and Harry B. Helmsley Charitable Trust grant G-1903-03793 and G-2103-05128, NSF CAREER 1452485, NSF 2040462, and in part using the resources of the Advanced Computing Center for Research and Education (ACCRE) at Vanderbilt University. This project was supported in part by the National Center for Research Resources, Grant UL1 RR024975-01, and is now at the National Center for Advancing Translational Sciences, Grant 2 UL1 TR000445-06, the National Institute of Diabetes and Digestive and Kidney Diseases, the Department of Veterans Affairs I01BX004366, and I01CX002171. The de-identified imaging dataset(s) used for the analysis described were obtained from ImageVU, a research resource supported by the VICTR CTSA award (ULTR000445 from NCATS/NIH), Vanderbilt University Medical Center institutional funding and Patient-Centered Outcomes Research Institute (PCORI; contract CDRN-1306-04869). This work is supported by NIH grant T32GM007347 and grant R01DK103831.

References

1. Aran, D., et al.: Reference-based analysis of lung single-cell sequencing reveals a transitional profibrotic macrophage. Nat. Immunol. **20**(2), 163–172 (2019)
2. Bao, S., et al.: A cross-platform informatics system for the gut cell atlas: integrating clinical, anatomical and histological data. In: Medical Imaging 2021: Imaging Informatics for Healthcare, Research, and Applications, vol. 11601, pp. 8–15. SPIE (2021)
3. Baumgart, D.C., Sandborn, W.J.: Crohn's disease. The Lancet **380**(9853), 1590–1605 (2012)
4. Berens, M.E., et al.: Multiscale, multimodal analysis of tumor heterogeneity in idh1 mutant vs wild-type diffuse gliomas. PLoS ONE **14**(12), e0219724 (2019)
5. Dahlhamer, J.M., Zammitti, E.P., Ward, B.W., Wheaton, A.G., Croft, J.B.: Prevalence of inflammatory bowel disease among adults aged ≥ 18 years-united states, 2015. Morb. Mortal. Wkly Rep. **65**(42), 1166–1169 (2016)
6. Dima, A.A., et al.: Comparison of segmentation algorithms for fluorescence microscopy images of cells. Cytometry A **79**(7), 545–559 (2011)
7. Feng, Y., Chai, X., Ba, Q., Yang, G.: Quality assessment of synthetic fluorescence microscopy images for image segmentation. In: 2019 IEEE International Conference on Image Processing (ICIP), pp. 814–818. IEEE (2019)
8. Janowczyk, A., Zuo, R., Gilmore, H., Feldman, M., Madabhushi, A.: HistoQC: an open-source quality control tool for digital pathology slides. JCO Clin. Cancer Inform. **3**, 1–7 (2019)
9. Kose, K., et al.: Utilizing machine learning for image quality assessment for reflectance confocal microscopy. J. Investig. Dermatol. **140**(6), 1214–1222 (2020)
10. Li, J., Sheng, Q., Shyr, Y., Liu, Q.: scMRMA: single cell multiresolution marker-based annotation. Nucleic Acids Res. **50**(2), e7–e7 (2022)
11. McKinley, E.T., et al.: Machine and deep learning single-cell segmentation and quantification of multi-dimensional tissue images. BioRxiv, p. 790162 (2019)
12. McKinley, E.T., et al.: MIRIAM: a machine and deep learning single-cell segmentation and quantification pipeline for multi-dimensional tissue images. Cytometry Part A (2022)
13. McKinley, E.T., et al.: Optimized multiplex immunofluorescence single-cell analysis reveals tuft cell heterogeneity. JCI Insight **2**(11) (2017)
14. Rashid, R., et al.: Highly multiplexed immunofluorescence images and single-cell data of immune markers in tonsil and lung cancer. Sci. Data **6**(1), 1–10 (2019)

15. Samplaski, M.K., Hernandez, A., Gill, I.S., Simmons, M.N.: C-index is associated with functional outcomes after laparoscopic partial nephrectomy. J. Urol. **184**(6), 2259–2263 (2010)
16. Sommer, C., Straehle, C., Koethe, U., Hamprecht, F.A.: Ilastik: interactive learning and segmentation toolkit. In: 2011 IEEE International Symposium on Biomedical Imaging: From Nano to Macro, pp. 230–233. IEEE (2011)
17. Yu, M., et al.: A resource for cell line authentication, annotation and quality control. Nature **520**(7547), 307–311 (2015)

A Pathologist-Informed Workflow
for Classification of Prostate Glands
in Histopathology

Alessandro Ferrero[1]([✉]), Beatrice Knudsen[2], Deepika Sirohi[2],
and Ross Whitaker[1]

[1] Scientific Computing and Imaging Institute, University of Utah,
72 S Central Campus Drive, Room 3750, Salt Lake City, UT 84112, USA
alessandro.ferrero@utah.edu, whitaker@cs.utah.edu
[2] University of Utah, 201 President Circle, Salt Lake City, UT 84112, USA
Beatrice.Knudsen@path.utah.edu, Deepika.Sirohi@hsc.utah.edu

Abstract. Pathologists diagnose and grade prostate cancer by examining tissue from needle biopsies on glass slides. The cancer's severity and risk of metastasis are determined by the Gleason grade, a score based on the organization and morphology of prostate cancer glands. For diagnostic work-up, pathologists first locate glands in the whole biopsy core, and—if they detect cancer—they assign a Gleason grade. This time-consuming process is subject to errors and significant inter-observer variability, despite strict diagnostic criteria. This paper proposes an automated workflow that follows pathologists' *modus operandi*, isolating and classifying multi-scale patches of individual glands in whole slide images (WSI) of biopsy tissues using distinct steps: (1) two fully convolutional networks segment epithelium versus stroma and gland boundaries, respectively; (2) a classifier network separates benign from cancer glands at high magnification; and (3) an additional classifier predicts the grade of each cancer gland at low magnification. Altogether, this process provides a gland-specific approach for prostate cancer grading that we compare against other machine-learning-based grading methods.

Keywords: Prostate cancer · Microscopy imaging · Segmentation · Classification

1 Introduction

Prostate cancer is the second most common cause of cancer death in men over 65 in the Unites States. A reliable diagnosis of prostate cancer can only be accomplished via a prostate needle biopsy. Pathologists examine the extracted tissue samples through a microscope and assign Gleason grades to cancerous regions as an indicator of cancer severity.

The main rationale for Gleason grading is to predict the risk of cancer progression and metastasis that informs treatment decisions. The Gleason grading

Y. Huo et al. (Eds.): MOVI 2022, LNCS 13578, pp. 53–62, 2022.
https://doi.org/10.1007/978-3-031-16961-8_6

system encompasses four grades: Gleason grades 2 and 3 are considered low grade and almost never lead to metastatic progression, while Gleason grades 4 and 5 are high grade and carry a risk of metastatic spread. Within the normal prostate tissue, cells organize in tube-like structures called glands. Pathologists use several morphological features to distinguish between cancerous and benign glands. Non-cancerous (i.e., benign) glands consist of basal and luminal cell layers that make up the wall of the tube. The inside of the tube is referred to as the lumen. In contrast, cancerous glands typically loose the basal cell layer, while cancer cell nuclei enlarge and display prominent nucleoli. In addition, the cancerous gland's luminal edge is straight compared to the undulated edge of benign glands.

While cancer diagnosis relies on the cells' organization and appearance, the Gleason grading scheme uses the growth pattern and structural complexity of glands to score the disease's severity. Cancerous glands with a single lumen are classified as low-grade cancer; glands within glands with multiple lumina, or glands that have lost the ability to form a lumen, are high-grade glands.

Building on deep learning successes in image classification and segmentation, researchers all over the world have turned to neural networks to develop Gleason grading algorithms. Fully convolutional networks [16], in particular, have proven useful in a variety of medical image analysis settings. Typically, a network is trained to recognize and classify structures of interest in the input image, *producing pixel-wise probability maps*, one per class, with each pixel assigned to the class with the highest probability. For instance, Silva-Rodríguez et al. [21] show that segmenting tumor areas through a neural network achieves better results than traditional algorithms, such as [8] and [2]. The U-net [20] is a special form of convolutional-neural-network architecture designed for image segmentation, and many Gleason grading methods such as [3,13,18,19] rely on variants of the U-net to process patches of a whole slide image (WSI) in order to produce a pixel-wise Gleason grade classification. Avinash et al. [15] designed their *Carcino-net's* architecture to include a pyramid pooling module [11] that employs different size convolutional kernels. They show their algorithm's high accuracy on low resolution images that include large cancer areas. However, this approach does not explicitly account for the gland-level patterns that define the pathology, and, as we will show in later sections, Carcino-net may arrive at incorrect conclusions on the gland's grade, even after summarizing pixel-level classification results. Other studies employ region-based convolutional neural networks (RCNNs) [9,10] to first identify bounding boxes around areas of interest in a prostate biopsy, and then segment and classify the epithelium within the boxes. The method in [14] demonstrates that these RCNNs can identify gland clusters, but struggles when glands with different grades are packed within cancer regions.

This paper aims to accurately reproduce the pathologist's grading process, breaking the gland classification problem into three sequential tasks: the segmentation of single glands, the identification of malignant glands based on cellular structure, and the classification of glands into low- and high-grade cancer based on the complexity of glandular morphology. In particular, the cancer identification step employs a novel set-based neural network that processes large collections of image patches, summarizing the information into histograms, to distinguish between benign and cancer glands. This *Histogram-based (HB)* workflow provides high gland segmentation accuracy with limited training data. It also allows clinicians and engineers to examine the results at every step of the analysis process. A self-supervised strategy [1,5,22] utilizes nuclear-staining properties to allow better generalization.

2   Data

The *training dataset*, described in [14], encompasses more than 40,000 glands, roughly equally distributed among the three classes of interest. The 2,200 tiles, of 1200 × 1200 pixels, that contain the glands were extracted from whole slide images (WSI) at magnification 20X, with a pixel size of $0.5\,\mu m \times 0.5\,\mu m$. Several pathologists hand-annotated polygons and assigned a label to the gland outline, marking benign glands, and low-grade (GG3) or high-grade (GG4, GG5) cancer glands. The stroma (ST) between glands is considered background. Through the same process, 10,000 additional glands from the same forty-one patients were gathered and labeled to form the *Internal test set* (537 tiles in total). Annotations mostly corresponded to glands, but clusters of small glands were often included in one outline, making an accurate segmentation difficult to learn. Therefore, 6100 polygons from the training set were later refined to separate all glands.

Fully testing the performance of ML-based histology-analysis algorithms requires generalization to data from *unseen patients*. As such, we created the *External test set* by selecting 14800 glands from WSIs in The Cancer Genome Atlas Program (TCGA). Two pathologists labeled the images from eighteen patients, initially at low resolution to identify regions of different Gleason grades. The 546 tiles extracted from these polygons were annotated a second time at high resolution, balancing the amount of tiles coming from each class.

For data augmentation, we used random rotation, flipping, and additive noise. As in [17], color augmentation is performed through histogram matching using color palettes from TCGA and PANDA [4] datasets as target color ranges.

3   Methods

3.1   *HB*-Workflow

The paper's workflow consists of three sequential stages: gland segmentation, cancer gland detection, and cancer grading.

Gland Segmentation and Processing. The close proximity of glands within the stroma presents a challenge in separating individual glands. To improve the segmentation, we propose a process that (1) performs epithelium (vs. stroma) segmentation, (2) finds the boundary of glands, (3) identifies the gland lumen to

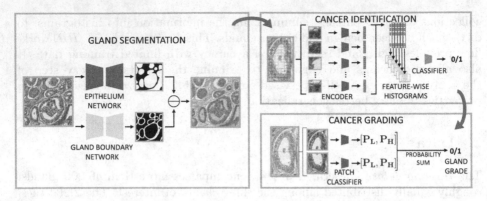

Fig. 1. *HB*-workflow. After segmentation, each gland is divided and processed in 32×32 pixel tiles by the cancer identification encoder. Features (n = 128) from each gland are placed into 128 histogram bins, which are used to classify between benign and cancerous glands. Next, 64×64 cancer gland pixel tiles are used to distinguish low- and high-grade cancer tiles (P_L, P_H). If a gland spans over multiple tiles, the sum of prediction results over all the tiles, normalized to the gland area, determines the gland's predicted grade.

form individual connected components, and (4) expands the connected components to the stromal boundaries to identify entire, distinct glands. Two identically structured U-net-like architectures perform the first two steps: one network recognizes the epithelium, and the second network finds boundaries around glands in input tiles. As shown by [6], short connections between layers increase the prediction accuracy when processing medical images; therefore we employ Resnet blocks [12] to capture relevant features. During the training phase, random 256×256 patches are extracted from the training tiles and the networks learn to minimize the cross-entropy loss between their predictions and the ground truth. The initial learning rate, set at 10^{-4}, decays every 10 epochs until the training stops at $2,000$ epochs. Pixel-wise subtraction of the epithelium and the gland boundary reveals the glands as individual, connected components. After removing small components, a region-growing algorithm ensures that gland instances include the entire epithelium.

Table 1. $mAP_{[0.5, 0.9]}$ on the gland segmentation

Internal test set	External test set (TCGA)
0.67 ± 0.02	0.77 ± 0.03

Cancer Gland Identification. Once the individual glands have been segmented, the next stage evaluates the fine-scale cell structure to separate benign and cancerous glands. Since glands may vary widely in size and shape, we design a neural network that accepts sets of image patches from each gland, and outputs a probability of cancer for the entire gland. To construct an appropriate set for analysis, each gland component is divided into 32×32 overlapping patches, each containing only a few luminal cells that span the thickness of the epithelium between the stroma and the lumen. The network is designed to extract useful cell features from each patch and properly aggregate that information, regardless of the gland size, helping the classifier output a probability of cancer.

Table 2. Results for CANCER IDENTIFICATION.

Internal test set						
	Pixel-wise			Gland-wise		
	F1	Sensitivity	Specificity	F1	Sensitivity	Specificity
ST	0.95 ± 0.01	0.96 ± 0.01	0.92 ± 0.01	N/A	N/A	N/A
BN	0.89 ± 0.01	0.91 ± 0.02	0.97 ± 0.01	0.95 ± 0.01	0.95 ± 0.01	0.95 ± 0.02
CN	0.89 ± 0.01	0.86 ± 0.01	0.98 ± 0.01	0.96 ± 0.01	0.93 ± 0.02	0.99 ± 0.01
External test set						
	Pixel-wise			Gland-wise		
	F1	Sensitivity	Specificity	F1	Sensitivity	Specificity
ST	0.97 ± 0.01	0.94 ± 0.01	0.98 ± 0.01	N/A	N/A	N/A
BN	0.74 ± 0.04	0.80 ± 0.06	0.93 ± 0.03	0.76 ± 0.04	0.81 ± 0.03	0.89 ± 0.06
CN	0.89 ± 0.01	0.88 ± 0.04	0.94 ± 0.01	0.96 ± 0.01	0.88 ± 0.04	0.83 ± 0.06

Inspired by the SetGAN discriminator's design in [7], the proposed NN architecture includes three modules: (1) an encoder that processes patches individually and generates a 128-dimensional feature vector; (2) a surrogate histogram function that summarizes each feature along all patches from a gland into a histogram with k bins (obtaining one histogram per feature), and (3) fully connected layers that use the resulting 128 histograms to output the gland classification. In this work, k is set to 5: empirically, fewer that 5 bins lead to an insufficiently descriptive latent representation, while more than 5 bins do not provide much additional information. This architecture has two advantages over a CNN: while the aggregating histogram function provides a rich representation of the whole gland, regardless of its size, the permutation invariance peculiar to the design (i.e., the patch order does not affect the classification) allows the network to study small cell groups, regardless of their location within the gland.

Cancer Gland Grading. The final step consists of classifying cancer glands into high or low grades. An analysis of the morphology of the entire gland, including its lumen, is necessary for this task. The above approach, developed for cancer detection, is not expected to work for cancer grading, since the unordered collection of small patches does not capture the complex morphology of high-grade cancer glands. Furthermore, Ma et al. [18] show that analyzing glands at a lower magnification yields better results when assigning Gleason grades. In order to format each malignant gland from the previous stage into a more appropriate set of NN inputs, we reduce the magnification to 10X via a down sampling by a factor of 2 and then use 64 × 64 patches. A Resnet architecture learns to assign each cancer patch as high- and low-grade class. While most glands can be contained in a single patch, glands that span multiple patches are graded based on a majority vote.

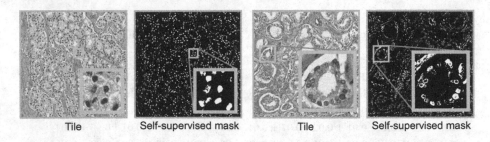

Tile   Self-supervised mask   Tile   Self-supervised mask

Fig. 2. Masks generated by thresholding the 10% darkest pixels.

3.2 Self-supervised Strategy

To further improve generalization, we employ a self-supervised strategy throughout the entire pipeline. When prostate tissue is stained with hematoxylin and eosin (H&E), cell nuclei acquire a purple/blue hue, usually the darkest color in prostate WSIs. The self-supervised task labels are obtained by thresholding the 10% darkest training tile pixels (see Fig. 2). The resulting mask highlights cell nuclei. All encoders train in association with a decoder that learns this coarse nuclear segmentation, encouraging encoders to learn nuclear features useful for segmenting and classifying glands. Altogether, our self-supervised approach is motivated by pathologist-defined diagnostic cues related to nuclear features.

4   Results

To quantitatively evaluate the model, the *HB*-workflow trained end-to-end ten times, using random validation sets of 2400 glands from the *External test set* and testing on the remaining samples. F1 scores, sensitivity and specificity are calculated per class (stroma - ST, benign - BN, low-grade - LG, high-grade - HG) to evaluate the pixel-wise and gland-wise performance. The *HB*-workflow's pixel-level data were generated using the gland-level classification labels. Gland-wise scores are obtained by majority vote of the corresponding pixels in the prediction mask, with the final score weight proportional to the gland's size.

Table 1 shows the mean average precision (mAP) between the manually segmented glands and the predicted glands. Although the *HB-workflow* tends to slightly oversegment glands (especially when the high-grade cancer consists of free cells), the mAP values are high. Experiments showed that gland oversegmentation is less detrimental to the final workflow's output than undersegmentation, where the binary classifiers tend to give class probabilities closer to 0.5

Table 3. F1 scores on the *Internal test set*, similar to the training set.

	Pixel-wise F1 scores			Gland-wise F1 scores		
Class	U-net	Carcino-net	3-stage	U-net	Carcino-net	3-stage
ST	0.92 ± 0.01	**0.95 ± 0.01**	0.95 ± 0.01	N/A	N/A	N/A
BN	0.84 ± 0.02	**0.93 ± 0.01**	0.89 ± 0.01	0.95 ± 0.01	**0.97 ± 0.01**	0.94 ± 0.01
LG	0.52 ± 0.02	**0.79 ± 0.01**	0.73 ± 0.01	0.71 ± 0.01	**0.91 ± 0.01**	0.86 ± 0.02
HG	0.68 ± 0.02	**0.89 ± 0.02**	0.86 ± 0.01	0.80 ± 0.01	**0.94 ± 0.01**	0.93 ± 0.01
	Pixel-wise Sensitivity			Gland-wise Sensitivity		
Class	U-net	Carcino-net	3-stage	U-net	Carcino-net	3-stage
ST	0.93 ± 0.01	**0.94 ± 0.01**	0.96 ± 0.01	N/A	N/A	N/A
BN	0.80 ± 0.02	**0.94 ± 0.01**	0.91 ± 0.01	0.94 ± 0.01	**0.97 ± 0.01**	0.95 ± 0.02
LG	0.81 ± 0.02	**0.76 ± 0.01**	0.75 ± 0.03	0.95 ± 0.01	**0.86 ± 0.01**	0.84 ± 0.02
HG	0.53 ± 0.02	**0.91 ± 0.01**	0.81 ± 0.02	0.67 ± 0.01	**0.96 ± 0.01**	0.90 ± 0.01
	Pixel-wise Specificity			Gland-wise Specificity		
ST	0.89 ± 0.01	**0.93 ± 0.01**	0.92 ± 0.01	N/A	N/A	N/A
BN	0.97 ± 0.01	**0.97 ± 0.01**	0.95 ± 0.02	0.98 ± 0.01	**0.98 ± 0.01**	0.95 ± 0.02
LG	0.90 ± 0.01	**0.98 ± 0.01**	0.97 ± 0.01	0.86 ± 0.01	**0.99 ± 0.01**	0.98 ± 0.01
HG	0.98 ± 0.01	**0.96 ± 0.01**	0.98 ± 0.01	0.99 ± 0.01	**0.98 ± 0.01**	0.98 ± 0.01

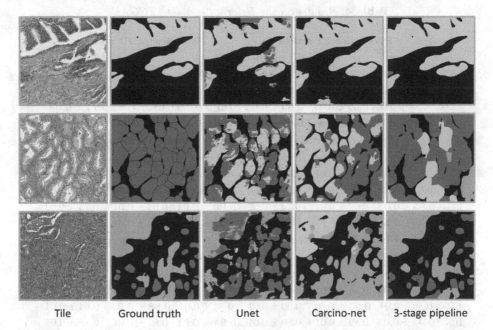

| Tile | Ground truth | Unet | Carcino-net | 3-stage pipeline |

Fig. 3. Classification results. H&E stained image tiles with manual ground truth labels are compared to U-net and Carcino-net pixel-level classification results and gland level classification from the *HB*-workflow (yellow - BN, red - LG, green - HG). (Color figure online)

when glands of different grades appear in the same segmented instance (i.e., the classifiers are less certain about their predictions and make more mistakes). The slight difference between the datasets' scores in Table 1 is mainly due to the gland conglomerates present in the *Internal test set*'s labels that decrease the mAP value. Despite this, the mAP values remain high.

Evaluations in Table 2 show that the cancer-identifying classifier distinguishes between benign and cancer glands with high accuracy, thanks to the rich representation provided by the learned histograms. Tables 3 and 4 compare U-net and Carcino-Net, trained as described in [15], to the *HB*-workflow.

Figure 3 confirms the high scores that the three architectures achieve in segmenting stroma. Panels displaying the U-net and Carcino-net pixel-level classification results demonstrate misclassified pixels within glands. These pixel labels are corrected by applying the majority voting scheme, resulting in a single label for each gland. The quantitative results in Tables 3 and 4 show that Carcino-Net performs better on the *Internal test set* (which is similar to the training data) than on the *External test set*, meaning that Carcino-Net is prone to overfitting. In contrast, the *HB*-workflow achieves higher F1 scores, pixel-wise and gland-wise, for all classes on the unseen data.

Table 4. Results on the *External test set (TCGA)*.

	Pixel-wise F1 scores			**Gland-wise F1 scores**		
Class	U-net	Carcino-net	*HB workflow*	U-net	Carcino-net	*HB workflow*
ST	0.89 ± 0.01	0.91 ± 0.01	$\mathbf{0.97 \pm 0.01}$	N/A	N/A	N/A
BN	0.58 ± 0.02	0.72 ± 0.11	$\mathbf{0.74 \pm 0.04}$	0.69 ± 0.05	0.74 ± 0.06	$\mathbf{0.76 \pm 0.04}$
LG	0.58 ± 0.04	0.66 ± 0.03	$\mathbf{0.69 \pm 0.03}$	0.67 ± 0.07	0.68 ± 0.08	$\mathbf{0.71 \pm 0.04}$
HG	0.39 ± 0.14	0.55 ± 0.06	$\mathbf{0.69 \pm 0.10}$	0.54 ± 0.18	0.68 ± 0.09	$\mathbf{0.72 \pm 0.01}$
	Pixel-wise Sensitivity			**Gland-wise Sensitivity**		
Class	U-net	Carcino-net	*HB workflow*	U-net	Carcino-net	*HB workflow*
ST	0.85 ± 0.01	0.87 ± 0.01	$\mathbf{0.94 \pm 0.01}$	N/A	N/A	N/A
BN	0.52 ± 0.02	$\mathbf{0.87 \pm 0.01}$	0.80 ± 0.06	0.55 ± 0.01	$\mathbf{0.88 \pm 0.01}$	0.81 ± 0.03
LG	$\mathbf{0.83 \pm 0.03}$	0.62 ± 0.01	0.73 ± 0.02	$\mathbf{0.90 \pm 0.01}$	0.64 ± 0.01	0.73 ± 0.02
HG	0.36 ± 0.14	0.58 ± 0.01	$\mathbf{0.65 \pm 0.04}$	0.41 ± 0.01	0.63 ± 0.01	$\mathbf{0.66 \pm 0.01}$
	Pixel-wise Specificity			**Gland-wise Specificity**		
Class	U-net	Carcino-net	*HB workflow*	U-net	Carcino-net	*HB workflow*
ST	0.93 ± 0.01	0.93 ± 0.01	$\mathbf{0.98 \pm 0.01}$	N/A	N/A	N/A
BN	$\mathbf{0.98 \pm 0.02}$	0.89 ± 0.01	0.93 ± 0.03	$\mathbf{0.98 \pm 0.01}$	0.86 ± 0.01	0.89 ± 0.06
LG	0.80 ± 0.04	$\mathbf{0.93 \pm 0.01}$	0.90 ± 0.01	0.53 ± 0.01	$\mathbf{0.88 \pm 0.01}$	0.84 ± 0.04
HG	$\mathbf{0.94 \pm 0.05}$	0.89 ± 0.01	0.89 ± 0.01	$\mathbf{0.94 \pm 0.01}$	0.86 ± 0.01	0.86 ± 0.06

5   Conclusions

Pathologists diagnose and grade prostate cancer glands based on vastly different morphological criteria. The *HB*-workflow presented in this paper mimics the pathologist's workflow by separating gland segmentation, cancer detection and cancer grading into three separate stages. The division of tasks allows each neural network to focus on the relevant features for the task at hand. In particular, the histogram aggregation function provides a permutation invariant way to process sets of small gland patches, allowing the cancer identification network to focus on the cell morphology. The *HB*-workflow shows higher quantitative and qualitative results per class than other state-of-the-art methods. Future work includes the training of this pipeline on larger, multi-cohort datasets, and its use for identifying high grade cancer regions to cost-effectively predict cancer stage and prognosis.

Acnowledgments. We acknowledge the generous support from the Department of Defense Prostate Cancer Program Population Science Award W81XWH-21-1-0725-. We also acknowledge that we received the training data from Cedars-Sinai Hospital in Los Angeles and we thank Dr. Akadiusz Gertych for his work on establishing the tiles. The results presented here are in part based upon data generated by the TCGA Research Network: https://www.cancer.gov/tcga.

References

1. Abbasi Koohpayegani, S., Tejankar, A., Pirsiavash, H.: Compress: self-supervised learning by compressing representations. In: Larochelle, H., Ranzato, M., Hadsell, R., Balcan, M.F., Lin, H. (eds.) Advances in Neural Information Processing Systems. vol. 33, pp. 12980–12992. Curran Associates, Inc. (2020). https://proceed ings.neurips.cc//paper/2020/file/975a1c8b9aee1c48d32e13ec30be7905-Paper.pdf
2. Avenel, C., Tolf, A., Dragomir, A., Carlbom, I.B.: Glandular segmentation of prostate cancer: an illustration of how the choice of histopathological stain is one key to success for computational pathology. Front. Bioeng. Biotechnol. **7**, 125 (2019). https://doi.org/10.3389/fbioe.2019.00125, https://www.frontiersin. org/article/10.3389/fbioe.2019.00125
3. Bulten, W., et al.: Epithelium segmentation using deep learning in H&E-stained prostate specimens with immunohistochemistry as reference standard. Sci. Rep. **9**, 864 (2019). https://doi.org/10.1038/s41598-018-37257-4
4. Bulten, W., et al.: The panda challenge: prostate cancer grade assessment using the Gleason grading system, March 2020. https://doi.org/10.5281/zenodo.3715938
5. Doersch, C., Zisserman, A.: Multi-task self-supervised visual learning. In: 2017 IEEE International Conference on Computer Vision (ICCV), pp. 2070–2079 (2017). https://doi.org/10.1109/ICCV.2017.226
6. Drozdzal, M., Vorontsov, E., Chartrand, G., Kadoury, S., Pal, C.: The importance of skip connections in biomedical image segmentation, August 2016. https://doi. org/10.1007/978-3-319-46976-8_19
7. Ferrero, A., Elhabian, S., Whitaker, R.: SetGANs: enforcing distributional accuracy in generative adversarial networks, June 2019

8. Gavrilovic, M., et al.: Blind color decomposition of histological images. IEEE Trans. Med. Imaging **32**(6), 983–994 (2013). https://doi.org/10.1109/TMI.2013.2239655
9. Girshick, R.: Fast R-CNN. In: 2015 IEEE International Conference on Computer Vision (ICCV), pp. 1440–1448 (2015). https://doi.org/10.1109/ICCV.2015.169
10. He, K., Gkioxari, G., Dollar, P., Girshick, R.: Mask R-CNN. In: 2017 IEEE International Conference on Computer Vision (ICCV), pp. 2980–2988 (2017). https://doi.org/10.1109/ICCV.2017.322
11. He, K., Zhang, X., Ren, S., Sun, J.: Spatial pyramid pooling in deep convolutional networks for visual recognition. IEEE Trans. Pattern Anal. Mach. Intell. **37**(9), 1904–1916 (2015). https://doi.org/10.1109/TPAMI.2015.2389824
12. He, K., Zhang, X., Ren, S., Sun, J.: Deep residual learning for image recognition. In: 2016 IEEE Conference on Computer Vision and Pattern Recognition (CVPR), pp. 770–778 (2016). https://doi.org/10.1109/CVPR.2016.90
13. Li, J., Sarma, K., Ho, K.C., Gertych, A., Knudsen, B., Arnold, C.: A multi-scale u-net for semantic segmentation of histological images from radical prostatectomies. In: AMIA Annual Symposium Proceedings, pp. 1140–1148. AMIA Symposium 2017, April 2018
14. Li, W., et al.: Path R-CNN for prostate cancer diagnosis and Gleason grading of histological images. IEEE Trans. Med. Imaging **38**(4), 945–954 (2019). https://doi.org/10.1109/TMI.2018.2875868
15. Lokhande, A., Bonthu, S., Singhal, N.: Carcino-net: A deep learning framework for automated Gleason grading of prostate biopsies. In: 2020 42nd Annual International Conference of the IEEE Engineering in Medicine Biology Society (EMBC), pp. 1380–1383 (2020). https://doi.org/10.1109/EMBC44109.2020.9176235
16. Long, J., Shelhamer, E., Darrell, T.: Fully convolutional networks for semantic segmentation. In: The IEEE Conference on Computer Vision and Pattern Recognition (CVPR), June 2015
17. Ma, J.: Histogram matching augmentation for domain adaptation with application to multi-centre, multi-vendor and multi-disease cardiac image segmentation (2020)
18. Ma, Z., Li, J., Salemi, H., Arnold, C., Knudsen, B., Gertych, A., Ing, N.: Semantic segmentation for prostate cancer grading by convolutional neural networks, p. 46, March 2018. https://doi.org/10.1117/12.2293000
19. Nagpal, K., et al.: Development and validation of a deep learning algorithm for improving Gleason scoring of prostate cancer. NPJ Digital Med. **2**, 48 (2019). https://doi.org/10.1038/s41746-019-0112-2
20. Ronneberger, O., Fischer, P., Brox, T.: U-net: convolutional networks for biomedical image segmentation. In: Navab, N., Hornegger, J., Wells, W.M., Frangi, A.F. (eds.) MICCAI 2015. LNCS, vol. 9351, pp. 234–241. Springer, Cham (2015). https://doi.org/10.1007/978-3-319-24574-4_28
21. Silva-Rodríguez, J., Payá-Bosch, E., García, G., Colomer, A., Naranjo, V.: Prostate gland segmentation in histology images via residual and multi-resolution U-NET. In: Analide, C., Novais, P., Camacho, D., Yin, H. (eds.) IDEAL 2020. LNCS, vol. 12489, pp. 1–8. Springer, Cham (2020). https://doi.org/10.1007/978-3-030-62362-3_1
22. Zheng, X., Wang, Y., Wang, G., Liu, J.: Fast and robust segmentation of white blood cell images by self-supervised learning. Micron **107**, 55–71 (2018). https://doi.org/10.1016/j.micron.2018.01.010

Leukocyte Classification Using Multimodal Architecture Enhanced by Knowledge Distillation

Litao Yang[1]([✉]), Deval Mehta[1], Dwarikanath Mahapatra[2], and Zongyuan Ge[1]

[1] Monash Medical AI, Monash University, Melbourne, Australia
litao.yang@monash.edu
[2] Inception Institute of Artificial Intelligence, Abu Dhabi, UAE
https://www.monash.edu/mmai-group

Abstract. Recently, a lot of automated white blood cells (WBC) or leukocyte classification techniques have been developed. However, all of these methods only utilize a single modality microscopic image i.e. either blood smear or fluorescence based, thus missing the potential of a better learning from multimodal images. In this work, we develop an efficient multimodal architecture based on a first of its kind multimodal WBC dataset for the task of WBC classification. Specifically, our proposed idea is developed in two steps - 1) First, we learn modality specific independent subnetworks inside a single network only; 2) We further enhance the learning capability of the independent subnetworks by distilling knowledge from high complexity independent teacher networks. With this, our proposed framework can achieve a high performance while maintaining low complexity for a multimodal dataset. Our unique contribution is twofold - 1) We present a first of its kind multimodal WBC dataset for WBC classification; 2) We develop a high performing multimodal architecture which is also efficient and low in complexity at the same time.

Keywords: WBCs classification · Multimodal · Knowledge distillation

1 Introduction

A complete blood count (CBC) test is the foremost requirement for diagnosing any health-related condition of a person [19], which consists of the count of red blood cells (RBCs), white blood cells (WBCs) and platelets [9,18]. Of these, WBCs are responsible to defend body organs and heal any damage to the biological structures [2]. Thus, it is vital for doctors to know the count of WBCs amongst the different categories to diagnose any specific disease or underlying health condition. Recently, due to the advent of machine learning and deep learning, there have been a plethora of methods developed for automated detection and classification of WBCs [13]. Most of these methods are based on blood

Supplementary Information The online version contains supplementary material available at https://doi.org/10.1007/978-3-031-16961-8_7.

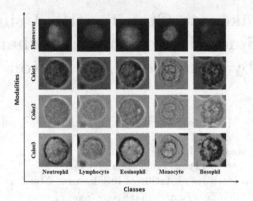

Fig. 1. WBC samples of our dataset which include four modalities and five classes

smear microscopic images which provide rich features about the morphology and structure of the cells but require manual preparation and staining of the slides by trained personnel [16]. More recently, the research community has developed image acquisition of cell images by mixing Acridine Orange (AO) dye with the blood samples and exposing them to different light source excitation yielding intense fluorescence like images [5]. The fluorescence based imaging is more efficient and can be integrated easily to some devices compared to the one based on blood smears [7]. Some fluorescence based imaging methods have also been developed for automated detection and classification of WBCs [5,20]. However, fluorescence based imaging suffers from phototoxicity and photobleaching, which makes the images less feature rich and the process of distinguishing between different cell types becomes more difficult as compared to the blood smear images [15]. Thus, we believe that multi-modal WBC images can be an effective solution for leveraging diverse features for making the models learn better and improve their classification performance [1]. To this end, we collect a unique WBC dataset with four light-sources - one from fluorescence and three from bright-field. Some samples from our dataset are shown in Fig. 1[1], where we represent the four modalities on the y-axis and the five WBC categories on the x-axis.

However, learning from a multi-modal dataset has its own challenges. One of the challenges is to devise a strategic fusion method that can leverage diverse features from the different modalities [1]. Based on the different possible locations of the fusion in an architecture, methods can be roughly divided into early and late fusion [6]. Early fusion [17] merges features from different modalities in the beginning and passes them to a single network to learn, whereas late fusion [17] employs separate networks for each modality and merges the features from each of them at the end. Both strategies have their pros and cons. While late fusion enables to increase the performance significantly by learning specific modality features using separate networks [8], it also increases the overall

---

[1] Please note that the colors of the images are for representation only and not the actual colors. The technical details of excitation lights and actual colours will be released once the disclosure has been filed.

framework complexity significantly. On the other hand, early fusion increases the framework complexity only slightly, however, it usually does not perform well as low-level fused features are not so effective for better learning by using a single network [14]. Apart from these two, there can be several different locations in the framework where fusion can be employed such as a halfway fusion [14] or middle fusion [4], but all these strategies will also have a trade-off between model complexity and performance.

In this work, for our multi-modal WBC dataset, we aim to address this trade-off of multimodal deep learning by developing low complexity networks which can achieve a higher performance. Specifically, we develop a framework for processing multimodal WBC images with tiny added cost of complexity compared with early fusion model while achieving an equivalent or even better performance than that of the late fusion strategy. We construct our framework in two steps (Fig. 3): First, we adapt the recently proposed Multi-input Multi-Output (MIMO) [11] architecture for our multi-modal dataset and develop a Multi-modal-MIMO (MM-MIMO) network for training modality specific independent subnetworks of a single deep learning network only. Second, on top of the MM-MIMO architecture, we further enhance its capability by employing knowledge distillation [12] to transfer the knowledge from late fusion strategy to MM-MIMO which helps to produce even better performance gains. We conduct extensive experiments to demonstrate the effectiveness of each part of our framework. To the best of our knowledge, we are the first to use a multi-modal dataset for WBC classification task, the first to adopt MIMO for multi-modal dataset, and the first to integrate knowledge distillation between different multimodal fusion methods. We believe our proposed idea can thus help to ease the trade-off between complexity and performance for multimodal datasets in general.

2   Method

2.1   Sample Preparation and Data Collection

We first collect blood samples from normal persons which are then exposed to the three different bright-field light sources and the resulting three different bright-field images are captured by a camera module. Then, we immediately stain the blood samples with Acridine Orange (AO) dye and expose them to another light source before collecting the resulting fluorescent images. Thus, we capture four different modal images of the blood samples (shown in Fig. 1), which are then given to two trained pathologist experts who then annotate and categorize the WBC cells images and build our multimodal WBC dataset.

2.2   Baseline Methods

For our multimodal dataset, we first train two baseline methods of early fusion and late fusion as shown in Fig. 2 (a) and (b). In early fusion, the four modal specific images from same WBC are concatenated in the channel dimension to

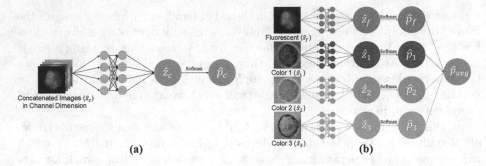

Fig. 2. Baseline fusion methods for our multimodal dataset (a): Early fusion; (b): Late fusion

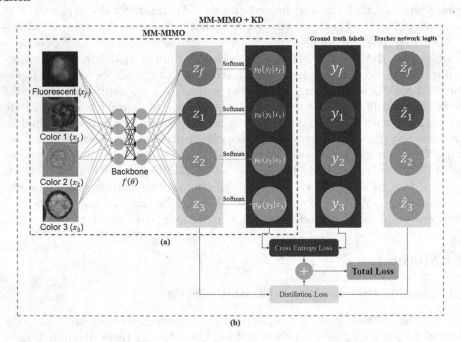

Fig. 3. The overview of our proposed framework. (a): Multi-modal Multi-input Multi-output Network architecture (MM-MIMO). We only use the cross entropy loss for training this part. (b): Multi-modal Knowledge Distillation (MM-MIMO + KD). We use combination of distillation loss and cross entropy loss for training this part.

$\widehat{x}_c$ which then passes through a single network to get the logits output $\widehat{z}_c$ and the probability prediction $\widehat{p}_c$. In late fusion, we train four single networks independently based on each modality then use the same WBC with four modalities as input during forward pass and average their probability prediction $\{\widehat{p}_f, \widehat{p}_1, \widehat{p}_2, \widehat{p}_3\}$ to get the final fusion prediction $\widehat{p}_{avg}$. All of the four single networks and early fusion are trained by using the standard cross entropy loss $\mathcal{L}_{CE}$.

2.3 Multi-modal Multi-input Multi-output Network (MM-MIMO)

Inspired by the sparse utilization of network parameters, a recently proposed architecture trained multiple subnetworks (MIMO) inside a single network for robust prediction of single modality datasets [11]. We believe that MIMO can thus be used to learn independent modality specific subnetworks and hence we adapt it to suit it for our multi-modal dataset and develop a Multi-modal MIMO (MM-MIMO). Figure 3 (a) shows the architecture of MM-MIMO. Our proposed architecture of MM-MIMO treats the independent subnetworks as the separate individual modalities networks similar to that of a late fusion and predicts the classification category in a similar way to that of late fusion. However, MM-MIMO itself only consists of a single network while late fusion strategy consists of N (N being 4 for our case) different separate networks thus having N times more complexity compared to MM-MIMO.

In the training process of MM-MIMO, the modal specific WBC images are concatenated in the channel dimension similar to that of early fusion. However, unlike early fusion, we randomly sample WBCs independently from the four modalities in MM-MIMO instead of using the same WBC as input. In other words, the input of MM-MIMO $\{x_f, x_1, x_2, x_3\}$ belong to different WBC categories and their four different corresponding WBC labels $\{y_f, y_1, y_2, y_3\}$ are used as the ground truth. The input data is then fed to a single backbone network $f(\theta)$ and corresponding four logit outputs $\{z_f, z_1, z_2, z_3\}$ are generated, which are then fed to a softmax layer to get the modal specific probability predictions $\{p_\theta(y_f|x_f), p_\theta(y_1|x_1), p_\theta(y_2|x_2), p_\theta(y_3|x_3)\}$. The overall loss L_M shown in Eq. 1 is the sum of the standard cross entropy loss $\mathcal{L}_{CE}$ for each of the four different modalities, which makes the whole network learn to classify the four different WBCs simultaneously and creating independent subnetworks within MM-MIMO. Since the input-output pairs are independent, the features derived from other modalities are not useful for predicting the corresponding modality output. During backpropagation, the corresponding subnetworks will learn to ignore the other modalities inputs and each output will consider and predict only the corresponding modality input. This way we get the independent subnetworks for each modality trained. During the testing phase, the four modality input images are from the same WBC category and the output predictions will be averaged to get the final prediction of that single WBC.

$$L_M = \sum_{i=f,1,2,3} \mathcal{L}_{CE}\left(y_i, p_\theta\left(y_i|x_i\right)\right) \tag{1}$$

2.4 Multi-modal Knowledge Distillation

Knowledge distillation (KD) has been widely used to transfer knowledge from teacher models to student models in order to improve the performance of student models [10]. Hinton et al. [12] first used the class probability derived from the teacher model as a soft label to guide the training of students. The teacher models are usually a high complexity network with higher performance than the compact student models. To further enhance the modality specific learning capability of MM-MIMO, we propose to utilize KD to transfer the knowledge from late fusion (acts as a high complexity teacher network) to MM-MIMO network (acts as a low complexity student network). Our inspiration comes from the idea that late fusion has separate powerful networks tailored to modality-specific features for the individual modalities, which have learnt the specific modality features better than those of low-complex individual subnetworks within MM-MIMO. We show the framework for training MM-MIMO with KD in Fig. 3 (b). Here our MM-MIMO model acts as the student network with logit outputs as $\{z_f, z_1, z_2, z_3\}$ which are to be guided from the teacher logit outputs $\{\widehat{z}_f, \widehat{z}_1, \widehat{z}_2, \widehat{z}_3\}$. These teacher logit outputs are produced from the four independent networks of the late fusion. During training, we enable independent subnetworks in MM-MIMO to learn from corresponding complex teachers in late fusion by employing KullbackLeibler divergence loss $\mathcal{L}_{KL}$ (given by Eq. 2) between the student and teacher logits.

$$L_{KD} = \sum_{i=f,1,2,3} \mathcal{L}_{KL}\left(p_s\left(\widehat{z}_i, T\right), p_s\left(z_i, T\right)\right) \tag{2}$$

where $p_s\left(z, T\right)$ are soft targets [12] which are the probabilities of inputs belonging to the classes and contain the informative dark knowledge from the model. They can be computed from the logits by a softmax function given by Eq. 3.

$$p_s\left(z_j, T\right) = \frac{\exp\left(z_j/T\right)}{\sum_k \exp\left(z_k/T\right)} \tag{3}$$

where z_j is the logit for the j-th class in logits z and T is the temperature hyperaparameter. The total loss L_T in multi-modal KD is the combination of distillation loss L_{KD} and cross entropy loss L_M in MM-MIMO, which is shown in Eq. 4. It is necessary to multiply distillation loss by T^2, since when producing the soft targets with Eq. 3, the magnitudes of the gradients are scaled by $\frac{1}{T^2}$. In this case, the relative contributions of hard and soft targets remain roughly the same and the independent subnetworks in MM-MIMO are learned under the supervision of both the ground truth and the cell-specific soft labels coming from the modality specific networks in late fusion framework.

$$L_T = L_M + T^2 L_{KD} \tag{4}$$

3   Experiment and Results

3.1   Dataset and Implementation

In this study, we use the multi-modal WBC dataset collected by the method described in Sect. 2.1. Our dataset consists of 14912 WBC samples with four modalities, which include 9616 Neutrophil (NEU), 4448 Lymphocyte (LYM), 677 Eosinophil (EOS), 124 Monocyte (MO), and 47 Basophil (BAS) in each modality.

We perform five-fold cross-validation to evaluate our methods and report our results. We use the standard data augmentation - RandAugment [3] with

Table 1. Comparison of performance and network complexity of different methods.

Backbone	Method	Performance Metrics				Complexity	
		F1-score	Sensitivity	Specificity	AUC	FLOPs	Params
Shufflenet V2	Fluorescent	93.61 0.97	93.73 0.94	93.06 1.47	98.41 0.26	147.79M	1.259M
	Color1	94.17 0.55	94.23 0.61	93.75 0.98	98.62 0.31	147.79M	1.259M
	Color2	94.60 0.42	94.66 0.45	93.81 1.35	98.70 0.32	147.79M	1.259M
	Color3	95.33 0.70	95.41 0.65	94.79 1.32	99.00 0.44	147.79M	1.259M
	Early fusion	95.43 0.36	95.52 0.35	94.91 0.63	99.04 0.28	172.17M	1.261M
	Late fusion	95.87 0.31	95.98 0.35	94.88 1.05	**99.43 0.22**	591.16M	5.036M
	MM-MIMO	95.65 0.46	95.84 0.44	94.64 0.93	99.35 0.12	172.19M	1.276M
	Early fusion + KD	95.68 0.49	95.80 0.46	94.96 0.85	99.10 0.40	172.17M	1.261M
	MM-MIMO + KD (Ours)	**95.99 0.52**	**96.10 0.50**	**95.00 0.95**	99.32 0.41	**172.19M**	**1.276M**
Resnet34	Fluorescent	93.67 0.81	93.78 0.73	93.14 0.97	98.24 0.29	3670.75M	21.287M
	Color1	94.32 0.90	94.41 0.87	93.15 1.72	98.68 0.20	3670.75M	21.287M
	Color2	94.82 0.57	94.87 0.57	94.43 1.19	98.76 0.30	3670.75M	21.287M
	Color3	95.48 0.52	95.55 0.47	94.89 1.23	99.04 0.22	3670.75M	21.287M
	Early fusion	95.56 0.63	95.65 0.58	94.89 1.05	99.08 0.48	4024.79M	21.315M
	Late fusion	96.04 0.48	96.14 0.43	95.00 1.02	**99.44 0.14**	14683.02M	85.148M
	MM-MIMO	95.81 0.64	95.94 0.63	94.76 1.39	99.28 0.20	4024.80M	21.323M
	Early fusion + KD	95.84 0.51	95.92 0.49	95.30 0.63	99.17 0.23	4024.79M	21.315M
	MM-MIMO + KD (Ours)	**96.13 0.28**	**96.24 0.28**	**95.33 0.47**	99.38 0.13	4024.80M	21.323M

N = 2 and M = 18 in all our experiments where N is the number of augmentation transformations to apply sequentially and M is the magnitude for all the transformations. Each WBC image is centercropped to a fixed size of 224×224. We **do not** use any other tricks for performance improvement in all experiments as we want to generalize our major contribution to the commonly employed strategies.

3.2 Quantitative Results

In this section, we report the weighted F1-score, sensitivity, specificity and AUC for performance evaluation, and number of parameters and FLOPs for complexity evaluation. For comprehensive experimentation and to justify our proposed ideas, we experiment on two backbone architectures - an efficient backbone - ShuffleNet V2 and a massive backbone - Resnet34. We report all our experimentation results in Table 1.

Baseline Performance. In Table 1, we first note that for both the backbones, the performance of bright-field based networks (Color1, Color2, Color3) is superior compared to the fluorescence based. This is due to the fact that fluorescent image has relatively inferior features. Specifically, we note that Color3 performs the best amongst all the modalities with highest F1-score of {95.33%, 95.48%} for Shufflenet V2 and Resnet34 respectively. Second, as expected, we note that late fusion increases the performance significantly compared to the early fusion. For late fusion, the f1-score is increased by {0.44%, 0.56%} for Shufflenet V2 and Resnet34 compared to the best performing modality of Color3 respectively.

Proposed Framework Performance. For our proposed strategies, first we note that MM-MIMO increases the performance compared to the early fusion

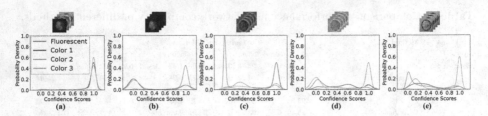

Fig. 4. Confidence score distributions of the four output heads in our MM-MIMO+KD framework with different input strategies (a): Four modalities; (b): Fluorescent only; (c): Color 1 only; (d): Color 2 only; (e): Color 3 only. (best viewed in zoom).

strategy, however, it cannot achieve a higher performance compared to late fusion. This is due to the fact that late fusion has highly complex independent networks for each modality whereas MM-MIMO has low complex independent subnetworks inside a single network. Thus, after integrating the KD with MM-MIMO, we can notice that the performance improves significantly which provides a comprehensive justification for utilizing KD to make the learning of the subnetworks within MM-MIMO stronger. Specifically, our overall strategy of MM-MIMO+KD achieves {0.12%, 0.09%} higher f1-score than that of the high-performing late fusion strategy and surpasses it for both the backbones of Shufflenet V2 and Resnet34 respectively.

The results depicted in Table 1 thus justify our proposed idea of combination of multiple modalities and also the specific advantages of each part of our overall proposed framework of MM-MIMO+KD for the task of WBC classification.

Complexity Comparison. It can be seen from the last column in Table 1 that late fusion increases the model complexity significantly (four times in our case) compared to the early fusion approach. It should also be noted that our proposed approaches only increase the model complexity slightly. To be specific, MM-MIMO+KD only uses {0.02M, 0.01M} more FLOPS compared to the early fusion strategy for Shufflenet V2 and Resnet34 respectively. This shows that our approach maintains a low complexity while achieving a high performance.

3.3   Visualization Results

To better analyse the subnetworks independence within our MM-MIMO+KD architecture, we show a visualization of confidence scores of the modality-specific output heads in Fig. 4. We adopt five different input strategies for this visualization. First, all the four modalities are concatenated and given as the input to our framework. In this case, it can be seen that (Fig. 4(a)) all the four output heads are highly confident in their predictions as they receive their modality-specific input images. However, once we start to feed in only one specific modality image by concatenating it along the dimensions, only the corresponding output head of that modality gives a high confidence. The confidence score of the rest of the modality-specific heads reduces drastically as can be noted for each of the modality in Fig. 4(b) to (e). Thus, this visualization provides a clear understanding of the independence of our individual subnetworks within our framework.

4 Conclusion

In this work, we present a first of its kind leukocyte classification based on a multimodal dataset. Our extensive experimental results conclude that our developed multimodal framework enhanced with knowledge distillation has the capability of achieving a performance equivalent or even more than that of late fusion strategy while only slightly increasing the complexity parameters than that of a single network baseline. Thus, our proposed approach helps to ease the performance-complexity trade-off for a multi-modal dataset significantly. We believe that our proposed framework can act as a guidance to the research community working with multimodal data to help create efficient multimodal networks.

References

1. Baltrušaitis, T., Ahuja, C., Morency, L.P.: Multimodal machine learning: a survey and taxonomy. IEEE Trans. Pattern Anal. Mach. Intell. **41**(2), 423–443 (2018)
2. Blumenreich, M.S.: The white blood cell and differential count. In: Clinical Methods: The History, Physical, and Laboratory Examinations. 3rd edn. (1990)
3. Cubuk, E.D., Zoph, B., Shlens, J., Le, Q.V.: Randaugment: practical automated data augmentation with a reduced search space. In: Proceedings of the IEEE/CVF Conference on Computer Vision and Pattern Recognition Workshops, pp. 702–703 (2020)
4. Damer, N., Dimitrov, K., Braun, A., Kuijper, A.: On learning joint multi-biometric representations by deep fusion. In: 2019 IEEE 10th International Conference on Biometrics Theory, Applications and Systems (BTAS), pp. 1–8. IEEE (2019)
5. Das, B., Bansal, S., Mohanta, G.C., Debnath, S.K., Bhatia, P.: Fluorescence imaging-based system for performing white blood cell counts. In: Singh, K., Gupta, A.K., Khare, S., Dixit, N., Pant, K. (eds.) ICOL-2019. SPP, vol. 258, pp. 617–620. Springer, Singapore (2021). https://doi.org/10.1007/978-981-15-9259-1_142
6. D'mello, S.K., Kory, J.: A review and meta-analysis of multimodal affect detection systems. ACM Comput. Surv. (CSUR). **47**(3), 1–36 (2015)
7. Forcucci, A., Pawlowski, M.E., Majors, C., Richards-Kortum, R., Tkaczyk, T.S.: All-plastic, miniature, digital fluorescence microscope for three part white blood cell differential measurements at the point of care. Biomed. Opt. Express **6**(11), 4433–4446 (2015)
8. Gadzicki, K., Khamsehashari, R., Zetzsche, C.: Early vs late fusion in multimodal convolutional neural networks. In: 2020 IEEE 23rd International Conference on Information Fusion (FUSION), pp. 1–6. IEEE (2020)
9. George-Gay, B., Parker, K.: Understanding the complete blood count with differential. J. Perianesth. Nurs. **18**(2), 96–117 (2003)
10. Gou, J., Yu, B., Maybank, S.J., Tao, D.: Knowledge distillation: a survey. Int. J. Comput. Vision **129**(6), 1789–1819 (2021)
11. Havasi, M., et al.: Training independent subnetworks for robust prediction. arXiv preprint arXiv:2010.06610 (2020)

12. Hinton, G., et al.: Distilling the knowledge in a neural network. arXiv preprint arXiv:1503.02531 **2**(7) (2015)
13. Khamael, A.D., Banks, J., Nugyen, K., Al-Sabaawi, A., Tomeo-Reyes, I., Chandran, V.: Segmentation of white blood cell, nucleus and cytoplasm in digital haematology microscope images: a review-challenges, current and future potential techniques. IEEE Rev. Biomed. Eng. **14**, 290–306 (2020)
14. Liu, J., Zhang, S., Wang, S., Metaxas, D.N.: Multispectral deep neural networks for pedestrian detection. arXiv preprint arXiv:1611.02644 (2016)
15. Ojaghi, A., et al.: Label-free hematology analysis using deep-ultraviolet microscopy. Proc. Natl. Acad. Sci. **117**(26), 14779–14789 (2020)
16. Ramesh, N., Dangott, B., Salama, M.E., Tasdizen, T.: Isolation and two-step classification of normal white blood cells in peripheral blood smears. J. Pathol. Inform. **3**, 13 (2012)
17. Snoek, C.G., Worring, M., Smeulders, A.W.: Early versus late fusion in semantic video analysis. In: Proceedings of the 13th Annual ACM International Conference on Multimedia, pp. 399–402 (2005)
18. Theml, H., Diem, H., Haferlach, T.: Color Atlas of Hematology: Practical Microscopic and Clinical Diagnosis. Thieme, Leipzig (2004)
19. Tkachuk, D.C., Hirschmann, J.V., Wintrobe, M.M.: Wintrobe's Atlas of Clinical Hematology. Lippincott Williams & Wilkins, Philadelphia (2007)
20. Yakimov, B.P., et al.: Label-free characterization of white blood cells using fluorescence lifetime imaging and flow-cytometry: molecular heterogeneity and erythrophagocytosis. Biomed. Opt. Express **10**(8), 4220–4236 (2019)

Deep Learning on Lossily Compressed Pathology Images: Adverse Effects for ImageNet Pre-trained Models

Maximilian Fischer[1]([✉]), Peter Neher[1], Michael Götz[1,4], Shuhan Xiao[1,2],
Silvia Dias Almeida[1,3], Peter Schüffler[5], Alexander Muckenhuber[5],
Rickmer Braren[5], Jens Kleesiek[6], Marco Nolden[1,7], and Klaus Maier-Hein[1,7]

[1] Division of Medical Image Computing, German Cancer Research Center (DKFZ),
Heidelberg, Germany
maximilian.fischer@dkfz-heidelberg.de
[2] Faculty of Mathematics and Computer Science, Heidelberg University,
Heidelberg, Germany
[3] Medical Faculty, Heidelberg University, Heidelberg, Germany
[4] Clinic of Diagnostics and Interventional Radiology,
Section Experimental Radiology, Ulm University Medical Centre, Ulm, Germany
[5] School of Medicine, Institute of Pathology, Technical University of Munich,
Munich, Germany
[6] Institute for AI in Medicine (IKIM), University Medicine Essen, Essen, Germany
[7] Pattern Analysis and Learning Group, Department of Radiation Oncology,
Heidelberg University Hospital, Heidelberg, Germany

Abstract. Digital Whole Slide Imaging (WSI) systems allow scanning complete probes at microscopic resolutions, making image compression inevitable to reduce storage costs. While lossy image compression is readily incorporated in proprietary file formats as well as the open DICOM format for WSI, its impact on deep-learning algorithms is largely unknown. We compare the performance of several deep learning classification architectures on different datasets using a wide range and different combinations of compression ratios during training and inference. We use ImageNet pre-trained models, which is commonly applied in computational pathology. With this work, we present a quantitative assessment on the effects of repeated lossy JPEG compression for ImageNet pre-trained models. We show adverse effects for a classification task, when certain quality factors are combined during training and inference.

Keywords: Whole Slide Imaging · Compression artifacts · Pathology image classification

1 Introduction

Computer-aided diagnosis (CAD) systems and particularly deep learning (DL) based algorithms for medical image analysis have shown to be extremely valuable tools for a wide range of tasks and are going to be a corner stone of modern

Y. Huo et al. (Eds.): MOVI 2022, LNCS 13578, pp. 73–83, 2022.
https://doi.org/10.1007/978-3-031-16961-8_8

radiology [17]. With the advent of digital Whole Slide Imaging (WSI) systems, this digital revolution has also arrived in the pathology domain with an increasing number of laboratories having digital imaging for image analysis implemented [21]. WSI scanners acquire virtual slides of tissue specimen, digitized at microscopic resolution, which results in tremendous storage requirements for WSI files and thus a common setting among vendors is the lossy JPEG compression to reduce file sizes [1]. Apart from still very large file sizes, even after compression, the development of efficient and scalable CAD systems for WSI files is further hampered by competing proprietary file formats from different WSI vendors [4]. One approach to overcome these competing file formats is the DICOM standard for digital pathology [12]. DICOM converters for proprietary WSI file formats enable access to large scale and vendor neutral image management systems and particularly in a scientific setting where multi-vendor data is quite common, DICOM conversion is applied regularly to enable uniform data handling [4,22]. During conversion, the DICOM standard allows the recompression of previously compressed vendor images using JPEG2000, JPEG-LS or lossy JPEG compression. While regularly applied, the effects of repeated lossy JPEG compression of pathology images on the performance of DL algorithms have not been thoroughly investigated.

Previous work evaluated the effects of image compression on DL algorithms for JPEG2000 compression of histopathological images [2,7,10]. In [2] a nuclei detection, a segmentation and a lymphocyte detection task is evaluated for JPEG2000 and lossy JPEG recompression of pathological images, while in [7,10] the effect of JPEG2000 compression is evaluated for an image classification task. A common finding across several studies is that WSI images can be compressed with JPEG2000 by up to 80% of the original file size with almost no loss in DL performance and JPEG2000 is generally preferred over lossy JPEG for recompressing WSI [2]. However, the majority of previous studies investigated the effects of image compression only for selected DL architectures and used the initially compressed WSI data for training, without further recompression.

In this manuscript, we deepen the previously conducted analyses on the effects of image compression on DL models and advance current state of the art knowledge in various aspects: (1) We consider lossy JPEG compression, which enables higher compression ratios and shorter conversion times than JPEG2000, which is more compute intensive. However, lossy JPEG also gives rise to irreversible image artifacts due to information loss and so far no comprehensive study investigating the effects of compression artifacts on the performance of DL algorithms has been conducted [12]; (2) We compare multiple state of the art model architectures on a standard image classification task in computational pathology, thereby shedding light on the generalizability of previous and new findings; (3) We implement models with pre-trained weights from ImageNet pre-training, which has so far not been quantitatively assessed by previous work. In [2,7], models were trained from scratch, which is often not possible for many clinical applications, where only few training data is available. In such scenarios, pre-training on large scale datasets, like ImageNet [18], often boosts the model performance, which has also been shown for downstream tasks in the pathology domain [3]. But so far the combined effects of pre-training on ImageNet and lossy JPEG recompression have not been fully investigated; (4) In contrast to previous research, we also train models on datasets that are compressed with different quality factors for the lossy JPEG recompression.

Our comprehensive experiments show that severe drops in the classification accuracy of DL models arise for certain combinations of quality factors during training and inference for ImageNet pre-trained models. Our results are particularly important for scenarios in which training and inference data are collected from different domains and compressed with different quality factors.

2 Methods and Experiments

Our experiments quantify the effects of lossy image compression artifacts for ImageNet pre-trained models by means of an image classification task in computational pathology. Image classification is a key element for histopathological image analysis and regularly applied to generate tumor heatmaps as support for pathologists [5]. While other tasks like semantic segmentation generate fine-grained pixel-level labels, image classification only predicts a global-level label. The most simple classification task is a binary classification, letting the model distinguish between two separate classes. If the different compression methods have an impact on this task, we hypothesize that effects will increase in more complex settings like multiclass classification or segmentation. Our experimental setup comprises seven commonly used deep learning architectures that are trained and tested in various data preprocessing scenarios. The actual classification task is the differentiation of metastatic and non-metastatic image patches in lymph node WSI of breast cancer patients. The following section describes technical considerations for lossy JPEG compression, our dataset, the preprocessing steps and our experimental setup during inference.

2.1 JPEG Compression

With high compression ratios that visibly do not affect the image quality, the JPEG format opened digital imaging for a wide range of applications, including the medical imaging domain [25]. The lossy JPEG compression algorithm exploits two principles of the human perceptual system: (1) the human perceptual system is more sensitive to changes in brightness than changes in color and (2) low-frequency components are more important than high-frequency components [20]. The lossy JPEG compression algorithm applies both ideas in turn. First, the RGB-image is converted to the YCbCr color space, a derived color space that separates brightness information (Y) from the blue-difference (Cb) and red-difference (Cr) chroma components. During compression, each of the Y, Cb and Cr components are divided into 8×8 blocks of pixels and for each individual block, the frequency spectrum is computed via a 2D discrete cosine transformation. Compression is achieved by dividing the 64 frequency components of each block by a quantization matrix. The factors in the quantization matrix are determined by the quality factor. For low quality factors, the coefficients in the quantization table are larger than for high quality factors, resulting in higher quantization. But, by default, high-frequency components are compressed stronger than low-frequency components, and the Cb and Cr components are compressed stronger than the Y component. For more details on the technical implementation of the JPEG standard please refer to [23,25]. Quality factors of 100 disable parts of the PIL[1] JPEG compression algorithm and yield hardly any gain in file size reduction, which is why we consider the quality factor $f = 95$ as the highest quality factor. Figure 1 shows an example of image artifacts caused by lossy JPEG compression.

2.2 Deep Learning Models

For the classification task, we implement the ResNet18 [11], ResNet50 [11], VGG19 [19], AlexNet [15], SqueezeNet [14], DenseNet [13] and a VisionTransformer [6] architecture. All architectures have achieved state of the art results in certain areas of DL. In contrast to the VisionTransformer, all architectures belong to the class of Convolutional Neural Networks (CNNs), which are considered as state of the art in image processing with DL. The VisionTransformer is a transformer based architecture that might have the potential to outperform CNNs also for image processing tasks within the next few years [6]. Each architecture was pre-trained on ImageNet and we used the pre-trained models from Torchvision, a machine learning framework from PyTorch[2].

Self Supervised Contrastive Pre-trained ResNet18. Ciga et al. showed that self supervised contrastive pre-trained models in the pathology domain outperform models on classification tasks that are pre-trained on ImageNet [3]. For comparison, we implement the pre-trained ResNet18 network from [3] as an approach with a pre-training different than that on ImageNet.

2.3 Dataset and Preprocessing

For training and inference of the models, we use the CAMELYON16 [8] WSI dataset, consisting of 270 training and 130 test-subjects. The dataset is divided on a subject level into the classes "metastasis" and "non-metastasis" for the train and test set. The train set consists of 110 patients with metastasis and 160 patients without metastasis. In the test set, 48 patients with metastasis and 82 patients without metastasis are available. From the WSI files $I \in \mathbb{R}^{m \times n \times 3}$ we extract a maximum of 500 non-overlapping patches $p_x \in \mathbb{R}^{s \times s \times 3}$ per class and patient at random positions $x \in \mathbb{R}^2$ with patch size $s = 224$ within the tissue

---

[1] https://pypi.org/project/Pillow/.
[2] https://pytorch.org/.

area of I. Metastatic tiles must at least contain at least 30% tumor tissue, so the maximum number of 500 patches is not necessarily extracted for each subject. With the provided ground truth in the dataset, we sample 28735 metastatic and 79418 non-metastatic tiles from the highest available magnification for the training dataset. The mentioned sampling strategy also applies for the test data, which results in 11097 metastatic tiles and 40500 non-metastatic tiles for testing.

Preprocessing. The WSI files from the CAMELYON16 challenge dataset are initially lossy JPEG compressed with a quality factor of 80% during image acquisition. For our use case, we are interested in the further lossy image compression of WSI files, e.g. for the DICOM conversion, so we consider the initial compression as baseline and refer to it as original data *"orig."*. Originating from the original training and test set, we create further lossy compressed representations for different quality factors, one for each of the quality factors $f = \{95; 90; 80; 70; 60; 50; 40; 30; 20; 10\}$. With the data that is extracted directly from the WSI files, we create 11 training and test datasets. Each copy contains the same images, but at a different compression ratio. Within one compressed copy, the degreee of compression is the same for all images. We use the Python package Pillow (see footnote 1) for the lossy image compression.

2.4 Experiments

As mentioned in Sect. 2.3, we use 11 different training datasets. Per DL architecture, we train one model on each of the 11 training dataset. For inference, we use the independent test data and according to the preprocessing steps Sect. 2.3, we also generate 11 test datasets. During inference we test one trained model on each quality factor in the inference data independently. Thus models that are trained on one specific quality factor are tested on each quality factor in the inference data. During training, each model is implemented with pre-trained weights from ImageNet. Without freezing any layer of the models, we train the models for our downstream task, which is the classification between metastatic and non-metastatic tiles. To meet the requirements for the binary classification task, we did some minor adjustments in each architecture. The last layer of each model was modified to output a probability of a given patch to belong to one of the classes metastasis or non-metastasis. All models are trained for 40 epochs with a four-fold cross-validation in the train data, and per fold, we train a separate model. During training, we augment our mean corrected data using random horizontal and vertical flips and random rotations of $\{0, 90, 180, 270\}$ degrees, as well as color jittering. Model weights are optimized with Stochastic Gradient Descent (SGD), during training we use CrossEntropy loss and we train with a learning rate $\mathrm{lr} = 10^{-3}$. All models are trained on Nvidia RTX2080 GPUs and we report the Area Under the ROC (Receiver Operating Characteristic) Curve (AUC) metric as a measure of the models' performance on the classification task. The models are implemented using Pytorch (see footnote 2).

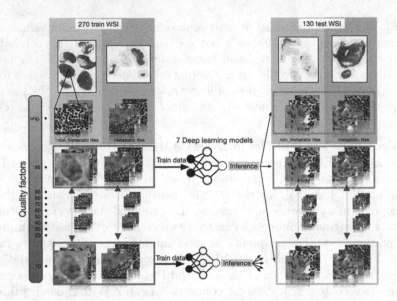

Fig. 1. Schematic overview of our approach. We extract tiles from the Camelyon16 WSI images. The patches are extracted from metastatic and non-metastatic regions. Based on the extracted tiles, we create lossy compressed copies of the data, indicated by the different quality factors on the left side. The figure also shows an enlarged area of a non-metastatic patch from the training data, visualizing lossy JPEG compression artifacts. For each of the seven DL architectures, we train one model on each quality factor in the training data. Each trained model is tested for the different quality factors in the test data.

3   Results

We report the performance of the models for various combinations of quality factors during training and testing. Within four-fold cross-validation, each fold is evaluated for each quality factor in the inference dataset and the averaged performance over all four folds is reported. Figure 1 shows a schematic overview of our approach. The results during inference for all model architectures are shown in Fig. 2.

As it can be seen from Fig. 2, severe drops in the performance of several architectures occur for inference data that was compressed with low quality factors. These drops occur especially for models that are trained on high quality factors, e.g. $f = \{orig.; 95; 90; 80\}$. This is shown by the far spread of the AUC curves for certain architectures, mainly in the left area of each plot. Moreover, it can be seen that the models that are trained on low quality factors perform slightly better on such low quality factors in the inference data. This can be seen by a smaller spread of the AUC curves in the right half of the plots for some architectures like the VGG19 architecture.

Figure 2 shows that the VGG19, both ResNets, AlexNet and the DenseNet architecture suffer most from these drops, while the SqueezeNet reveals only small drops. In contrast to these models, the accuracy of the Vision Transformer and the self-supervised contrastive pre-trained ResNet18 does not drop for any of the tested compression ratios. However, the classification accuracy of the transformer architecture also remains far beyond the accuracy of the CNN architectures, while the contrastive pre-trained ResNet18 achieves a stable classification accuracy for almost each quality factor in the test data.

Figure 2 also reveals a drop in the performance for architectures, when models are trained on $f = 70, 60$, shown in the middle of each plot. These drops occur for almost each quality factor in the inference data. Only for the same quality factor in the inference data, these models achieve stable accuracy. Again, the transformer model and the contrastive pre-trained model remain unaffected by these drops.

From the plots in Fig. 2, it can be seen that the drop that occurs for models that are trained on quality factors $f = \{60; 70\}$, which divide the AUC-plots for the architectures in two components. On the left side of this drop, models are located that are trained on high quality factors. These models perform bad on inference data that is highly compressed, while good classification accuracy is achieved for high quality factors in the inference data. On the right side of this drop, models are located that are trained with highly compressed training data. On low quality factors in the inference data, these models perform better than models that are trained on high quality factors.

For certain architectures we also compared the performance of the models when no pre-training on ImageNet is applied. Our preliminary results for a classification task are so far consistent with the literature [2,10] and the results show that without pre-training on ImageNet no drops occur, while the overall accuracy is decreased.

4   Discussion

In this work we analyze the combined effects of ImageNet pre-training and lossy JPEG compression on DL-based classification of pathology images, which is a common scenario in computational pathology. It has been shown in previous research [2,7,10] that pathological images can, in principle, be highly compressed without affecting the performance of DL algorithms. However, these findings mainly apply for models that are trained from scratch. We reveal adverse effects of certain combinations of quality factors during training and inference for the classification accuracy of ImageNet pre-trained models.

Our findings are especially relevant when training and inference data are from different domains, which is very common in DL application for digital pathology, since publicly available training data is limited and therefore training and testing data are often collected from two different data sources. Data bases like the Imaging Data Commons (IDC) [9] address this problem and provide training data for many clinical downstream tasks. However the IDC relies on the DICOM WSI data format and data might thus be repeated lossy JPEG compressed. Collecting training and testing data from two different data collections on such

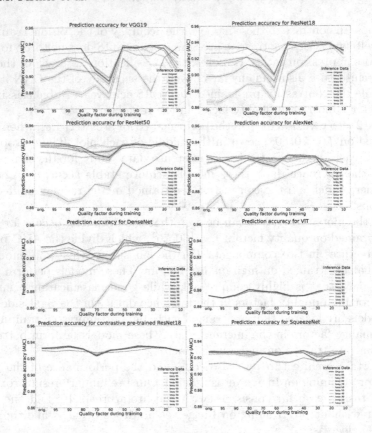

Fig. 2. Plots of the AUC-values during inference for the tested DL architectures. The plots visualize the quality factor in the training data along the x-axis, while the AUC-score shows the achieved accuracy during inference along the y-axis. Each colored line represents the accuracy of the model on one of the quality factors in the inference data. Color coding, as well as the shown segment from the y-axis is consistent for all plots. The shaded area around each curve indicates the standard deviation along the folds.

data bases can result in the adverse combination of two different quality factors in the training and testing data for ImageNet pre-trained models.

Our comparison also has some limitations. We want to highlight that the self-supervised contrastive pre-trained model by [3] was also trained on the Camelyon16 dataset. Although the model was not trained with that data on the binary classification task, it cannot be guaranteed that the different behavior of this model, compared to all other models arises only from the different pre-training. Further experiments should exclude the CAMELYON16 data set for the self-supervised contrastive pre-training in the pathology domain. Also other tasks, like a segmentation task, should be considered in further experiments. Future work might also include more recent image compression algorithms, since the lossy JPEG algorithm is mainly developed for the human perceptual system and might therefore be not ideally suited to compress images for DL applications. Other compression schemes like WebP[3] might be more suitable for DL applications, even if they are not yet supported by the DICOM WSI standard. Another further extension of our experiments is the impact of stain normalization [16,24] together with lossy JPEG compression, which has not yet been investigated.

Our experiments show that for certain combinations of quality factors during training and inference ImageNet pre-training is not always beneficial. We show that models trained on low quality factors perform generally better or comparably on low quality factors in the test data than models trained on high quality factors, while for high quality factors in the test data, both training on low and high quality factors achieve comparable classification performance. Depending on the application, the further compression of the training data should be thus considered.

Acknowledgements. This work was partially supported by the DKTK Joint Funding UPGRADE, Project "Subtyping of pancreatic cancer based on radiographic and pathological features" (SUBPAN), and by the Deutsche Forschungsgemeinschaft (DFG, German Research Foundation) under the grant 410981386. Furthermore, we thank Tassilo Wald from the German Cancer Research Center for his feedback on the manuscript.

References

1. Abels, E.,et al.: Computational pathology definitions, best practices, and recommendations for regulatory guidance: a white paper from the digital pathology association. J. Pathol. **249**(3), 286–294 (2019). https://doi.org/10.1002/path.5331, https://onlinelibrary.wiley.com/doi/10.1002/path.5331
2. Chen, Y., Janowczyk, A., Madabhushi, A.: Quantitative assessment of the effects of compression on deep learning in digital pathology image analysis. JCO Clin. Cancer Inform. **4**, 221–233 (2020). https://doi.org/10.1200/CCI.19.00068
3. Ciga, O., Xu, T., Martel, A.L.: Self supervised contrastive learning for digital histopathology. arXiv:2011.13971 [cs, eess] (2021)
4. Clunie, D.A.: DICOM format and protocol standardization-a core requirement for digital pathology success. Toxicol. Pathol. **49**(4), 738–749 (2020). https://doi.org/10.1177/0192623320965893, https://journals.sagepub.com/doi/10.1177/0192623320965893
5. Cui, M., Zhang, D.Y.: Artificial intelligence and computational pathology. Lab. Invest. **101**(4), 412–422 (2021). https://doi.org/10.1038/s41374-020-00514-0, https://www.nature.com/articles/s41374-020-00514-0
6. Dosovitskiy, A., et al.: An image is worth 16 × 16 words: transformers for image recognition at scale. arXiv:2010.11929 [cs] (2021)
7. Doyle, S., et al.: Evaluation of effects of JPEG2000 compression on a computer-aided detection system for prostate cancer on digitized histopathology. In: 2010 IEEE International Symposium on Biomedical Imaging: From Nano to Macro, pp. 1313–1316. IEEE (2010). https://doi.org/10.1109/ISBI.2010.5490238, https://ieeexplore.ieee.org/document/5490238/

---

[3] https://developers.google.com/speed/webp.

8. Ehteshami Bejnordi, B., et al.: The CAMELYON16 consortium: diagnostic assessment of deep learning algorithms for detection of lymph node metastases in women with breast cancer. JAMA **318**(22), 2199 (2017). https://doi.org/10.1001/jama.2017.14585, https://jama.jamanetwork.com/article.aspx?doi=10.1001/jama.2017.14585

9. Fedorov, A., et al.: NCI imaging data commons. Can. Res. **81**(16), 4188–4193 (2021). https://doi.org/10.1158/0008-5472.CAN-21-0950, https://aacrjournals.org/cancerres/article/81/16/4188/670283/NCI-Imaging-Data-CommonsNCI-Imaging-Data-Commons

10. Ghazvinian Zanjani, F., Zinger, S., Piepers, B., Mahmoudpour, S., Schelkens, P.: Impact of JPEG 2000 compression on deep convolutional neural networks for metastatic cancer detection in histopathological images. J. Med. Imaging **6**(2), 1 (2019). https://doi.org/10.1117/1.JMI.6.2.027501

11. He, K., Zhang, X., Ren, S., Sun, J.: Deep residual learning for image recognition. arXiv:1512.03385 [cs] (2015)

12. Herrmann, M.D., et al.: Implementing the DICOM standard for digital pathology. J. Pathol. Inform. **9**, 37 (2018). https://doi.org/10.4103/jpi.jpi_42_18

13. Huang, G., Liu, Z., van der Maaten, L., Weinberger, K.Q.: Densely connected convolutional networks. arXiv:1608.06993 [cs] (2018)

14. Iandola, F.N., Han, S., Moskewicz, M.W., Ashraf, K., Dally, W.J., Keutzer, K.: SqueezeNet: AlexNet-level accuracy with 50× fewer parameters and <0.5 mb model size. arXiv:1602.07360 [cs] (2016)

15. Krizhevsky, A., Sutskever, I., Hinton, G.E.: ImageNet classification with deep convolutional neural networks. Commun. ACM **60**(6), 84–90 (2017). https://doi.org/10.1145/3065386

16. Macenko, M., et al: A method for normalizing histology slides for quantitative analysis. In: 2009 IEEE International Symposium on Biomedical Imaging: From Nano to Macro, pp. 1107–1110 (2009). https://doi.org/10.1109/ISBI.2009.5193250

17. McBee, M.P., et al.: Deep learning in radiology. Acad. Radiol. **25**(11), 1472–1480 (2018). https://doi.org/10.1016/j.acra.2018.02.018, https://linkinghub.elsevier.com/retrieve/pii/S1076633218301041

18. Russakovsky, O., et al.: ImageNet large scale visual recognition challenge (2015). arxiv.org/abs/1409.0575

19. Simonyan, K., Zisserman, A.: Very deep convolutional networks for large-scale image recognition. arXiv:1409.1556 [cs] (2015)

20. Sreelekha, G., Sathidevi, P.: An improved JPEG compression scheme using human visual system model. In: 2007 14th International Workshop on Systems, Signals and Image Processing and 6th EURASIP Conference focused on Speech and Image Processing, Multimedia Communications and Services, pp. 98–101 (2007). https://doi.org/10.1109/IWSSIP.2007.4381162

21. Stathonikos, N., Nguyen, T.Q., van Diest, P.J.: Rocky road to digital diagnostics: implementation issues and exhilarating experiences. J. Clin. Pathol. **74**(7), 415–420 (2021). https://doi.org/10.1136/jclinpath-2020-206715, https://onlinelibrary.wiley.com/doi/10.1111/his.13953

22. Stathonikos, N., Nguyen, T.Q., Spoto, C.P., Verdaasdonk, M.A.M., Diest, P.J.: Being fully digital: perspective of a Dutch academic pathology laboratory. Histopathology **75**(5), 621–635 (2019). https://doi.org/10.1111/his.13953, https://onlinelibrary.wiley.com/doi/10.1111/his.13953

23. Telegraph, T.I., Committee, T.C.: Digital compression and coding of continuous-tone still images - requirements and guidelines. https://www.w3.org/Graphics/JPEG/itu-t81.pdf

24. Vahadane, A., et al.: Structure-preserving color normalization and sparse stain separation for histological images. IEEE Trans. Med. Imaging **35**(8), 1962–1971 (2016). https://doi.org/10.1109/TMI.2016.2529665, https://ieeexplore.ieee.org/document/7460968/

25. Wallace, G.: The JPEG still picture compression standard. IEEE Trans. Consum. Electron. **38**(1), 18–34 (1992). https://doi.org/10.1109/30.125072

Profiling DNA Damage in 3D Histology Samples

Kristofer E. delas Peñas[1,3,4(✉)], Ralf Haeusler[1,3], Sally Feng[5],
Valentin Magidson[5], Mariia Dmitrieva[1,3], David Wink[6], Stephen Lockett[5],
Robert Kinders[5], and Jens Rittscher[1,2,3]

[1] Department of Engineering Science, University of Oxford, Oxford, UK
kristofer.delaspenas@wolfson.ox.ac.uk,
{mariia.dmitrieva,jens.rittscher}@eng.ox.ac.uk
[2] Nuffield Department of Medicine, University of Oxford, Oxford, UK
[3] Big Data Institute, University of Oxford, Li Ka Shing Centre for Health
Information and Discovery, Oxford, UK
[4] Department of Computer Science, University of the Philippines, Quezon City,
Philippines
[5] Frederick National Laboratory for Cancer Research, National Cancer Institute,
Frederick, USA
[6] Center for Cancer Research, National Cancer Institute, Frederick, USA

Abstract. The morphology of individual cells can reveal much about
the underlying states and mechanisms in biology. In tumor environments,
the interplay among different cell morphologies in local neighborhoods
can further improve this characterization. In this paper, we present an
approach based on representation learning to capture similarities and
subtle differences in cells positive for γH2AX, a common marker for DNA
damage. We demonstrate that texture representations using GLCM and
VAE-GAN enable profiling of cells in both singular and local neighborhood contexts. Additionally, we investigate a possible quantification of
immune and DNA damage response interplay by enumerating CD8+ and
γH2AX+ on different scales. Using our profiling approach, regions in
treated tissues can be differentiated from control tissue regions, demonstrating its potential in aiding quantitative measurements of DNA damage and repair in tumor contexts.

Keywords: Cell morphology · DNA damage · 3D histology ·
Representation learning

1 Introduction

The analysis of cell morphology is an important task in biology and is an active
area of research where techniques are being developed for different imaging
modalities and domains [6]. The characterization of morphology can give clues
on cell functions and responses [9,15]. Different cellular processes can alter the
morphology of the cell. Importantly, morphology allows assignment of biological

Y. Huo et al. (Eds.): MOVI 2022, LNCS 13578, pp. 84–93, 2022.
https://doi.org/10.1007/978-3-031-16961-8_9

effects due to, for example, drug treatment, to be assigned to specific cell types in a tissue under study. This process is performed by pathologists and automated methods that can help them profile morphology of cells and tissues can have big impact in experimental medicine.

One cell process that manifests differently, in terms of morphology, due to many underlying factors is DNA damage and repair. Normally, a DNA-damaged cell will initiate repair once it detects alterations such as breaks, fragmentation, translocation and deletions in the DNA. If excessive damage has occurred, programmed cell death can be triggered. In tumor contexts, studying DNA repair mechanisms is specially important as evidences of impaired repairing capability in tumor cells have been presented [1]. Dysregulation of DNA damage response (DDR) promotes genomic instability, increased mutation rate, and intra-tumor heterogeneity [3,4]. Inhibition of DNA repair by targeting specific repair enzymes, e.g. topoisomerases and PARP, has proven to be a useful strategy for treating patients with solid tumors, and a number of drugs are widely used in clinical practice.

Our understanding of DDR defects in tumors is not yet complete but several anti-cancer therapies already exploit this mutation. Ionizing radiation and chemotherapy aim to induce cell death by damaging DNA. This process however is not guaranteed as tumor cells can still initiate DNA repair pathways and become resistant to these therapies. Inhibiting such pathways and specific targeting of tumor cells can therefore enhance the anticancer effect of DNA damage-based therapy [17].

To further efforts in this area, the quantification of DNA damage is the subject of many previous studies. DNA damage in cells is frequently investigated through imaging with a marker for γH2AX [7,8,13,20,24]. Traditionally, the quantification is done by counting the foci in cells either manually or automatically, or by counting the number of cells in an image field that are positive for γH2AX signal above some cutoff value assigned on a per cell basis [2,23].

In this work, we investigated the use of representation learning and texture features computed from fluorescence intensity statistics (gray-level co-occurrence matrices, GLCM) and latent encoding using a deep learning model (VAE-GAN) towards building profiles of cells in 3D histology. Representation learning reduces the need for manual counting and measurements to capture similarities and dissimilarities in data points. Using these discovered features from representation learning in an unsupervised manner enables building phenotypes without the need for annotation or additional fluorescent markers. We deviate from previous works by profiling DNA damage using visual texture, instead of directly computing for foci density. We analyzed 3D volumes of 125 μm thick 4T1 tissue sections, identified cells and cell clusters with DNA damage, and extended the characterization to local neighborhoods of cells, looking at proximity of immune cells (CD8+) and γH2AX+ cells in both control and treated samples.

We highlight the contribution of this work as follows:

1. State-of-the-art artificial intelligence methods are integrated with thick 3D histology analysis by developing a seamless pipeline, from segmentation of

3D 4T1 histology volumes to profiling DNA damage in local neighborhoods of cells.
2. Representations of morphological variations of DNA damage in cells are constructed using a VAE-GAN model and GLCM features.
3. Clustering on the extracted features using GLCM and VAE-GAN provided pseudo-labels for texture classes that can be used to characterize tissue regions.
4. Local neighborhood profiles that were constructed using our analysis pipeline and the proximity information on CD8+ and γH2AX+ cells reveal differences between control and treated classes, demonstrating potential in refining quantification of experiments.

2 Methods

2.1 Data

In our experiments, we analyzed four 4T1 mouse tumor tissue samples. Thick tissue biopsy sections (125 μm) were cleared and imaged using standard confocal microscopy at 63× magnification. Tissues were treated with irradiation, indomethacin, and L-NAME. Cells were stained for γH2AX, CD8, pan proteins, and DAPI.

From the acquired 3D confocal images, regions of size 302px × 302px × 130px (W × H × D) with high level of fluorescence for γH2AX and CD8 were manually curated and extracted. Twelve sub-volumes were selected from the control and 14 sub-volumes were selected from the treated samples. The number of cells in each selected region ranged from 500 to 900.

2.2 Segmentation

The first step in our analysis is to isolate individual nuclei in the 3D volumes, one of which is shown in Fig. 1A. We used a pre-trained Cellpose [22] model for this segmentation task. Cellpose is a segmentation model for biological images based on deep learning. The segmentation is done by estimating flow gradients from cell centroids and reconstructing cell outlines by tracking these gradients. The model has been demonstrated to generalize well to many different microscopy data and can be used without the need for retraining. Figure 1E shows a slice of a 3D Cellpose nuclei segmentation of a histology volume using its DAPI channel (shown in Fig. 1B).

After segmenting the nuclei using Cellpose, we wanted to focus on cells positive for γH2AX (see Fig. 1C). We observed that simple thresholding on the γH2AX channel is sufficient to segment γH2AX+ nuclei and using the Cellpose model on the γH2AX channel actually resulted in "hallucinated" nuclei, false segmentations in areas without nuclei. One drawback of the thresholding, however, is that cell outlines are rougher compared to the Cellpose output. To solve this, we superimposed the thresholded γH2AX volumes with the previous nuclei segmentation. Cells with a significant overlap in this superimposition are retained in the final γH2AX segmentation mask. Figure 1F shows segmented γH2AX+ nuclei.

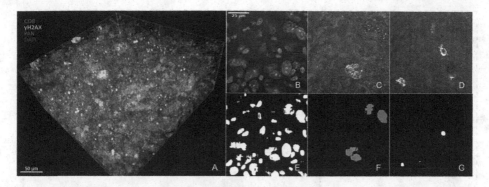

Fig. 1. A 3D image volume (A) from the dataset used in this work (CD8 in red, γH2AX in yellow, pan protein in green, DAPI in blue), z-slices of individual channels (B–D) and nuclei segmentation (E–G). Using the DAPI channel (B), Cellpose was used to generate segmentation of all nuclei (E). Using this segmentation and threshold masks on the γH2AX channel (C) and the CD8 channel (D), γH2AX+ cells and CD8+ are identified (F, G). (Color figure online)

For each of the identified γH2AX+ nuclei, we extracted bounding boxes to be used for the computation of texture feature representation. A total of 372 γH2AX+ nuclei were extracted with high confidence. Augmentation was done to increase this number for training our model.

We also applied a similar segmentation approach to the CD8 channel (see Figs. 1D and 1G) to isolate CD8+ cells. As the immunomarker for CD8 binds on the cell membrane, the nuclei segmentation was dilated first before superimposition to ensure overlap.

2.3 Building Cell Profiles of DNA Damage

Techniques that look solely at shape like in [18] exist and were demonstrated to capture the heterogeneity and variations of cells in tissues. However, they rely heavily on segmentation. In our case, as γH2AX+ is primarily analyzed for its distribution across nuclei, texture more than shape would capture this information.

Statistical Texture Features. A popular way to quantify texture in images is to compute and analyze gray-level co-occurrence matrices (GLCM). GLCM is a second-order statistic that captures pairwise relationship of intensity levels within a specific neighborhood size in an image. Its use in medical image analysis is widespread, ranging from brain magnetic resonance images [21] to liver ultrasound [25]. From the computed matrices, features encapsulating the intensity co-occurrences in different ways can be measured [12]. In this work, we used the following GLCM features: energy, contrast, prominence, and correlation.

Latent Features. We also explored the use of latent features from deep learning methods to characterize the morphology of DNA-damaged and apoptotic

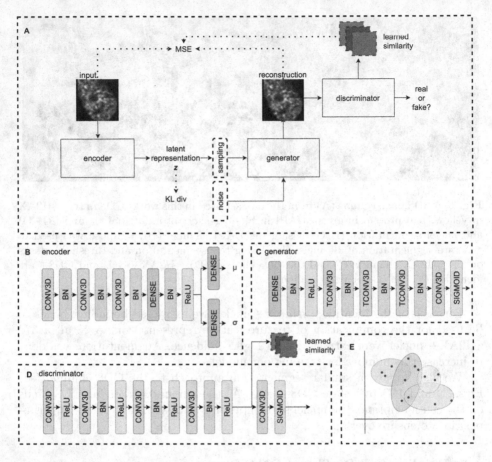

Fig. 2. The VAE-GAN architecture (A) used to construct the manifold of DNA damage in cells. The network is composed of three components: encoder, generator, and discriminator. The encoder (B) maps input images to 16-dimensional Gaussian distributions with diagonal covariance. The generator (C) produces a reconstruction from sampled points in the latent space. The discriminator (D) forces the generator to output images as similar to the input as possible. Latent encoding of the image volumes are then clustered to form pseudo-classes of DNA damage subtypes (E).

cells. Data representations in latent spaces have been applied to many biological domains and were demonstrated to capture subtle similarities and dissimilarities in imaging data [5, 19]. In this work, we used a type of a variational autoencoder [14].

VAE-GAN [16] is a type of a variational autoencoder that adds a discriminator to the network to further improve decoding and stabilize the training process. It borrows the discriminator concept from generative adversarial networks (GAN) [10], another generative deep learning technique. Further, it utilizes a learned similarity metric derived from feature maps from the discriminator in addition to the pixel-wise MSE loss. As capturing good representations of DNA damage-induced morphology and not faithful reconstructions of image data is the primary task, a high level similarity test is desirable. For this reason, we employed the VAE-GAN architecture to construct a manifold for DNA damage. Figure 2 shows the structure of our model. Our model's encoder contains three convolutional layers with batch normalization, followed by a series of dense feed-forward layers. For all our experiments, the dimension of the latent space is set to 16. The generator/decoder mirrors the encoder with three transposed convolutional layers. For the discriminator, a network with five convolutional layers with batch normalization was constructed. Feature maps after the fourth convolutional layer are extracted and used for the learned similarity metric. For training, the images of segmented γH2AX nuclei were resized to and centered on 64×64 patches, and scaled to the $[0, 1]$ range. All network modules are trained with ADAM optimizers with learning rate of 0.0001 for 500 epochs.

2.4   Pseudo-class Labels

Extracted representations for individual cells were clustered into 5 pseudo texture classes using KMeans. These clusters are then projected and visualized into 2D using principal components analysis. Since our data lacks expert annotation for repair and apoptotic classes, we aimed to use the formed clusters to find texture similarities in foci across individual cells, acting as class label surrogates.

2.5   Comparing Cell Profiles in Control and Treated Tissues

The last step in our analysis is to form profiles of local neighborhoods of cells to distinguish between regions from treated and control samples. Constructing spherical neighborhoods of various radii lengths, centered on identified γH2AX+ cells, we looked at the proximity of other γH2AX+ from different texture classes. We also counted the number of identified CD8+ cells within the vicinity. This colocalization of γH2AX+ and CD8+ cells follows the results of studies establishing links between immune response and DNA repair in tumor microenvironments [11].

3   Results and Discussion

Using the texture subtypes identified by clustering on GLCM-based features, we constructed heatmaps for control and treated samples. Shown in Fig. 3 are co-occurrence heatmaps of texture subtypes. Visually, there seems to be a clear difference between control and treated tissues. Clusters of γH2AX+ cells with labels 0 and 3 are more prominent in treated tissues. On the other hand, control tissues exhibit clusters of γH2AX+ cells with labels 0 and 2. We also observed difference in heatmaps using pseudo-class labels generated from clustering VAE-GAN encodings as shown in Fig. 3. The number of neighboring γH2AX+ cells with labels 2 and 4 are elevated in control tissues while prominence in treated is

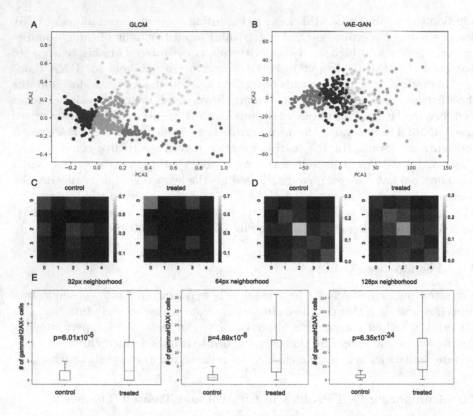

Fig. 3. Clustering on GLCM representations (A) and VAE-GAN encodings (B). Heatmaps, using pseudo-classes from GLCM (C) and VAE-GAN (D), show differences in γH2AX profiles in neighborhoods in control and treated samples. Proximity analysis shows a higher number of γH2AX+ cells near CD8+ cells in treated samples (E).

in γH2AX+ cells with labels 1 and 2. Both representations resulted in distinct profiles for control and treated regions. This demonstrates that the identified texture subtypes capture information that can be utilized for a more refined analysis of tissue sections. Lacking annotation for the data used in this work, however, explaining the profile differences will be difficult. It will be worth exploring how these texture subtypes correspond to DNA damage response types.

Lastly, we looked at the proximity of identified CD8+ cells to γH2AX cells. Our understanding of the links between immune response and DNA repair still contain gaps and tools that can provide quantitative measurements have the potential to accelerate current studies in this area. In Fig. 3, we enumerated γH2AX+ cells within the neighborhood of CD8+ cells. We computed this on various scales (32px (10.28 μm), 64px (20.56 μm), 128px (41.13 μm)). In general, we see an increase in the number of γH2AX+ cells near CD8+ cells. While further tests are needed for increased immune response to be claimed with certainty, quantifying the proximity of these two cell types can be useful in establishing baseline levels and investigating the heterogeneity in tumor tissues.

4   Conclusion

Here we presented a pipeline for the analysis and profiling of 3D histology samples. We demonstrated using a 4T1 dataset that texture representations using GLCM and VAE-GAN have a potential impact on DNA repair analysis on tissue microenvironments. Using our approach, we identified γH2AX+ and CD8+ nuclei and constructed profiles describing local cell neighborhoods of different scales. The learned texture subtypes and the neighborhood profiles show notable differences between control and treated tissues. This can enable a more precise quantification of experiments, particularly response to anti-cancer drugs and therapies.

In future work, we aim to validate the texture clusters formed from GLCM and VAE-GAN features against morphological manifestation of DNA repair and apoptosis types. While the pseudo-class labels from these clusters are demonstrated to be useful in showing differences between regions in treated and control tissues, it is desirable to improve the explainability of the labels and ground them on current biological and pathological knowledge. This, however, would entail curating individual cells and incorporating additional markers to determine the specific types. Moreover, we envision to extend our profiling to other specific cell targets such as immune cells and to support further studies looking at links between immune response and DNA repair in tumor contexts.

Acknowledgements. This project has been funded in whole or in part with Federal funds from the National Cancer Institute, National Institutes of Health, under Task Order No. HHSN26100055 under Contract No. HHSN261201500003I. The content of this publication does not necessarily reflect the views or policies of the Department of Health and Human Services, nor does mention of trade names, commercial products, or organizations imply endorsement by the U.S. Government. The computational aspects of this research were supported by the Wellcome Trust Core Award Grant Number 203141/Z/16/Z and the NIHR Oxford BRC. The views expressed are those of the author(s) and not necessarily those of the NHS, the NIHR or the Department of Health. K.D. is supported by EPSRC and MRC (EP/L016052/1), the University of the Philippines, and the Philippine Department of Science and Technology (ERDT). M.D. and J.R. were funded by a Wellcome Collaborative award (203285/C/16/Z) from Wellcome Trust.

References

1. Alhmoud, J.F., Woolley, J.F., Al Moustafa, A.E., Malki, M.I.: DNA damage/repair management in cancers. Cancers **12**(4), 1050 (2020). https://doi.org/10.3390/cancers12041050
2. Brunner, S., et al.: Analysis of ionizing radiation induced DNA damage by super resolution dSTORM microscopy. Pathol. Oncol. Res. **27**, 1069971 (2021). https://doi.org/10.3389/pore.2021.1609971

3. Burrell, R.A., McGranahan, N., Bartek, J., Swanton, C.: The causes and conse-
   quences of genetic heterogeneity in cancer evolution. Nature 501(7467), 338–345
   (2013). https://doi.org/10.1038/nature12625
4. Chae, Y.K., et al.: Genomic landscape of DNA repair genes in cancer. Oncotarget
   7(17), 23312 (2016). https://doi.org/10.18632/oncotarget.8196
5. Chartsias, A., et al.: Disentangled representation learning in cardiac image analysis.
   Med. Image Anal. 58, 101535 (2019). https://doi.org/10.1016/j.media.2019.101535
6. Chen, S., Zhao, M., Wu, G., Yao, C., Zhang, J.: Recent advances in morphological
   cell image analysis. Comput. Math. Methods Med. 2012, 101536 (2012). https://
   doi.org/10.1155/2012/101536
7. Do, K., et al.: Phase I study of single-agent AZD1775 (MK-1775), a wee1 kinase
   inhibitor, in patients with refractory solid tumors. J. Clin. Oncol. 33(30), 3409
   (2015). https://doi.org/10.1200/JCO.2014.60.4009
8. Dull, A.B., et al.: Development of a quantitative pharmacodynamic assay for
   apoptosis in fixed tumor tissue and its application in distinguishing cytotoxic
   drug-induced DNA double strand breaks from DNA double strand breaks associated with apoptosis. Oncotarget 9(24), 17104 (2018). https://doi.org/10.18632/
   oncotarget.24936
9. Essen, D., Kelly, J.: Correlation of cell shape and function in the visual cortex of
   the cat. Nature 241(5389), 403–405 (1973). https://doi.org/10.1038/241403a0
10. Goodfellow, I., et al.: Generative adversarial nets. In: Ghahramani, Z., Welling, M.,
    Cortes, C., Lawrence, N.D., Weinberger, K.Q. (eds.) Advances in Neural Informa-
    tion Processing Systems, vol. 27, pp. 2672–2680. Curran Associates, Inc. (2014).
    http://papers.nips.cc/paper/5423-generative-adversarial-nets.pdf
11. Green, A.R., et al.: Clinical impact of tumor DNA repair expression and T-cell
    infiltration in breast cancers. Cancer Immunol. Res. 5(4), 292–299 (2017). https://
    doi.org/10.1158/2326-6066.CIR-16-0195
12. Haralick, R.M., Dinstein, I., Shanmugam, K.: Textural features for image classifi-
    cation. IEEE Trans. Syst. Man Cybern. SMC 3(6), 610–621 (1973). https://doi.
    org/10.1109/TSMC.1973.4309314
13. Kinders, R.J., et al.: Development of a validated immunofluorescence assay for
    γH2AX as a pharmacodynamic marker of topoisomerase I inhibitor activity. Clin.
    Cancer Res. 16(22), 5447–5457 (2010). https://doi.org/10.1158/1078-0432.CCR-
    09-3076
14. Kingma, D.P., Welling, M.: An Introduction to Variational Autoencoders. CoRR
    abs/1906.0 (2019). http://arxiv.org/abs/1906.02691
15. Labouesse, C., Verkhovsky, A.B., Meister, J.J., Gabella, C., Vianay, B.: Cell shape
    dynamics reveal balance of elasticity and contractility in peripheral Arcs. Biophys.
    J. 108(10), 2437–2447 (2015). https://doi.org/10.1016/j.bpj.2015.04.005
16. Larsen, A.B.L., Sønderby, S.K., Larochelle, H., Winther, O.: Autoencoding beyond
    pixels using a learned similarity metric. In: Proceedings of the 33rd International
    Conference on International Conference on Machine Learning, vol. 48, pp. 1558–
    1566. ICML 2016, JMLR.org (2016)
17. Li, L.Y., Guan, Y.D., Chen, X.S., Yang, J.M., Cheng, Y.: DNA repair pathways in
    cancer therapy and resistance. Front. Pharmacol. 11, 629266 (2021). https://doi.
    org/10.3389/fphar.2020.629266
18. Phillip, J.M., Han, K.S., Chen, W.C., Wirtz, D., Wu, P.H.: A robust unsupervised
    machine-learning method to quantify the morphological heterogeneity of cells and
    nuclei. Nat. Protoc. 16(2), 754–774 (2021). https://doi.org/10.1038/s41596-020-
    00432-x

19. Rappez, L., Rakhlin, A., Rigopoulos, A., Nikolenko, S., Alexandrov, T.: DeepCycle reconstructs a cyclic cell cycle trajectory from unsegmented cell images using convolutional neural networks. Mol. Syst. Biol. **16**(10), e9474 (2020)
20. Redon, C.E., et al.: Histone γH2AX and poly(ADP-ribose) as clinical pharmacodynamic biomarkers. Clin. Cancer Res. **16**(18), 4532–4542 (2010). https://doi.org/10.1158/1078-0432.CCR-10-0523
21. Sivapriya, T.R., Saravanan, V., Ranjit Jeba Thangaiah, P.: Texture analysis of brain MRI and classification with BPN for the diagnosis of dementia. In: Communications in Computer and Information Science, vol. 204. CCIS (2011). https://doi.org/10.1007/978-3-642-24043-0_56
22. Stringer, C., Wang, T., Michaelos, M., Pachitariu, M.: Cellpose: a generalist algorithm for cellular segmentation. Nat. Methods **18**(1), 100–106 (2021). https://doi.org/10.1038/s41592-020-01018-x
23. Varga, D., Majoros, H., Ujfaludi, Z., Erdélyi, M., Pankotai, T.: Quantification of DNA damage induced repair focus formation: via super-resolution dSTORM localization microscopy. Nanoscale **11**(30), 14226-14236 (2019). https://doi.org/10.1039/c9nr03696b
24. Wilsker, D.F., et al.: Evaluation of pharmacodynamic responses to cancer therapeutic agents using DNA damage markers. Clin. Cancer Res. **25**(10), 3084–3095 (2019). https://doi.org/10.1158/1078-0432.CCR-18-2523
25. Xian, G.M.: An identification method of malignant and benign liver tumors from ultrasonography based on GLCM texture features and fuzzy SVM. Expert Syst. App. **37**(10), 6737–6741 (2010). https://doi.org/10.1016/j.eswa.2010.02.067

Few-Shot Segmentation of Microscopy Images Using Gaussian Process

Surojit Saha[1][(✉)], Ouk Choi[2], and Ross Whitaker[1]

[1] Scientific Computing and Imaging Institute, University of Utah,
Salt Lake City, USA
{surojit,whitaker}@cs.utah.edu
[2] Department of Electronics Engineering, Incheon National University,
Incheon, Republic of Korea
ouk.choi@inu.ac.kr

Abstract. Few-shot segmentation has received recent attention because of its promise to segment images containing novel classes based on a handful of annotated examples. Few-shot-based machine learning methods build generic and adaptable models that can quickly learn new tasks. This approach finds potential application in many scenarios that do not benefit from large repositories of labeled data, which strongly impacts the performance of the existing data-driven deep-learning algorithms. This paper presents a few-shot segmentation method for microscopy images that combines a neural-network architecture with a Gaussian-process (GP) regression. The GP regression is used in the latent space of an autoencoder-based segmentation model to learn the distribution of functions from the encoded image representations to the corresponding representation of the segmentation masks in the support set. This regression analysis serves as the prior for predicting the segmentation mask for the query image. The rich latent representation built by the GP using examples in the support set significantly impacts the performance of the segmentation model, demonstrated by extensive experimental evaluation.

Keywords: Few-shot segmentation · Gaussian process · Microscopy images

1 Introduction

Recent advances in deep learning technology have accelerated the automation of medical image segmentation. Deep learning models deliver good results with a sufficiently large training data set consisting of pairs of medical images and their manual annotations. However, obtaining sufficient training data for a specific domain is challenging. Algorithms that quickly learn the target task from a

---

Supplementary Information The online version contains supplementary material available at https://doi.org/10.1007/978-3-031-16961-8_10.

Y. Huo et al. (Eds.): MOVI 2022, LNCS 13578, pp. 94–104, 2022.
https://doi.org/10.1007/978-3-031-16961-8_10

limited number of labeled examples without overfitting address this issue. This learning paradigm is known as the few-shot learning.

Microscopy image is an important modality in the field of medical imagining. Segmentation of the microscopy image for nuclei, mitochondria, and cells [1,3,7, 18,21,32] enables scientists to quantitatively analyze cell counts, size, and shape over time. Availability of annotated examples in large numbers has always been a challenge in this domain. Supervised methods apply data augmentation [21,32] or rely on synthetic data [32] in the scenarios of limited data. The use of semi-supervised and unsupervised methods [7,13,18,30] are potential workarounds to deal with limited labeled data.

Although a domain-specific data set may not be sufficient to train a deep neural network, we can utilize a variety of data sets of different but related domains to enhance the generalization power of the models. Few-shot learning is a meta-learning method based on this principle. Few-shot learning is a two-stage algorithm, where in the first stage, known as *meta-training*, the model is trained with a large amount of annotated examples from domains related to but different from the target domain for solving tasks different from the target task. For example, if the target task is to learn the segmentation of spleens from MRI images, the model can undergo meta-training for segmentation of different organs (other than the spleen) using both MRI and CT images. Then there is a *fine-tuning* stage where very few examples from the target task are used to update the model parameters for better performance. Fine-tuning is not essential on every occasion, as many algorithms developed for classification and segmentation of natural images [9,20,23,28] can achieve reasonably good performance with the meta-trained models. However, the fine-tuning stage has proved to be beneficial for medical imaging data [3,15,24]. Few-shot learning algorithms can be broadly categorized as model-based (black-box) [20,22], metric-based (non-parametric) [11,25,28] or optimization-based methods [5,17]. Training for all these methods is performed using *support* and *query* examples, except for optimization-based methods [5,17] which do not require *query* examples.

Among the few-shot image segmentation methods, [3,9,23,27,29,31,34,35], the method of [9], DGPNet, which relies on Gaussian processes in the latent space, is particularly promising, because of the high degree of adaptivity (to the number of training examples) and the estimates of uncertainty provided by the GP regression [19,26,33]. Chen et al. [2] introduced a GP in in their formulation of the scalable functional Bayesian neural network for estimation of the uncertainty in the segmentation output, which is critical in the medical imaging community.

In this paper, we present a few-shot segmentation method for microscopy images using a GP in the latent space, named as the GP-UNet. The GP-UNet, illustrated in Fig. 1, uses a GP in the latent space of the UNet-based backbone network. This is motivated by the method introduced by Johnander [9]. Our choice of the U-Net [21] as the backbone network is due to its impressive performance in segmenting medical images. The GP-UNet, similar to other medical imaging applications [3,15,24], also does fine-tuning on examples from the target tasks. Through extensive empirical evaluation, we showcase the strength of the GP-UNet over other competing methods.

2 Method

For the discussion of few-shot learning, we denote the source data set containing N different classes as $D_{source} = \{D_{source}^1, D_{source}^2, .., D_{source}^N\}$, where $D_{source}^c = \{(x,y)^i\}_{i=1}^{|D_{source}^c|}$ are the annotated examples for class c. Likewise, the target data set containing M different classes is defined as $D_{target} = \{D_{target}^1, D_{target}^2, .., D_{target}^M\}$, where $D_{target}^d = \{(x,y)^i\}_{i=1}^{|D_{target}^d|}$ are the annotated examples for class d. The source and target data contain examples from completely different data sets or types with no overlap. The *support* set is produced following the N-way K-shot structure, where N and K represent the number of classes and examples (or shots) from each class, respectively. For the segmentation tasks in this paper, we use $N = 1$ as in [23], i.e., for a task, we select a class at random and sample K examples from the selected class as the *support* set and a single example from the same class as the *query* set.

For a given task in the K-shot segmentation algorithm, the *support* set is denoted as $S = \{(x_s, y_s)^i\}_{i=1}^K$, where $x_s^i \in R^{H \times W \times 3}$ is a *support* image and $y_s^i \in \{0,1\}^{H \times W}$ is its corresponding mask. The *query* set is denoted as $Q = \{(x_q, y_q)\}$, where $x_q \in R^{H \times W \times 3}$ is the *query* image and $y_q \in \{0,1\}^{H \times W}$, its corresponding mask.

The GP-UNet has three trainable blocks, the image encoder (IE), mask encoder (ME), and mask decoder (D), shown in Fig. 1. The image encoder is used to encode both the *support* and *query* images. The mask encoder is used for only the *support* masks because the *query* image mask is treated as unknown. The mask decoder predicts the segmentation mask for the *query* image using the output of the GP regression and skip connections.

The encoded representation of a *support* image and its corresponding mask, denoted as z_s and z_s', respectively, are defined as follows:

$$z_s = IE(x_s) \in R^{H' \times W' \times C} \text{ and } z_s' = ME(y_s) \in R^{H' \times W' \times C'} \tag{1}$$

Similarly, the encoded representation of a *query* image is defined as follows:

$$z_q = IE(x_q) \in R^{H' \times W' \times C} \tag{2}$$

The GP regression used only in the bottleneck layer of the GP-UNet learns a distribution of functions that regress from the encoded image space $\in R^C$ to the encoded mask space $\in R^{C'}$. For an encoded query input, z_q, parameters of the posterior distribution, $\mu_{q|S}$(mean) and $\Sigma_{q|S}$ (co-variance), computed using the encoded representation of all examples in the support set (z_S, z_S') as the prior, are defined as follows [19]:

$$\mu_{q|S} = K_{Sq}^T (K_{SS} + \sigma_z^2 \mathbf{I})^{-1} z_S' \in R^{H' \times W' \times C'} \tag{3}$$

$$\Sigma_{q|S} = K_{qq} - K_{Sq}^T (K_{SS} + \sigma_z^2 \mathbf{I})^{-1} K_{Sq} \in R^{H' W' \times H' W'}, \tag{4}$$

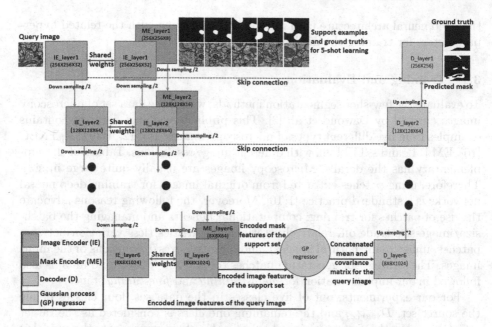

Fig. 1. Architecture of the GP-UNet model for few-shot segmentation of microscopy images. Shared weights indicate the use of the same IE for both source and query inputs. Each block has the details of the output size.

where K_{SS}, K_{qq}, and K_{Sq} are the co-variance matrices computed using $KH'W'$ examples from z_S and $H'W'$ examples from z_q in the encoded space. The noise in the labeled data is represented by σ_z. Considering, the influence of the spatial neighbors$(O \times O)$, $\Sigma_{q|S}$ is reshaped to $R^{H' \times W' \times (O^2)}$ as in [9]. Each entry in the co-variance matrices $\in R$ is a measure of similarity between the pairs of encoded points $\in R^C$ which is computed using the widely used squared exponential kernel, defined as follows:

$$Kernel_{SE}(z_1, z_2) = \sigma^2 \exp \frac{-\|z_2 - z_1\|_2^2}{2l^2} \qquad (5)$$

In Eq. 5, l and σ represent the kernel bandwidth and scaling factor, respectively. The decoder predicts the final mask $\in R^{H \times W}$ using the mean ($\mu_{q|S}$) and co-variance ($\Sigma_{q|S}$) of the posterior distribution (concatenated along the channel axis $\in R^{H' \times W' \times (C' + O^2)}$) and encoding of the query image at different levels obtained through the skip connections. The estimated mask for the query image and its ground truth is used for computing the weighted cross entropy loss to update the trainable model parameters using stochastic gradient descent.

3 Experimental Setup

In this section, we discuss the data set and its use in training and evaluating the competing methods for a $K-$shot experimental setup. In addition, we discuss the deep neural architecture used in the GP-UNet along with the related hyper-parameters for training the models.

3.1   Training and Evaluation

To evaluate the few-shot segmentation methods, we use the data set of microscopy images curated by Dawoud et al. [3]. This publicly available data set contains examples from five different types of microscopy images, B5 [12], B39 [12], TNBC [16], EM [14], and ssTEM [6], with different image resolutions. Table 1 of the supplementary has the details. Microscopy images are usually quite large in size. Therefore, using patches extracted from original images for training deep neural networks is a standard practice [1,10]. Moreover, the following reasons advocate the use of patches for training: computational benefits and managing the batch-size/image-size trade off, relatively stationary statistics (less variation between patches, unlike many natural images), and different sizes/resolutions of the input images. The strategy for generating patches (of size 256×256) used in [3] is also followed in our implementation for *meta-training* and *fine-tuning* stage.

For our experiments, out of five classes in the data set, four classes define the source set, D_{source}, and the remaining one class is considered as the target set, D_{target}. In the meta-training stage of a $K-$shot experiment, the model is trained on patches extracted from all the images in D_{source}, following the strategy outlined in Sect. 2. In the fine-tuning stage, the model is trained on patches extracted only from K images in D_{target} (containing N images) for adapting it to the target task, following the same training procedure. Average number of patches extracted from K images in D_{target} (for the fine-tuning operation) are reported in Table 4 for all the target classes in the data set. Typical values of K used in our experiments are $K \in \{1, 5, 10\}$. However, for the evaluation of a model, full-sized images are used instead of patches. The use of patches in the training stages (meta-training and fine-tuning) and full-sized images for evaluation [10] is a typical setup used in the study of microscopy images, unlike natural images. The architecture of the GP-UNet is capable of handling different settings used in the training and evaluation phase.

For evaluation of a model for the K-shot setup, K full-sized images in D_{target} (containing N images) form the *support* set (which are also used in the fine-tuning stage) and prediction of the segmentation mask is done for the remaining $N - K$ examples (*query* set) in D_{target}. We use mean intersection over union (mIoU) for evaluating the performance (higher is better). For statistical significance of the mIoU evaluated for a target class, 10 different sets of K examples are constructed.

3.2   Implementation Details

The U-Net [21] architecture adapted for the image encoder and decoder in the GP-UNet has 6 layers in the encoder-decoder structure (increased from 5 layers in the U-Net [21]) with 32 and 1024 channels in the first convolution and bottleneck layer, respectively. The channel depth of the mask encoder for the first double

Table 1. Performance of the GPUNet with and without fine-tuning in terms of the mIoU.

Target class	1−shot		5−shot	
	Without fine-tuning	With fine-tuning	Without fine-tuning	With fine-tuning
B5	0.460 ± 0.128	**0.842 ± 0.139**	0.232 ± 0.000	**0.884 ± 0.022**
B39	0.635 ± 0.000	**0.870 ± 0.052**	0.571 ± 0.001	**0.907 ± 0.006**
TNBC	0.140 ± 0.002	**0.370 ± 0.060**	0.133 ± 0.004	**0.455 ± 0.017**
EM	0.246 ± 0.000	**0.736 ± 0.041**	0.374 ± 0.001	**0.857 ± 0.007**
ssTEM	0.265 ± 0.002	**0.741 ± 0.033**	0.333 ± 0.007	**0.838 ± 0.007**

Table 2. Comparison of the GP-UNet with DGPNet+ initialized randomly or with pre-trained model parameters in terms of the mIoU.

Target class	1−shot			5−shot		
	DGPNet+ (random)	DGPNet+ (pre-trained)	GP-UNet	DGPNet+ (random)	DGPNet+ (pre-trained)	GP-UNet
B5	0.392 ± 0.102	0.496 ± 0.167	**0.842 ± 0.139**	0.320 ± 0.025	0.452 ± 0.044	**0.884 ± 0.028**
B39	0.255 ± 0.094	0.379 ± 0.144	**0.870 ± 0.052**	0.313 ± 0.054	0.751 ± 0.022	**0.907 ± 0.006**
TNBC	0.150 ± 0.063	0.200 ± 0.112	**0.370 ± 0.060**	0.190 ± 0.037	0.313 ± 0.042	**0.455 ± 0.017**
EM	0.015 ± 0.013	0.647 ± 0.025	**0.736 ± 0.041**	0.006 ± 0.004	0.756 ± 0.012	**0.857 ± 0.007**
ssTEM	0.028 ± 0.010	0.641 ± 0.069	**0.741 ± 0.033**	0.025 ± 0.011	0.772 ± 0.026	**0.838 ± 0.007**

convolution block is 8, which is doubled in successive layers with the maximum channel depth of 64 in the bottleneck layer. We replaced the max pool layers in the image and mask encoder, used for down sampling, with strided convolution layers. In the *meta-training* stage, we trained the models for 20 epochs using the Adam optimizer with the learning rate of $1e − 03$ (weight decay $= 5e − 04$) and a batch size of 8. In the *fine-tuning* stage, we set the learning rate to $1e − 04$ (weight decay $= 5e − 04$), and train the model for 20 epochs with a batch size of 8. Since there is a chance of over-fitting in the fine-tuning stage, we use the model with the best validation loss for evaluation. The hyper-parameters of the GP used in all the experiments are as follows: $\sigma_z = 0.1, \sigma = 1, l = \sqrt{C}$, and $O = 5$. Table 2 of the supplementary has additional implementation details.

4 Results

In this section, we first study the effect of fine-tuning on the performance of GP-UNet. Results reported in Table 1 for 1−, and 5−shot segmentation tasks clearly demonstrates the effectiveness of the fine-tuning operation. This observation is consistent with other few-shot applications in the medical imaging community [3,15,24]. We observe similar behavior in the performance of the DGPNet [9] (refer to results reported in Table 3 of the supplementary), which in its original formulation did not adopt the refinement policy. Hence, we consider the DGPNet [9] with *fine-tuning* stage as a potential method for segmentation of microscopy images, and named it as the DGPNet+.

Table 3. Comparison of the GP-UNet with GBMLCS [3] in terms of the mIoU.

Target class	1−shot		5−shot		10−shot	
	GBMLCS*	GP-UNet	GBMLCS*	GP-UNet	GBMLCS*	GP-UNet
B5	**0.85**	0.842 ± 0.139	**0.90**	0.884 ± 0.028	**0.95**	0.917 ± 0.016
B39	0.85	**0.870 ± 0.052**	0.88	**0.907 ± 0.006**	0.90	**0.919 ± 0.002**
TNBC	**0.41**	0.370 ± 0.060	**0.47**	0.455 ± 0.017	**0.52**	0.512 ± 0.017
EM	0.56	**0.736 ± 0.041**	0.65	**0.857 ± 0.007**	0.70	**0.869 ± 0.006**
ssTEM	0.47	**0.741 ± 0.033**	0.65	**0.838 ± 0.007**	0.70	**0.847 ± 0.013**

We use the ResNet [8], pretrained on ImageNet data set [4], as the backbone for the DGPNet+. To evaluate its effect, we initialized the ResNet parameters randomly, similar to the other blocks of the DGPNet+. From the results reported in Table 2 for 1− and 5−shot setup, we can infer that random initialization has adverse effects on the performance of the DGPNet+.

We can see in Table 2 that the GP-UNet outperforms DGPNet+ in all the scenarios. Therefore, though DGPNet+ and GP-UNet both use the GP regression in the latent space, the backbone architecture of the GP-UNet is a better fit for the segmentation of microscopy images.

Comparison of the GP-UNet with GBMLCS is reported in Table 3. For the GBMLCS [3], approximate mIoU scores (indicated by *) for different experimental setups are obtained from the bar-graphs of the UNet-based model. For a typical setup, say 5−shot learning for the target class, EM, we have considered the mIoU score of the best performing model out of all the regularized few-shot learning models proposed in [3]. For all but a couple of the target classes, the GP-UNet outperforms GBMLCS in all scenarios, with significant improvement observed for the EM and ssTEM classes. Bar graphs in Fig. 2(a) that report the average mIoU over all the shots for the target classes in the data set corroborate our observation. Figure 2(b), summarizing the results for different shots, shows that the performance of the GP-UNet is better than GBMLCS in all the scenarios, with an average overall gain of **+7.4** mIoU. Poor performance for the target class, TNBC [16], could be attributed to the high variability in the data. Moreover, we did not do any post-processing as in [16]. Figure 3 shows the segmentation masks predicted by the GP-UNet for the 5−shot experiment. The supplementary material has the prediction of the segmentation masks for 1−shot and 10−shot learning.

In an ablation study, we removed the GP from the latent space of the GP-UNet. This represents a model similar to the encoder-decoder architecture used in the vanilla U-Net [21] with skip connections where we perform transfer learning, referred to herein as the TL-UNet. For a K-shot setup, we train the network on patches extracted from all the images in D_{source} and then *fine-tune* the model on the patches extracted from K images in D_{target}. From the results reported in

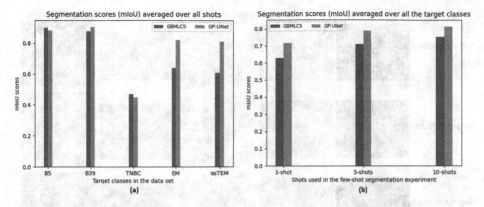

Fig. 2. Comparison of the GP-UNet with GBMLCS (a) segmentation scores (mIoU) averaged over 1−, 5−, and 10−shot experiments (b) segmentation scores (mIoU) averaged over all the target classes.

Table 4. Comparison of the GP-UNet with TL-UNet in terms of the mIoU. The average number of patches (over 10 different sets) used in the *fine-tuning* stage is reported under the column Patches.

Target class	1−shot			5−shot		
	Patches	TL-UNet	GP-UNet	Patches	TL-UNet	GP-UNet
B5	135	**0.843 ± 0.109**	0.842 ± 0.139	660	0.879 ± 0.032	**0.884 ± 0.028**
B39	102	0.850 ± 0.090	**0.870 ± 0.052**	495	**0.908 ± 0.006**	0.907 ± 0.006
TNBC	100	0.367 ± 0.060	**0.370 ± 0.060**	490	**0.469 ± 0.015**	0.455 ± 0.017
EM	390	**0.747 ± 0.034**	0.736 ± 0.041	1910	**0.857 ± 0.007**	0.857 ± 0.007
ssTEM	525	0.726 ± 0.023	**0.741 ± 0.033**	2680	0.836 ± 0.006	**0.838 ± 0.007**

Table 4 for 1−shot and 5−shot setup, we can say that the GP-UNet mostly outperforms this conventional approach when the amount of data in the target set (D_{target}) is limited (i.e., fewer shots or fewer patches for fine-tuning). However, the difference in performance decreases with increasing training data. This observation is consistent with [3]. Comparable performance by the TL-UNet could be attributed to the sufficient number of patches used in the fine-tuning stage. The average number of patches extracted from K full-sized images in D_{target} (used in the *fine-tuning* stage) are reported in Table 4.

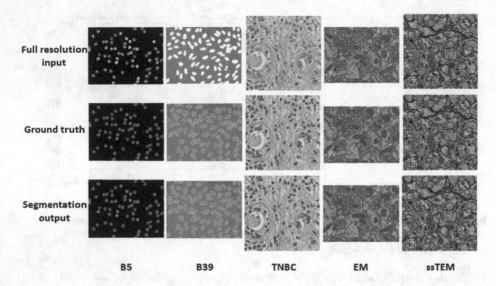

Fig. 3. Segmentation output of the 5−shot GP-UNet for different target classes.

5 Conclusion

In this paper, we present a few-shot segmentation method for microscopy images using a GP in the latent space, GP-UNet. We demonstrate that the *fine-tuning* stage of the few-shot learning framework is beneficial for microscopy images. The GP-UNet outperforms the DGPNet+ in all scenarios. The overall performance of the GP-UNet is better than the GBMLCS. The ablation study manifests the strength of the GP-UNet to produce compelling results in scenarios having a limited amount of data. The GP-UNet sets a new state-of-the-art for the few-shot segmentation of the complex target classes, EM and ssTEM, in the microscopy image data set [3], considered in this work. We plan to investigate more microscopy image data sets and extend this method to other challenging modalities in medical imaging.

References

1. Al-Kofahi, Y., Zaltsman, A., Graves, R., Marshall, W., Rusu, M.: A deep learning-based algorithm for 2-d cell segmentation in microscopy images. BMC Bioinform. **19**(365), 1050–1065 (2018)
2. Chen, X., Zhao, Y., Liu, C.: Medical image segmentation using scalable functional variational Bayesian neural networks with gaussian processes. Neurocomputing **500**, 58–72 (2022)
3. Dawoud, Y., Hornauer, J., Carneiro, G., Belagiannis, V.: Few-shot microscopy image cell segmentation. In: Dong, Y., Ifrim, G., Mladenić, D., Saunders, C., Van Hoecke, S. (eds.) ECML PKDD 2020. LNCS (LNAI), vol. 12461, pp. 139–154. Springer, Cham (2021). https://doi.org/10.1007/978-3-030-67670-4_9

4. Deng, J., Dong, W., Socher, R., Li, L.J., Li, K., Fei-Fei, L.: ImageNet: a large-scale hierarchical image database. In: IEEE Conference on Computer Vision and Pattern Recognition (2009)
5. Finn, C., Abbeel, P., Levine, S.: Model-agnostic meta-learning for fast adaptation of deep networks. In: International Conference on Machine Learning, vol. 70, pp. 1126–1135 (2017)
6. Gerhard, S., Funke, J., Martel, J., Cardona, A., Fetter, R.: Segmented anisotropic ssTEM dataset of neural tissue. In: figshare (2013)
7. Han, L., Yin, Z.: Unsupervised network learning for cell segmentation. In: de Bruijne, M., et al. (eds.) MICCAI 2021. LNCS, vol. 12901, pp. 282–292. Springer, Cham (2021). https://doi.org/10.1007/978-3-030-87193-2_27
8. He, K., Zhang, X., Ren, S., Sun, J.: Deep residual learning for image recognition. In: IEEE Conference on Computer Vision and Pattern Recognition, pp. 770–778 (2016)
9. Johnander, J., Edstedt, J., Felsberg, M., Khan, F.S., Danelljan, M.: Dense Gaussian processes for few-shot segmentation (2021)
10. Kassim, Y.M., Glinskii, O.V., Glinsky, V.V., Huxley, V.H., Palaniappan, K.: Patch-based semantic segmentation for detecting arterioles and venules in epifluorescence imagery. In: IEEE Applied Imagery Pattern Recognition Workshop (AIPR), pp. 1–5 (2018)
11. Koch, G.: Siamese neural networks for one-shot image recognition. Master's thesis, University of Toronto (2015)
12. Lehmussola, A., Ruusuvuori, P., Selinummi, J., Huttunen, H., Yli-Harja, O.: Computational framework for simulating fluorescence microscope images with cell populations. IEEE Trans. Med. Imaging 26(7), 1010–1016 (2007)
13. Liu, D., et al.: Unsupervised instance segmentation in microscopy images via panoptic domain adaptation and task re-weighting. In: IEEE/CVF Conference on Computer Vision and Pattern Recognition, pp. 4243–4252 (2020)
14. Lucchi, A., Li, Y., Fua, P.: Learning for structured prediction using approximate subgradient descent with working sets. In: IEEE/CVF Conference on Computer Vision and Pattern Recognition, pp. 1987–1994. IEEE (2013)
15. Mahajan, K., Sharma, M., Vig, L.: Meta-dermdiagnosis: few-shot skin disease identification using meta-learning. In: Computer Vision and Pattern Recognition Workshops. IEEE (2020)
16. Naylor, P., Laé, M., Reyal, F., Walter, T.: Segmentation of nuclei in histopathology images by deep regression of the distance map. IEEE Trans. Med. Imaging 38(2), 448–459 (2019)
17. Nichol, A., Achiam, J., Schulman, J.: On first-order meta-learning algorithms (2018)
18. Nishimura, K., Ker, D.F.E., Bise, R.: Weakly supervised cell instance segmentation by propagating from detection response. In: Shen, D., et al. (eds.) MICCAI 2019. LNCS, vol. 11764, pp. 649–657. Springer, Cham (2019). https://doi.org/10.1007/978-3-030-32239-7_72
19. Rasmussen, C.E., Williams, C.K.I.: Gaussian Processes for Machine Learning. The MIT Press, Cambridge (2006)
20. Ravi, S., Larochelle, H.: Optimization as a model for few-shot learning. In: International Conference on Learning Representations (2017)
21. Ronneberger, O., Fischer, P., Brox, T.: U-net: convolutional networks for biomedical image segmentation. In: Navab, N., Hornegger, J., Wells, W.M., Frangi, A.F. (eds.) MICCAI 2015. LNCS, vol. 9351, pp. 234–241. Springer, Cham (2015). https://doi.org/10.1007/978-3-319-24574-4_28

22. Santoro, A., Bartunov, S., Botvinick, M., Wierstra, D., Lillicrap, T.: Meta-learning with memory-augmented neural networks. In: International Conference on Machine Learning (2016)
23. Shaban, A., Shray, Liu, B.Z., Essa, I., Boots, B.: One-shot learning for semantic segmentation. In: British Machine Vision Conference. BMVA Press (2017)
24. Singh, R., Bharti, V., Purohit, V., Kumar, A., Singh, A.K., Singh, S.K.: MetaMed: few-shot medical image classification using gradient-based meta-learning. Pattern Recogn. **44**(2), 1050–1065 (2021)
25. Snell, J., Swersky, K., Zemel, R.: Prototypical networks for few-shot learning. In: Advances in Neural Information Processing Systems, vol. 30 (2017)
26. Snell, J., Zemel, R.S.: Bayesian few-shot classification with one-vs-each pólya-gamma augmented gaussian processes. In: International Conference on Learning Representations (2021)
27. Tian, Z., Zhao, H., Shu, M., Yang, Z., Li, R., Jia, J.: Prior guided feature enrichment network for few-shot segmentation. IEEE Trans. Pattern Anal. Mach. Intell. **44**(2), 1050–1065 (2022)
28. Vinyals, O., Blundell, C., Lillicrap, T., Kavukcuoglu, K., Wierstra, D.: Matching networks for one shot learning. In: Advances in Neural Information Processing Systems, vol. 29 (2016)
29. Wang, K., Liew, J.H., Zou, Y., Zhou, D., Feng, J.: PANet: Few-shot image semantic segmentation with prototype alignment. In: IEEE/CVF International Conference on Computer Vision, pp. 9196–9205 (2019)
30. Wu, H., Wang, Z., Song, Y., Yang, L., Qin, J.: Cross-patch dense contrastive learning for semi-supervised segmentation of cellular nuclei in histopathologic images. In: IEEE/CVF Conference on Computer Vision and Pattern Recognition, pp. 11666–11675 (2022)
31. Xie, G.S., Liu, J., Xiong, H., Shao, L.: Scale-aware graph neural network for few-shot semantic segmentation. In: IEEE/CVF Conference on Computer Vision and Pattern Recognition, pp. 5471–5480 (2021)
32. Xie, W., Noble, J.A., Zisserman, A.: Microscopy cell counting and detection with fully convolutional regression networks. Comput. Methods Biomech. Biomed. Eng. Imaging Visual. **6**(3), 283–292 (2018)
33. Ze, W., Zichen, M., Xiantong, Z., Qiang, Q.: Learning to learn dense gaussian processes for few-shot learning. In: Advances in Neural Information Processing Systems (2021)
34. Zhang, C., Lin, G., Liu, F., Guo, J., Wu, Q., Yao, R.: Pyramid graph networks with connection attentions for region-based one-shot semantic segmentation. In: IEEE/CVF International Conference on Computer Vision, pp. 9586–9594 (2019)
35. Zhang, C., Lin, G., Liu, F., Yao, R., Shen, C.: CANet: Class-agnostic segmentation networks with iterative refinement and attentive few-shot learning. In: IEEE/CVF Conference on Computer Vision and Pattern Recognition, pp. 5212–5221 (2019)

Adversarial Stain Transfer to Study the Effect of Color Variation on Cell Instance Segmentation

Huaqian Wu[1], Nicolas Souedet[1], Camille Mabillon[1], Caroline Jan[1], Cédric Clouchoux[2], and Thierry Delzescaux[1(✉)]

[1] CEA-CNRS-UMR 9199, MIRCen, Fontenay-aux-Roses, France
thierry.delzescaux@cea.fr
[2] WITSEE, Paris, France

Abstract. Stain color variation in histological images, caused by a variety of factors, is a challenge not only for the visual diagnosis of pathologists but also for cell segmentation algorithms. To eliminate the color variation, many stain normalization approaches have been proposed. However, most were designed for hematoxylin and eosin staining images and performed poorly on immunohistochemical staining images. Current cell segmentation methods systematically apply stain normalization as a preprocessing step, but the impact brought by color variation has not been quantitatively investigated yet. In this paper, we produced five groups of NeuN staining images with different colors. We applied a deep learning image-recoloring method to perform color transfer between histological image groups. Finally, we altered the color of a segmentation set and quantified the impact of color variation on cell segmentation. The results demonstrated the necessity of color normalization prior to subsequent analysis.

Keywords: Histological images · Microscopy · Stain transfer · Generative Adversarial Network · Cell segmentation

1 Introduction

Cell segmentation is the first step of many biological applications in preclinical research. For example, neuron instance segmentation is the prerequisite for quantitative studies of neuron population, morphology and distribution to investigate brain aging and neurodegenerative diseases. Advances in Whole Slide Imaging (WSI) techniques allow scanning entire tissue sections at the cellular level, while processing such a massive amount of data is still challenging. To reduce the manual workload, many automatic segmentation approaches have been proposed. In particular, Deep Learning (DL) based methods have demonstrated higher accuracy and robustness than traditional segmentation methods [7,15]. Although DL methods are considered more robust, the inconsistency of stain color in the

© The Author(s), under exclusive license to Springer Nature Switzerland AG 2022
Y. Huo et al. (Eds.): MOVI 2022, LNCS 13578, pp. 105–114, 2022.
https://doi.org/10.1007/978-3-031-16961-8_11

histological images exists as a critical issue. This problem is related to many factors in the staining procedure, such as dye type, solution concentration, staining duration, and room temperature. Even if the staining procedure is strictly standardized, variation may still occur during the digitization. The DL models often underperform when applied to images with colors different from the training dataset [12]. To this end, most DL-based segmentation methods systematically applied color normalization as a preprocessing step [4,6]. In contrast, the impact of the color variation on the segmentation is still not fully understood and inadequately quantified.

Many stain normalization methods have been proposed, which can be divided into two categories: conventional and deep learning-based. Histogram matching [3] maps the histogram of the source image to that of the target image, treating color distribution independently of image content. The color transfer method [10] converts the image into $l\alpha\beta$ color space and matches mean and standard deviation of histograms. However, they perform badly when the color of the source and target images differ significantly. The fringing method [8] and the structure-preserving color normalization [13] normalize the stain vectors in the optical density (OD) space separately for each staining channel. They were developed specifically for color variation in hematoxylin-eosin (H&E) staining histological images. Neurons are often stained with NeuN, which is a biomarker evidenced by using immunohistochemistry (IHC). Color normalization in IHC-stained histological images is a less explored research area. Recently, several DL-based approaches have been proposed. These approaches generally address the color normalization as a style transfer problem, using Generative Adversarial Networks (GANs) [2,11] to learn the color distribution of the reference stain and apply it on the source image. Nevertheless, the trained model can only deal with the specific stain of the training set and it is not suitable for images with multiple stains. GANs were often used as "black boxes", in which we had no explicit control over the image details until the invention of SyleGAN [5]. By feeding the generator gradually with latent style vectors, StyleGAN can control the style and appearance of the generated image. Furthermore, they show that the color-related features are mainly determined in the fine layers (superior layers). Inspired by StyleGAN, Afifi et al. proposed HistoGAN [1], which controls the color of GAN generated images by feeding the desired color histogram in the last two blocks of the generator. In particular, a variant of HistoGAN, named ReHistoGAN, is designed to generate a realistic image with the color of the target image and the content of the input source image.

In this paper, we created a dataset dedicated to exploring color transfer, containing five histological image groups of a mouse brain with controlled color variations. For the first time, we applied ReHistoGAN to recolor histological images while keeping the image content. The trained ReHistoGAN is not limited to a single stain target, which was the main drawback of previous GAN-based normalization methods. We recolored a cell segmentation test set of a macaque brain with the trained ReHistoGAN, using images of different colors as references, including five from the mouse set and one from the macaque set as a

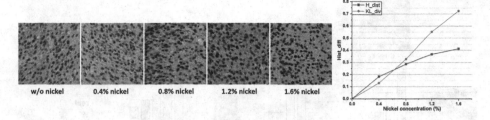

Fig. 1. Neuron microscopic images with five nickel concentrations. Left: image examples of different nickel groups. Right: correlation of histogram difference and nickel concentration (with the nickel-free group as reference).

control group. To our knowledge, this is the first study to quantify the effect of color change on cell segmentation of the DL model. The results revealed that the segmentation degradation of the DL model was linked to the color difference between the training and test sets. The segmentation performance in groups with significant color variation was considerably reduced. On the contrary, the control group remains at the same level as the initial group. Thus, color normalization prior to inference is mandatory for robust and accurate segmentation.

2   Material and Method

2.1   Dataset

The data used for the color transfer study are mouse neuron microscopic images. Histological sections of a mouse brain were stained using IHC: sections were incubated with NeuN antibody, then treated with Diaminobenzidine (DAB) chromogen and nickel (a DAB enhancer) to develop color. DAB staining is usually brown, and the addition of nickel helps the staining become darker and easier to recognize. The DAB amount stayed constant throughout the staining process, and the only variable was the nickel concentration. This procedure yielded five section groups with different color representations, one of which was nickel-free and the other four were enhanced with nickel concentrations of 0.4%, 0.8%, 1.2% and 1.6%, respectively. The nickel concentration in this study is estimated by the proportion of nickel solution to DAB solution. Figure 1 left illustrates image examples from the five groups. The higher the concentration of nickel, the darker the color of neurons. We manually extracted 10 images (3k × 3k pixels) of the cortex from each section group to build our dataset, including a training set of 13k 256 × 256 images and a test set of five 512 × 512 images, which represented five color groups.

The cell segmentation dataset and a trained DL segmentation model were retrieved from [14]. Microscopic images were extracted from a macaque brain section stained with NeuN and nickel concentration of 1.6%, knowing that the distribution and staining of neurons in mouse and macaque cortex are similar. This dataset was independent of the mouse color transfer dataset. In this study, we used only a subset of cortex, containing 36 1024 × 1024 images, on which we altered the stain color to examine the effect on segmentation.

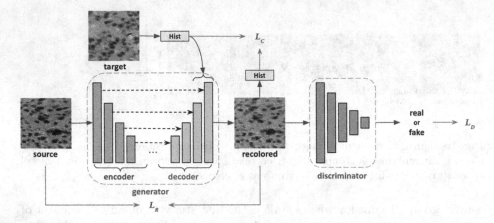

Fig. 2. ReHistoGAN architecture.

2.2 Histogram Feature

We converted images from RGB to log-chroma space and calculated the histograms in this space. The intensity of each channel was normalized by the other two channels to make the histogram differentiable and insensitive to illumination changes. For example, the conversion of the R channel is defined as [1]:

$$I_{uR} = log(\frac{I_R + \epsilon}{I_G + \epsilon}), I_{vR} = log(\frac{I_R + \epsilon}{I_B + \epsilon}) \tag{1}$$

where I_K is the intensity of the K channel of image I, ϵ is added for numeric stability, and the u and v are the K channel normalized by the other two channels, respectively. The G and B channels are also projected into log-chroma space to compute I_uG, I_vG, I_uB, I_vB. Binning is performed in u and v dimensions for each channel, resulting in a histogram with the shape of $n \times n \times 3$, where n equals 64, is the number of bins.

The difference between the two histograms was measured using Hellinger distance (H dist) and Kullback-Leibler divergence (KL div) [1]. They are usually used to quantify the similarity between two probability distributions. The more similar the distributions are, the closer the value is to 0. Previous studies suggested that H dist had a better sensibility to minor deviations, whereas KL div was more responsive to large deviations [1,9]. In this study, they were used to assess the color variation in different nickel groups and compare the color transfer performance of different normalization methods. In particular, the H dist was also employed to train the neural network as the color matching loss.

2.3 ReHistoGAN

The objective of ReHistoGAN was to generate a realistic image, preserving both the content of the source image and the color information of the target image.

As shown in Fig. 2, the network consisted of a generator to recolor the input image and a discriminator. The generator network was modified from a U-Net-like structure with skip connections. The target histogram features were projected into latent space and inserted in the last two blocks of the decoder to control the color of the output image. The generator was trained to generate an image having the same content as the source image and a color distribution similar to the target image. It is worth noting that the ReHistoGAN was trained in a fully unsupervised manner since the only ground truth needed was the histogram features, which were computed as described in Sect. 2.2. The goal of the discriminator was to distinguish the generated image from the real one. The loss function of the entire network is defined as [1]:

$$L = \alpha L_C(H_t, H_r) + \beta L_R(I_t, I_r) + \gamma L_D \qquad (2)$$

where t, s and r are target, source and recolored images respectively. H is the histogram. L_C is the color matching loss computed with Hellinger distance. I is perceptual detail (without color information), which was obtained with the Laplacian operator. L_R is the reconstruction loss computed with the L1 norm. The discriminator loss L_D is used to measure how realistic the generated image is. α, β and γ are hyperparameters equal to 32, 1.5 and 4, respectively, which were defined empirically in [1] to control the weight of each term.

The ReHistoGAN model was then applied to recolor each image of the cell segmentation dataset using itself and five images in the mouse color transfer test set as targets. This procedure yielded six supplementary groups with continuous color changes. The first was a control group where no color changes were expected (same source image as target image), which was added to measure possible artifacts brought by the GAN network during encoding and decoding. The remaining five groups inherited the color distributions from the color transfer dataset, which were different from the segmentation set. Six colors on the same set allowed us to study the effect of color variation on cell segmentation.

2.4 Cell Segmentation

We utilized the segmentation method proposed in [14], which consisted of a neural network to predict the cell, the inter-cell contour and the background, followed by a post-processing scheme based on mathematical morphology to individualize each cell instance. Color augmentation techniques were applied during the training to improve the robustness of the model to color inconsistencies. After training, we applied the network on the segmentation test set as well as the six GAN-recolored sets to study the impact of color variation.

2.5 Evaluation Metrics

In this study, the color variation between images was assessed by the difference between color histograms (H dist and KL div). A good color transfer method should provide a recolored image with low H dist and KL div matching the target.

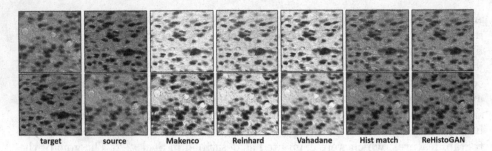

target   source   Makenco   Reinhard   Vahadane   Hist match   ReHistoGAN

Fig. 3. Stain color transfer results from different methods. The first row presents recolored results of a 1.6% nickel image using a nickel-free image as reference. The second row shows recolored results after switching the source and target.

Table 1. Comparison of color transfer methods. The H dist and KL div are reported to show the color difference between recolored results and target images

Metrics	Macenko	Reinhard	Vahadane	Hist match	ReHistoGAN
H_dist	0.239 ± 0.038	0.284 ± 0.223	0.383 ± 0.131	0.043 ± 0.031	$\mathbf{0.052 \pm 0.006}$
KL_div	0.258 ± 0.076	0.42 ± 0.458	0.557 ± 0.284	0.011 ± 0.012	$\mathbf{0.011 \pm 0.002}$

The cell segmentation was evaluated using three metrics: F1 score, Aggregated Jaccard Index (AJI) and Dice [12]. F1 score evaluated the cell instance segmentation, a segmented cell was considered a true positive when it overlapped the ground truth with an intersection over union greater than 0.5. AJI was a stricter metric to evaluate the instance segmentation since it penalized false segmentations. We also computed the Dice score to evaluate the semantic segmentation.

3   Results and Discussion

We measured the color histogram similarity between the nickel-free group versus other nickel groups using H dist and KL div. As shown in Fig. 1 right, color variation becomes more significant as nickel concentration gets higher. In the tested range, the KL div curve was roughly linear, whereas the H dist saturated as nickel concentration increased.

3.1   Color Transfer Performance of ReHistoGAN and Other Methods

We compared ReHistoGAN with four state-of-the-art color transfer methods: Macenko *et al.* [8], Reinhard *et al.* [10], Vahadane *et al.* [13] and histogram matching [3]. Each image in the mouse test set was recolored using all color groups as color references, resulting in 25 combinations in total. Figure 3 shows the visual comparison of two extreme cases from the nickel-free group (brown) and the highest-nickel group (dark). Macenko *et al.* [8] changed the stain color while it introduced artifacts, especially when recoloring the dark stain to brown. Reinhard *et al.* [10] was unable to retain all color information of the target image, with the stain color in the results still affected by the source images. Vahadane *et al.* [13] achieved better results visually, however both Macenko *et al.* [8] and Vahadane *et al.* [13] suffered intensity issues, the recolored images were unnaturally too bright compared to the source and target images. The possible explanation for this might be that the IHC stain is a scatterer of light rather than an absorber. Therefore the Beer-Lambert law of absorption used for color space conversion is no longer applicable [13]. The dark stain was successfully recolored into brown using the histogram matching [3]. On the other hand, it did not perform well in converting brown stains to dark (brown spots still exist, see Fig. 3), and the resulting stain colors were absent from both the source and target images. Compared to other methods, ReHistoGAN showed better performance and robustness, and it worked well in all cases, transferring the target color without losing the source content.

Table 1 reports the quantitative comparison of ReHistoGAN and other methods on mouse data. H dist and KL div of color histograms were measured between the recolored images and their target images. Histogram matching had the best average H dist and KL div since the objective was to produce similar color histograms. However, the high standard deviation suggests that this method lacks robustness. This finding is consistent with visual results in Fig. 3, where the method performed poorly when the source and target images had very dissimilar statistics. On the other hand, besides comparable quantitative results as histogram matching (same KL div and slightly higher H dist), ReHistoGAN had the lowest standard deviations, which indicates its robustness. Despite bringing illumination changes, Macenko *et al.* [8], Reinhard *et al.* [10] and Vahadane *et al.* [13] were unable to correctly adjust color variation in IHC stained images. Compared to Histogram matching [3] and ReHistoGAN, these methods resulted in recolored images with more significant color differences from the target images.

3.2   Impact of Color Variation on Cell Segmentation

We applied ReHistoGAN to recolor images of the macaque segmentation test set, as illustrated in Fig. 4. The second column is the control group recolored using the same macaque image as the target, which allowed us to investigate the possible effect of encoding and decoding. The following columns show recolored images using five nickel mouse groups as the target, respectively. In total, six additional sets were produced, including one set without color change (control) and five with continuous color variations from brown to dark (recolored 1–5). Surprisingly, experts estimated that the original macaque images were closest in color to recolored-3 (0.8%), although the nickel concentration used for macaque images was the same as recolor-5 (1.6%). This inconsistency may be due to factors other than nickel concentration during the staining process.

We evaluated the segmentation network on the original and six additional sets of macaque images. Table 2 reports the segmentation results and the color

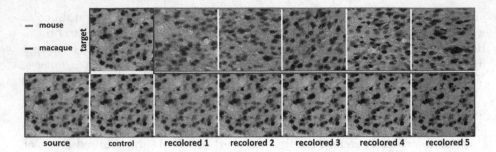

Fig. 4. Macaque segmentation dataset recolored by ReHistoGAN. First row: target images, second row: source macaque image and recolored results. From left to right: GAN-recolored images using the macaque image (control), nickel-free (recolored-1), 0.4%, 0.8%, 1.2% and 1.6% nickel mouse images (recolored-2–5) as targets.

Table 2. Comparison of segmentation performances (F1, AJI and Dice) on segmentation dataset without and with color variations inherited from the different groups in the color transfer dataset. Color variations between the two datasets are quantified using H dist and KL div.

Metrics	Original	Control	Recolored-1	Recolored-2	Recolored-3	Recolored-4	Recolored-5
H_dist	-	-	0.257	0.093	**0.05**	0.132	0.182
KL_div	-	-	0.27	0.035	**0.01**	0.075	0.135
F1	0.91	0.899	0.842	0.892	**0.898**	0.893	0.867
AJI	0.754	0.734	0.628	0.711	**0.733**	0.729	0.7
Dice	0.972	0.961	0.909	0.951	**0.962**	0.956	0.936

variation between the test sets and the training set. Despite the fact that the model was trained using color augmentation techniques, segmentation performance has been negatively impacted by color variations. The scores of the original set were the best since they came from the same data as the training set. They were used as references to show the performance degradation due to GAN artifacts and color variation. The scores of the control group were comparable to the reference but slightly lower, indicating that almost all information of the original image was preserved during encoding and decoding. The group with the most degradation in segmentation was the recolored-1 set, which had the most significant color variation compared to the original set (KL div: 0.27). In particular, the AJI of this set decreased by 17% when compared to the reference. The recolored-3 set, on the other hand, scored similarly to the control group as it had similar color distributions both visually and quantitatively (KL div: 0.01). It suggests that the DL segmentation model is robust to slight color variation. Overall, the findings suggest that the segmentation performance decreases more in test sets with higher color variation. Surprisingly, the segmentation in the recolored-4 set was better than that in recolored-2, even though the former had a more visually distinct color variance. This might be due to the fact that despite the color variation, the contrast between cell and tissue is also essential for neural networks to segment cells. In our case, the darker stained images in the recolored-4 set presented a more significant contrast than lighter stained images in the recolored-2 set, providing a better condition for cell segmentation.

4   Conclusion and Perspectives

In this paper, we created an original dataset with five controlled color changes, which is well-suited for evaluating the performance of color transfer methods. We applied the ReHistoGAN method to perform the stain color transfer on IHC staining histological images. The results demonstrated its superiority and robustness compared with other state-of-the-art methods. Using ReHistoGAN, we intentionally altered the color of the macaque segmentation test set, which enabled us for the first time to quantitatively investigate the impact of color variation on IHC stained cell segmentation (semantic and instance) using neural networks. Experiments showed that the cell segmentation negatively correlated to the color variation between the test and the training sets. However, for a given color variation, the segmentation was better on images with darker stains. (see recolored-2 and recolored-4 in Table 2). Previous GAN-based approaches [2,11] have not been assessed due to their lack of flexibility. Further studies are needed to validate the color transfer performance of ReHistoGAN compared to these methods. As a preliminary study, we only investigated NeuN staining images in the cortex region. Further work is needed to establish a strategy for the automatic selection of appropriate target images in various anatomical regions, which will allow us to expand this study to the entire brain. Moreover, additional study on images with other stainings (*e.g.*, H&E) would also be worthwhile.

Acknowledgements.. This work was supported by DIM ELICIT grants from Région Ile-de-France, by the French National Research Agency (project SUMMIT ANR-21-CE45-0022-01) and by the European Union's Horizon 2020 research and innovation program under the grant agreement No. 945539 (Human Brain Project SGA3).

References

1. Afifi, M., Brubaker, M.A., Brown, M.S.: HistoGAN: controlling colors of GAN-generated and real images via color histograms. In: Proceedings of the IEEE/CVF Conference on Computer Vision and Pattern Recognition, pp. 7941–7950 (2021)
2. BenTaieb, A., Hamarneh, G.: Adversarial stain transfer for histopathology image analysis. IEEE Trans. Med. Imaging **37**(3), 792–802 (2017)
3. Coltuc, D., Bolon, P., Chassery, J.M.: Exact histogram specification. IEEE Trans. Image Process. **15**(5), 1143–1152 (2006)
4. Cui, Y., Zhang, G., Liu, Z., Xiong, Z., Hu, J.: A deep learning algorithm for one-step contour aware nuclei segmentation of histopathology images. Med. Biol. Eng. Comput. **57**(9), 2027–2043 (2019). https://doi.org/10.1007/s11517-019-02008-8
5. Karras, T., Laine, S., Aila, T.: A style-based generator architecture for generative adversarial networks. In: Proceedings of the IEEE/CVF Conference on Computer Vision and Pattern Recognition, pp. 4401–4410 (2019)

6. Kumar, N., Verma, R., Sharma, S., Bhargava, S., Vahadane, A., Sethi, A.: A dataset and a technique for generalized nuclear segmentation for computational pathology. IEEE Trans. Med. Imaging **36**(7), 1550–1560 (2017)
7. Liu, D., Zhang, D., Song, Y., Huang, H., Cai, W.: Panoptic feature fusion net: a novel instance segmentation paradigm for biomedical and biological images. IEEE Trans. Image Process. **30**, 2045–2059 (2021)
8. Macenko, M., et al.: A method for normalizing histology slides for quantitative analysis. In: 2009 IEEE International Symposium on Biomedical Imaging: from Nano to Macro, pp. 1107–1110. IEEE (2009)
9. Mocnik, F.B.: Benford's law and geographical information-the example of open-streetmap. Int. J. Geograph. Inf. Sci. **35**(9), 1746–1772 (2021)
10. Reinhard, E., Adhikhmin, M., Gooch, B., Shirley, P.: Color transfer between images. IEEE Comput. Graph. Appl. **21**(5), 34–41 (2001)
11. Shaban, M.T., Baur, C., Navab, N., Albarqouni, S.: StainGAN: stain style transfer for digital histological images. In: 2019 IEEE 16th International Symposium on Biomedical Imaging (ISBI 2019), pp. 953–956. IEEE (2019)
12. Tellez, D., et al.: Quantifying the effects of data augmentation and stain color normalization in convolutional neural networks for computational pathology. Med. Image Anal. **58**, 101544 (2019)
13. Vahadane, A., et al.: Structure-preserving color normalization and sparse stain separation for histological images. IEEE Trans. Med. Imaging **35**(8), 1962–1971 (2016)
14. Wu, H., Souedet, N., Jan, C., Clouchoux, C., Delzescaux, T.: A general deep learning framework for neuron instance segmentation based on efficient UNet and morphological post-processing. arXiv preprint arXiv:2202.08682 (2022)
15. Wu, H., Wang, Z., Song, Y., Yang, L., Qin, J.: Cross-patch dense contrastive learning for semi-supervised segmentation of cellular nuclei in histopathologic images. In: Proceedings of the IEEE/CVF Conference on Computer Vision and Pattern Recognition, pp. 11666–11675 (2022)

Constrained Self-supervised Method with Temporal Ensembling for Fiber Bundle Detection on Anatomic Tracing Data

Vaanathi Sundaresan[1]([✉]), Julia F. Lehman[2], Sean Fitzgibbon[3], Saad Jbabdi[3], Suzanne N. Haber[2,4], and Anastasia Yendiki[1]

[1] Athinoula A. Martinos Center for Biomedical Imaging, Massachusetts General Hospital and Harvard Medical School, Charlestown, MA, USA
vsundaresan1@mgh.harvard.edu
[2] Department of Pharmacology and Physiology, University of Rochester School of Medicine, Rochester, NY, USA
[3] Wellcome Centre for Integrative Neuroimaging, FMRIB Centre, Nuffield Department of Clinical Neurosciences, University of Oxford, Oxford, UK
[4] McLean Hospital, Belmont, MA, USA

Abstract. Anatomic tracing data provides detailed information on brain circuitry essential for addressing some of the common errors in diffusion MRI tractography. However, automated detection of fiber bundles on tracing data is challenging due to sectioning distortions, presence of noise and artifacts and intensity/contrast variations. In this work, we propose a deep learning method with a self-supervised loss function that takes anatomy-based constraints into account for accurate segmentation of fiber bundles on the tracer sections from macaque brains. Also, given the limited availability of manual labels, we use a semi-supervised training technique for efficiently using unlabeled data to improve the performance, and location constraints for further reduction of false positives. Evaluation of our method on unseen sections from a different macaque yields promising results with a true positive rate of ∼0.90. The code for our method is available at https://github.com/v-sundaresan/fiberbundle_seg_tracing.

Keywords: Anatomic tracing · Fiber bundle detection · Self-supervised · Contrastive loss

1 Introduction

Diffusion MRI (dMRI) allows us to probe the macroscopic organization and the microscopic features of white matter (WM) pathways *in vivo*, and to study their role in psychiatric and neurological disorders [1,2]. However, dMRI can only provide indirect measurements of axonal orientations based on water diffusion, and only at the mm scale. As a result, dMRI tractography sometimes fails,

Y. Huo et al. (Eds.): MOVI 2022, LNCS 13578, pp. 115–125, 2022.
https://doi.org/10.1007/978-3-031-16961-8_12

particularly in areas of complex fiber configurations, such as branching, fanning, or sharp turns [2–4]. In contrast, anatomic tracing in non-human primates enables us to follow the trajectory of individual axons. As the fibers travel from an injection site, split into different fiber bundles and reach their terminal fields, they provide in-depth knowledge of how the brain is actually wired [5–8]. Example tracer data from an injection site at the frontopolar cortex of a macaque monkey are shown in Fig. 1. Anatomic tracing has been used to visualize tracts that are challenging for dMRI tractography [3,7,9]. For instance, WM fibers from prefrontal cortex travel through the gray matter of the striatum in small fascicles before entering the internal capsule (IC) [7,9]. From the IC, these fibers also enter anterior commissure perpendicular to the its main fiber tract orientation [9]. These discontinuities and tortuous trajectories of fibers confound dMRI tractography, but can be visualized clearly with anatomic tracing. However, the manual charting of fiber bundles on histological slides is extremely time consuming and labor-intensive, limiting the availability of annotated tracer data for large-scale validation studies.

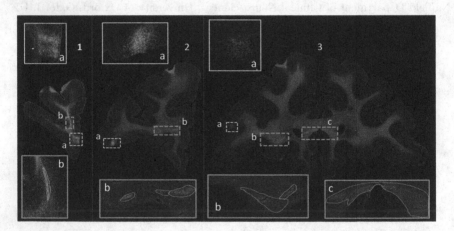

Fig. 1. Photomicrographs showing coronal sections (1–3); (1a, 2a, 3a) terminal fields at different cortical locations. In the rostrocaudal direction, a fiber bundle stalk (1b) branches into two fiber bundles in prefrontal white matter (2b) and travels laterally in the external capsule (3b) and medially in the corpus callosum (3c). Manual chartings of dense and moderate bundles shown in green and orange respectively. (Color figure online)

The goal of this work is to accelerate this process by developing an accurate, automated method for detecting fiber bundles in histological sections. Existing work on automated fiber bundle segmentation on tracer data is quite scarce, and has been done primarily in marmoset brains [10]. In contrast with these new world primates, the cortex of old world primates, (i.e. macaques) is evolutionarily much closer to humans and, as such the trajectory of fibers are more similar [5,11]. In general, automated fiber bundle detection on anatomic tracing data is challenging due to various confounding structures (e.g., terminal fields), sectioning distortions, localized and speckle artifacts and varying background intensities/textures. In this work, we propose a deep learning-based method for fully automated, accurate fiber bundle detection for the first time on tracer data from macaque brains, using only a few manually labeled sections. We use a multi-tasking model with anatomy-constrained self-supervised loss and utilise continuity priors to ensure accurate detection and to avoid false positives (FPs). So far, various semi/self-supervised and ensembling techniques have been shown to work well on noisy data and limited labels with uncertainties [12–16]. Given the shortage of manually annotated tracer data, we successfully adapt a semi-supervised training technique to improve fiber bundle detection. We also evaluate the robustness of fiber bundle detection by validating our method on unseen sections from a different macaque brain.

In addition to segmenting fiber bundles, our automated tool can also provide further quantification of fibers (e.g., density, volume). It is publicly available and we plan to deploy it for quantitative analyses of tracer data, and for large-scale validation studies where the accuracy of tractography algorithms will be evaluated across multiple seed areas.

2 Method

The aim of this work is end-to-end automatic segmentation of the fiber bundles (regions indicated by manual chartings in Fig. 1) on anatomic tracing data from macaque brains. For training our method, we used (1) an encoder-decoder architecture for segmenting fiber bundles, while simultaneously discriminating fiber bundles from background using self-supervised contrastive loss, and (2) a temporal ensembling framework to efficiently use sections without manual charting from different brains.

2.1 Self-supervised, Temporal Ensembling Framework

Anatomy-Constrained Self-supervised Learning: We used a 2D U-Net [17] to build a multi-tasking model as shown in Fig. 2, since U-Net is one of the most successful architectures for medical image segmentation tasks [18]. The multi-tasking model consists of a U-Net backbone (F_{Seg}) for segmenting the fiber regions/bundles and an auxiliary classification arm (F_{Class}) for discriminating fiber patches from background patches. We provided randomly sampled RGB patches of size $256 \times 256 \times 3$ as input. F_{Class} is connected to the bottleneck of the encoder of F_{Seg}, where the feature maps are passed through a downsampling module followed by two fully connected layers ($fc1024$, $fc256$) and an output layer with 2 nodes (fiber bundle vs background). The downsampling module consists of 2 max-pooling layers, each followed by two 3×3 convolution layers to extract high-level global features in the patches. We used focal loss (Eq. 1) for training F_{Seg}, since it handles class imbalance well [19]. The focal loss is given by:

$$FL(p_t) = -\alpha_t(1 - p_t)^\gamma log(p_t), \quad p_t = \begin{cases} p, & \text{if } y = 1 \\ (1 - p), & \text{otherwise} \end{cases} \quad (1)$$

where α and γ are weighing and focusing parameters, respectively, and $p \in [0,1]$ is the predicted probability for the fiber bundle class. As mentioned earlier, the manual charting of fiber bundles does not include all fiber regions and might not be precise along the boundaries. Moreover, we have texture variations and noise in the background. Therefore, we used a self-supervised technique for training F_{Class} that learns intrinsic texture/intensity variations in addition to the fiber features from the manual charting alone. We used a contrastive loss function based on SimCLR [12], where augmented data from each sample constitute the positive example to the sample while the rest were treated as negatives for the loss calculation. In SimCLR, random cropping and color distortions were shown to perform well. In our case we adapted the learning method by choosing augmentations better suited to our problem: (i) random cropping of patches closer to the input patch (<20 μm), constrained within the white matter (by iterative sampling of patches until mean intensity criterion is satisfied), (ii) noise injection + Gaussian blurring (with randomly chosen $\sigma \in [0.05, 0.3]$). The self-supervised loss with the above augmentations has two advantages: (1) effective separation between fiber and non-fiber background patches and (2) identification of fiber patches correctly even in the presence of artifacts, aided by the shared weights in the encoder of F_{Seg}. We used the contrastive loss [12] (Eq. 2) between positive pairs of patches (i, j) of F_{Class}, given by:

$$CL(i,j) = \frac{exp(sim(f_i, f_j)/\tau)}{\sum_{k=1}^{2N} I_{k \neq i}\, exp(sim(f_i, f_k)/\tau)}, \quad sim(x,y) = \frac{x^T y}{||x|| ||y||} \quad (2)$$

where f is the output of F_{Class}, $sim(.)$ is the cosine similarity function, $I_{k \neq i} = 1$ if $k \neq i$, else 0 is the indicator function and τ is the temperature parameter.

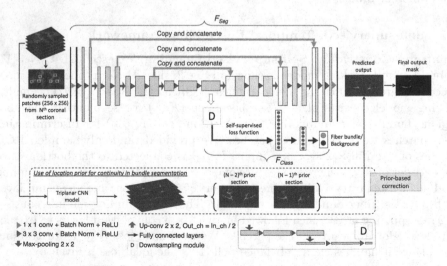

Fig. 2. Network architecture used for fiber segmentation, and the use of location priors from rostral sections for false positive reduction.

Temporal Ensembling (TE) Training: Only ~6% of sections were manually charted, which would be insufficient for this challenging detection problem. Hence, after initially pretraining the model for Np epochs using the manually charted samples alone, we used the additional unlabeled samples for training both F_{Seg} and F_{Class}, using the temporal ensembling technique [15], where predictions from the previous r epochs ($[P_{N-r}, ..., P_{N-1}]$) were averaged and thresholded to obtain the target label for the current epoch N (we empirically set $r = 3$). We used focal loss for pretraining the encoder-decoder of F_{Seg}, since contrastive loss was calculated at patch-level in F_{Class}. For the first 3 epochs after pretraining, predictions from the pretrained model P_{N_p} were used for label generation. Averaging predictions reduced segmentation noise and aided in adapting the model to data from different brains.

Inference on Test Brain Sections: We obtained the predictions by applying the segmentation part F_{Seg} of the model on the whole coronal sections (or patches of size 1024 × 1024 in the case of sections with dimensions larger than 1024 voxels).

2.2 Continuity Prior for False Positive Removal

We used the spatial continuity of fibers from the injection site to remove obvious FPs (e.g., in cortical regions). We downsampled the sections by a factor of 10 and aligned the sections along the ventricles (or along the lateral edges of the brain for sections without ventricles) to roughly form 3D histological volumes. We applied a triplanar U-Net architecture used in [20] to obtain a 3D priormap containing a crude segmentation of main dense fiber bundles and later upsampled it to the original dimensions. For each section, we computed the average of the segmented fiber bundle masks from the two nearest neighboring priormap sections (in rostral and/or caudal directions, if available). We removed any detected fiber bundle region in the current section, whose distance from the averaged bundles of prior sections was >0.2 mm.

Postprocessing: We further reduced noisy regions and FPs by automated rejection of the predicted regions with area <2 mm² and those near the brain outline.

3 Experiments

Dataset Used: We used digitized, coronal histological sections from 12 macaques, with a slice thickness 50 μm and in-plane resolution of 0.4 μm. We considered every 8th section, resulting in a slice gap of 400 μm (refer to [6,8,21] for more details on tracer injection, immunocytochemistry and histological processing). Manual charting of fiber bundles labeled under 'dense' and 'moderate' bundles (examples shown in Fig. 1) had been done previously by an expert neuroanatomist under dark-field illumination with a 4.0 or 6.4× objective, using Neurolucida software (MBF Bioscience). Manually charted region masks were registered with the tracing data using similarity (affine) transform with 6

DOF. Manual chartings were available for 2 macaques (61 sections). *Dataset 1 (DS1)* consists of 465 sections, including 25 charted sections (out of 61) from one macaque and 440 unlabeled sections from 10 macaques for training. *Dataset 2 (DS2)* consists of 36 charted sections from the other annotated macaque for testing. Both datasets were downsampled in-plane by a factor of 4 for training and testing.

Implementation Details: For training, we used the Adam optimizer [22] ($\epsilon = 10^{-3}$), batch size $= 8$, pretraining epochs (N_p) $= 100$ and trained with TE for 100 epochs with a patience value of 25 epochs for early stopping (converged at $\sim$90 epochs). For focal loss, we used $\alpha = 0.25$; $\gamma = 2$, and for contrastive loss, we used $\tau = 0.5$. The hyperparameters were chosen empirically. For F_{Seg}, we augmented data using translation (offset $\in [-50, 50]$ voxels), rotation ($\theta \in [-20°, 20°]$), horizontal/vertical flipping and scaling ($s \in [0.9, 1.2]$). The model was implemented using PyTorch 1.10.0 on Nvidia GeForce RTX 3090, taking $\sim$10 mins/epoch for $\sim$22,000 samples (training:validation $= 90{:}10$).

Experimental Setup and Evaluation Metrics: We performed 5-fold cross-validation on 465 sections (440 unlabeled + 25 labeled) from DS1 with a training-validation-testing split ratio of 80-13-5 sections (for each fold, only manually charted sections were used for testing). We then trained the model on the DS1 and tested it on the unseen dataset DS2 (sections from a macaque different from the training one). We also performed an ablation study of the method on DS2. We studied the detection performance for dense and moderate bundles with the addition of individual components of the method: (i) F_{Seg} with cross-entropy loss (CE loss), (ii) F_{Seg} with focal loss, (iii) F_{Seg} with addition of F_{Class} with contrastive loss (focal loss + ss_con loss), (iv) F_{Seg} and F_{Class} with TE (focal loss + ss_con loss + TE). We used the same postprocessing for all cases (i-iv), since our main aim is to study the effect of addition of F_{Seg}, ss_con loss and TE, rather than postprocessing. For evaluation, we used the following metrics: (1) True positive rate (TPR): number of true positive bundles/total number of true bundles charted manually, (2) Average number of FPs (FP_{avg}): number of false positive bundles/number of test sections and (3) Fiber density ratio (fib_dens): ratio between fiber voxels (obtained from fiber binary map) and the total bundle area. We obtained the fiber binary map by considering fibers within the bounding box of the bundle, enhancing the contrast using contrast-limited adaptive histogram equalization [23] and thresholding at the 95th percentile of intensity values (sample fiber maps shown in Fig. 4). We calculated the difference in the ratio (δ_{fib_dens}) between the manual charting and the detected bundles.

4   Results and Discussion

Cross-Validation (CV) on DS1: On performing 5-fold CV on DS1, we obtained better performance in the detection of dense bundles than moderate ones due to the contrast, increased fiber density and texture differences of the former with respect to the background. Fig. 3(a) shows FROC curves for

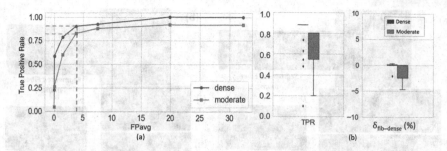

Fig. 3. Results of cross-validation on DS1. (a) FROC curves for fiber bundle detection. (b) boxplots of TPR and δ_{fib_dens} at $FP_{avg} = 2$ FPs/section, after applying continuity constraints and postprocessing. (Color figure online)

Table 1. Results of 5-fold cross-validation and ablation study. CE loss - Cross-entropy loss, Focal loss - F_{Seg} with focal loss, ss_con loss - F_{Class} with self-supervised contrastive loss, TE - temporal ensembling. (*) indicates significant improvements in the results compared to the previous row, determined using paired two-tailed T-tests. The best performance in the ablation study is highlighted in bold. ↑/↓ indicate that higher/lower values lead to better results.

	TPR ↑		$|\delta_{fib\_dens}|$ (%) ↓		FP_{avg} ↓
	Dense	Moderate	Dense	Moderate	
5-fold cross-validation	0.90 ± 0.20	0.82 ± 0.17	1.5 ± 0.45	3.5 ± 1.67	2.0
Ablation study					
CE loss	0.76 ± 0.33	0.65 ± 0.29	4.1 ± 0.39	5.8 ± 1.09	7.5
Focal loss	$*0.85 \pm 0.31$	$*0.71 \pm 0.34$	$*3.0 \pm 0.48$	$*4.6 \pm 1.01$	$*4.0$
Focal loss + ss_con loss	$*0.88 \pm 0.20$	$*0.78 \pm 0.23$	2.8 ± 0.21	$*4.0 \pm 0.86$	3.5
Focal loss + ss_con loss + TE	$\mathbf{*0.89 \pm 0.21}$	$\mathbf{0.79 \pm 0.30}$	$\mathbf{*2.0 \pm 0.21}$	$\mathbf{*3.7 \pm 0.80}$	$\mathbf{*2.5}$

dense and moderate fiber bundle detection. We obtained a TPR of 0.92/0.84 for dense/moderate bundles at 3.7 FPs/section at the *elbow point* (shown in dotted lines) for a threshold value of 0.4.

Figure 3(b) shows the boxplots of TPR and δ_{fib_dens} values after postprocessing (performance values reported in Table 1). We observed a significant reduction of FP_{avg} ($p < 0.05$) after postprocessing, mainly due to continuity constraints, for much lower changes in TPR values. Typically, fiber density ratios fib_dens ranged between ∼6–20% and ∼2–10% for dense and moderate bundles respectively. We obtained mean $\delta_{fib\_dens} = -1.5\%$ and -3.5% for dense and moderate bundles, respectively. While % values closer to 0 are better, the negative values indicate more fibers in the predicted regions than manual charting in most cases, indicating that predicted regions recover most of the fibers within the bundle.

Ablation Study Results on DS2: We trained the method on dataset DS1 for ablation study cases (i–iv), tested on DS2 (from different brain) and used a threshold of 0.4 to obtain binary maps. We used the same postprocessing for all cases (i–iv) of the study. Table 1 reports the results of the study and Fig. 4 shows

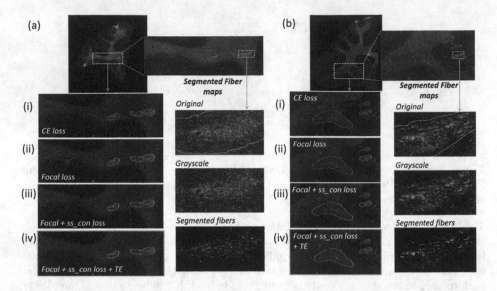

Fig. 4. Two sample results of the ablation study, with the profile of fibers within detected bundles. (a, b) Sections with ROIs enlarged (white dotted box); (i–iv) Ablation study results on the ROIs - TP, FP and FN bundles shown in yellow, red and blue outlines respectively (the proposed method highlighted in green box (iv)). Further enlarged ROIs (orange dotted box) containing fibers in the original RGB, grayscale and fiber binary maps. (Color figure online)

sample results of the ablation study for a dense bundle in the prefrontal white matter (a) and a moderate bundle in the IC (b). Among all the methods, experiments using focal loss (ii–iv) gave significantly better performance than the CE loss (case i), showing that focal loss was better at handling the heavy class imbalance. Also, using the self-supervised contrastive loss (ss_con loss) significantly improved TP regions (especially moderate fiber bundles) and reduced FP_{avg} due to the better discrimination between subtle variations in the background intensity and texture. We also observed a significant reduction in δ_{fib_dens} for focal loss + ss_con loss (case iii) in moderate fiber bundles (where the fibers are sparser than dense bundles). This shows that contrastive loss function not only reduced FPs, but also improved the segmentation of predicted regions. Using TE (case iv) further improved the detection, especially increasing the TPR of dense bundles and reducing FP_{avg}. We observed that the value of r (number of prior epochs to predict the target labels) in TE played a crucial role in the reduction of prediction noise. We set $r = 3$ because it significantly reduced FP_{avg} over $r = 1$ ($p < 0.01$), but provided FP_{avg} values not significantly different from those with higher $r = 5$ ($p = 0.52$).

The direct comparison of our results with prior work is currently not possible since fiber bundle segmentation on macaque brains has not been explored before. The work done in [10], perhaps the closest to ours, segmented fibers on marmoset brain tracer data and achieved a voxel-wise TPR of 0.7.

The main source of FPs included terminal fields (shown in Fig. 1), artifacts such as glare or dust particles, and other structures with similar intensity profiles. Use of continuity priors and ss_con loss was highly useful in removing these spurious regions. Currently, inclusion of such priors in the training framework was not possible due to the lack of sufficient number of manual chartings for consecutive sections. Hence, a future direction of this work could explore the possibility of integrating the priors within the training framework for further reduction of FPs, and improving the method to reduce the variation (indicated by standard deviation) in our results. Also, testing on additional sections from different brains could be done to expand the statistical analysis of the work and further validation of the multi-tasking model design with SimCLR method. Another area for further study is the quantification of fiber-level characteristics (e.g., fiber density and orientation).

5 Conclusions

In this work, we proposed an end-to-end automated, anatomy-constrained self supervised learning tool for accurate detection of fiber bundles on macaque tracer data. With only ~6% of training data manually charted, we achieved TPR of 0.90/0.80 for dense/moderate fiber bundles on different macaque brain sections. Our tool could be used for generating voxel visitation maps to analyse the precise route of axon bundles and their densities along fiber trajectories for voxel-level validation of dMRI tractography across multiple seed regions. The code for our method is available at https://github.com/v-sundaresan/fiberbundle_seg_tracing.

Acknowledgements. This work was supported by the National Institute of Mental Health (R01-MH045573, P50-MH106435), the National Institute of Neurological Disorders and Stroke (R01-NS119911), and the National Institute of Biomedical Imaging and Bioengineering (R01-EB021265).

References

1. Yendiki, A., Aggarwal, M., Axer, M., Howard, A.F., van Walsum, A.M.V.C., Haber, S.N.: Post mortem mapping of connectional anatomy for the validation of diffusion MRI. NeuroImage 119146 (2022)
2. Grisot, G., Haber, S.N., Yendiki, A.: Diffusion MRI and anatomic tracing in the same brain reveal common failure modes of tractography. Neuroimage **239**, 118300 (2021)
3. Maffei, C., et al.: Insights from the IronTract challenge: optimal methods for mapping brain pathways from multi-shell diffusion MRI. Neuroimage **257**, 119327 (2022)
4. Schilling, K.G., Gao, Y., Stepniewska, I., Janve, V., Landman, B.A., Anderson, A.W.: Anatomical accuracy of standard-practice tractography algorithms in the motor system-a histological validation in the squirrel monkey brain. Magn. Reson. Imaging **55**, 7–25 (2019)

5. Haber, S.N., Liu, H., Seidlitz, J., Bullmore, E.: Prefrontal connectomics: from anatomy to human imaging. Neuropsychopharmacology **47**(1), 20–40 (2022)
6. Lehman, J.F., Greenberg, B.D., McIntyre, C.C., Rasmussen, S.A., Haber, S.N.: Rules ventral prefrontal cortical axons use to reach their targets: implications for diffusion tensor imaging tractography and deep brain stimulation for psychiatric illness. J. Neurosci. **31**(28), 10392–10402 (2011)
7. Safadi, Z., et al.: Functional segmentation of the anterior limb of the internal capsule: linking white matter abnormalities to specific connections. J. Neurosci. **38**(8), 2106–2117 (2018)
8. Haynes, W.I., Haber, S.N.: The organization of prefrontal-subthalamic inputs in primates provides an anatomical substrate for both functional specificity and integration: implications for basal ganglia models and deep brain stimulation. J. Neurosci. **33**(11), 4804–4814 (2013)
9. Jbabdi, S., Lehman, J.F., Haber, S.N., Behrens, T.E.: Human and monkey ventral prefrontal fibers use the same organizational principles to reach their targets: tracing versus tractography. J. Neurosci. **33**(7), 3190–3201 (2013)
10. Woodward, A., et al.: The nanozoomer artificial intelligence connectomics pipeline for tracer injection studies of the marmoset brain. Brain Struct. Funct. **225**(4), 1225–1243 (2020)
11. Preuss, T.M., Wise, S.P.: Evolution of prefrontal cortex. Neuropsychopharmacology **47**(1), 3–19 (2022)
12. Chen, T., Kornblith, S., Norouzi, M., Hinton, G.: A simple framework for contrastive learning of visual representations. In: International Conference on Machine Learning, pp. 1597–1607. PMLR (2020)
13. Wu, H., Wang, Z., Song, Y., Yang, L., Qin, J.: Cross-patch dense contrastive learning for semi-supervised segmentation of cellular nuclei in histopathologic images. In: Proceedings of the IEEE/CVF Conference on Computer Vision and Pattern Recognition, New Orleans, pp. 11666–11675 (2022)
14. Lai, Z., Wang, C., Hu, Z., Dugger, B.N., Cheung, S.C., Chuah, C.N.: A semisupervised learning for segmentation of gigapixel histopathology images from brain tissues. In: 2021 43rd Annual International Conference of the IEEE Engineering in Medicine & Biology Society (EMBC), pp. 1920–1923. IEEE (2021)
15. Perone, C.S., Ballester, P., Barros, R.C., Cohen-Adad, J.: Unsupervised domain adaptation for medical imaging segmentation with self-ensembling. Neuroimage **194**, 1–11 (2019)
16. Huang, R., Noble, J.A., Namburete, A.I.L.: Omni-supervised learning: scaling up to large unlabelled medical datasets. In: Frangi, A.F., Schnabel, J.A., Davatzikos, C., Alberola-López, C., Fichtinger, G. (eds.) MICCAI 2018. LNCS, vol. 11070, pp. 572–580. Springer, Cham (2018). https://doi.org/10.1007/978-3-030-00928-1_65
17. Ronneberger, O., Fischer, P., Brox, T.: U-Net: convolutional networks for biomedical image segmentation. In: Navab, N., Hornegger, J., Wells, W.M., Frangi, A.F. (eds.) MICCAI 2015. LNCS, vol. 9351, pp. 234–241. Springer, Cham (2015). https://doi.org/10.1007/978-3-319-24574-4_28
18. Panayides, A.S., et al.: AI in medical imaging informatics: current challenges and future directions. IEEE J. Biomed. Health Inform. **24**(7), 1837–1857 (2020)
19. Lin, T.Y., Goyal, P., Girshick, R., He, K., Dollár, P.: Focal loss for dense object detection. In: Proceedings of the IEEE International Conference on Computer Vision, Venice, pp. 2980–2988 (2017)
20. Sundaresan, V., Zamboni, G., Rothwell, P.M., Jenkinson, M., Griffanti, L.: Triplanar ensemble U-Net model for white matter hyperintensities segmentation on MR images. Med. Image Anal. **73**, 102184 (2021)

21. Haber, S.N., Kim, K.S., Mailly, P., Calzavara, R.: Reward-related cortical inputs define a large striatal region in primates that interface with associative cortical connections, providing a substrate for incentive-based learning. J. Neurosci. **26**(32), 8368–8376 (2006)
22. Kingma, D.P., Ba, J.: Adam: a method for stochastic optimization. arXiv preprint arXiv:1412.6980 (2014)
23. Zuiderveld, K.: Contrast limited adaptive histogram equalization. Graph. Gems 474–485 (1994)

Sequential Multi-task Learning for Histopathology-Based Prediction of Genetic Mutations with Extremely Imbalanced Labels

Haleh Akrami[1,2]([⊠]), Tosha Shah[2], Amir Vajdi[2], Andrew Brown[2],
Radha Krishnan[2], Razvan Cristescu[2], and Antong Chen[2]([⊠])

[1] University of Southern California, Los Angeles, CA, USA
akrami@usc.edu
[2] Merck & Co., Inc., Rahway, NJ, USA
antong.chen@merck.com

Abstract. H&E images can be utilized to predict genetic mutations as biomarkers to potentially substitute many molecular biomarker assays in order to aid patients. Having a single model built by conducting prediction tasks simultaneously can save computation resources and provide a more generalizable model for future usage. A basic technique for generating such a comprehensive and efficient model is to employ a multi-task learning approach. However, overfitting the model to the trivial answers can occur in training for multiple tasks with extremely imbalanced class labels where resampling and rebalancing for all minor classes simultaneously are prohibited. Herein we propose a sequential multi-task learning approach to train a single model capable of predicting multiple genetic mutations while avoiding overfitting to trivial answers for imbalanced classes. We compared our strategy to the baseline multi-task training, as well as two more advanced approaches: (1) using weighted loss and (2) using self-supervised pre-training. We also used a trimming method to deal with noisy labels. To assess our methods, we trained models to predict 10 genetic mutations on the H&E images of the TCGA-LUAD dataset. AUROC and F1 score are reported, while we demonstrate that F1 score may be a more suitable metric for multi-task learning with imbalanced labels. It is shown that our proposed trimming strategy combined with sequential learning could improve the predictions on all of the mutations compared with other multi-task learning approaches. Also, we investigated the application of continual learning.

Keywords: Multi-task learning · Imbalanced label · Genetic mutation · Trimming

1 Introduction

Demands for predicting genetic mutations for assisting targeted or biomarker-based therapies [3,5,9] are growing. Deep learning techniques for predicting

H. Akrami—Work done as intern at Merck & Co., Inc., Rahway, NJ, USA.

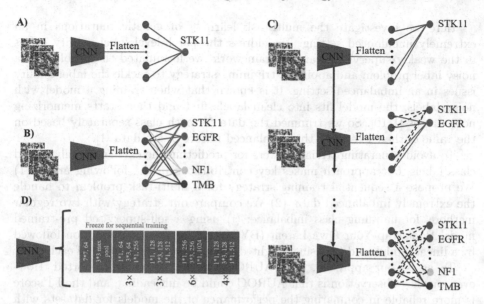

Fig. 1. A) Single-task model. B) Multi-task model. C) Sequential training. Non-trainable parameters are shown with dash lines. D) Resnet50 model where the first 20 layers are freezing for sequential training and transfer learning.

genetic mutations based on diagnostic histopathology images have reached success in recent years. This is generally regarded as a weakly supervised learning problem, as patches derived from hematoxylin and eosin (H&E)-stained whole-slide images (WSI) are fed into deep convolutional neural networks (CNN) carrying the corresponding WSI-level labels in the training phase. In the testing phase, WSI-level prediction results are aggregated from patch-level results using max or mean pooling or more sophisticated techniques e.g. weighted sum [21], or self-attention [11]. Recent findings show that learned computational histopathological features are associated with a wide range of recurrent genetic aberrations across cancer types [5,9]. Using a single model that can predict many genetic properties may be preferable for its lower computational overhead and better generalizability.

Here our goal is to train a single CNN model capable of predicting multiple molecular biomarkers using H&E WSI. In order to generate such a model, efforts have been made to assemble many digital pathology datasets in supervised or self-supervised multi-task learning frameworks [2,6,9]. However, we might encounter optimization challenges in multi-task learning emerging from varying learning speeds of different tasks and plateaus in the optimization landscape, or even gradients conflict in the learning procedure [18]. Moreover, histopathological datasets are extremely imbalanced for some gene mutation labels. It is nearly impossible to use augmentation/re-sampling techniques to reach meaningful ratios between positive/negative samples for all labels simultaneously in a multi-task learning framework. Most of the time, results converge to trivial answers for extremely imbalanced labels.

Here we investigate the multi-task learning of genetic mutations in an extremely imbalanced setting. To address the patch-level label quality issues in the weakly supervised learning framework, we formulated the problem as a noisy label problem and applied a trimming strategy to tackle the label quality issues in an imbalanced setting. It is known that when training a model with noisy labels, the model fits into clean labels first and then starts memorizing noisy labels [1,10]. So we trimmed the data for each class separately based on the value of their loss to fit the imbalanced nature of the data [1].

To avoid generating trivial answers for predicting the extremely imbalanced class labels, our approach makes key contributions in the following areas: (1) We propose a sequential training strategy for a multi-task problem to handle the extremely imbalanced data. (2) We compare our strategy with two regular methods for handling class imbalance: (i) using a self-supervised pre-trained model Bootstrap Your Own Latent (BYOL) [7] for feature extraction followed by a linear model, and (ii) using weighted loss based on the portion of each class.

To assess our approach, both AUROC and F1 scores are reported. However, our key observation is that AUROC could be misleading, and the F1 score is more reliable in comparing the performance of the models for datasets with extremely imbalanced class labels [2]. Our proposed trimming strategy combined with sequential learning could improve the predictions on all of the genetic mutations. In addition, we investigated applying continual learning (CL) to mitigate the effect of the task order and improve the performance of the model for the tasks at the beginning of the sequence.

2   Methods

A total of 670 WSIs were downloaded from TCGA-LUAD[1] dataset. We trained the network to predict ten binary genetic mutation labels. The number of positive (1) and negative (0) class samples are shown in Fig. 2(A) for each label, which are STK11 (92/490), EGFR (87/495), SETPB1 (71/511), TP53 (307/275), FAT1 (74/508), KRAS (175/407), KEAP1 (111/471), LRP1B (211/371), NF1 (88/494), and tumor mutation burden (TMB) (258/320). A threshold of 175 was applied to classify the WSIs into TMB-H (1) and TMB-L (0). Less than 5 WSIs were used for each of the 370 unique subjects.

Patches of 512×512 pixels were extracted at the $20\times$ magnification ratio, and only patches with more than 85% content as tissue were used. Example WSIs and patches are shown in Fig. 2(B). The dataset is split into a 70/10/20 ratio for training/validation/testing at the subject level. First, we compared the performance of single-task learning with different strategies to handle weak and imbalanced labels in terms of AUROC and F1 score. These methods under the single-task training framework could be considered as a set of strong baseline solutions. Then we compared the performance of various methods under the multi-task training framework.

---

[1] https://portal.gdc.cancer.gov/projects/TCGA-LUAD.

2.1   Single-Task Training

Here we started with training a separate neural network for each of the 10 binary classification tasks, as shown in Fig. 1(A). We used a ResNet50 model and compared the baseline model, denoted "regular", with four different techniques to handle weak and imbalanced labels: (i) Training with re-sampling to have a similar number of samples for both classes. This method is denoted "reSample". (ii) Start from a pre-trained model BYOL [7] trained for 80 epochs with a batch size of 256, followed by re-sampling. BYOL does not explicitly use negative samples and Instead consists of two parallel networks and predicts the projection or encoding of an augmented view of the input passed from a target and an averaging network. According to [7], BYOL's performance is comparable to its counterparts requiring negative samples but needs a smaller batch size compared to other contrastive learning models. After training the BYOL model, we freeze the first 20 layers of the pre-trained Resnet50 and train each task separately with re-sampling. Since it is out of the scope of this work, we did not particularly optimize the number of trainable parameters for this model. This method is denoted "reSample+BYOL". (iii) Starting from the previous task and freezing the first 20 layers of the Resnet50 for the training and applying re-sampling. This method is denoted "transfer". (iv) Trimming with under-sampling the dominant class. In each batch, we trimmed the data for each class separately based on the value of their loss. Different percentages (0%, 10%, 20%, 50%) of samples with the highest error were removed from the training in each batch. The trimming percentage is chosen based on the F1 score performance on the validation set. This method is denoted "trim" in subsequent sections.

The F1 score is calculated following the equations below:

$$Precision = True\ Positive/(True\ Positive + False\ Positive) \qquad (1)$$

$$Recall = True\ Positive/(True\ Positive + False\ Negative) \qquad (2)$$

$$F1 = 2 * Precision * recall/(precision + recall) \qquad (3)$$

The Micro F1 score is calculated as the average of F1 scores for all tasks.

2.2   Multi-Task Training

Following the framework in [3], we trained a ResNet50 with 10 parallel binary classification heads, namely a multi-head layer, as it is shown in Fig. 1(B). The loss was the sum of binary cross-entropy loss for each classification task. This baseline method is denoted "mutli-task". To mitigate the effect of class imbalance, we tried two strategies under the multi-task framework: (i) We used a weighted loss where weights were the ratio of positive labels in the training set. This method is denoted "multi-task-weighted". (ii) We used pre-trained weights trained with ImageNet and only continued to train the multi-head layer for one epoch. This method is denoted pre-trained-ImageNet". (iii) We trained the network using the self-supervised learning method BYOL for 80 epochs and then only fine-tuned the multi-head layer using the labels for one epoch. This method is "denoted pre-trained-BYOL" in subsequent sections.

2.3 Sequential Training

In sequential training, we started with a pre-trained BYOL model and froze the first 20 layers of the Resnet50 for the rest of the training to have more generalizable features. Then we trained the model sequentially for tasks 1 to 10 based on the sequence of genetic mutation labels introduced at the beginning of the section, i.e. trained the model for task 1 predicting STK11 for 10 epochs and kept the best weights based on the F1 score of validation data, then continued to train the model for task 2 predicting EGFR, and followed the same procedure for the remaining tasks until the model was fully trained for all subsequent tasks. We evaluated the performance of the model on the testing dataset for all 10 labels after the sequential training finished, which is different from the single-task training in Sect. 2.1 where models were only trained/tuned for the current task, and the best testing results on the current mutation label were reported. To mitigate the effect of imbalanced classes on each task, we resampled the data for each batch in a way to have a similar number of samples for both classes, which is denoted "sequential-resample". Additionally, we tried a trimming strategy to handle the noisy labels at the tile level. For each task, we had 0%, 10%, 20%, and 50% trimming based on the validation of WSI's F1 score. The trimming was applied for each batch by keeping p% of samples with less error after warming up the model. We also did under-sampling from the majority class to take care of class imbalance. The method is denoted "sequential-trimming" in subsequent sections.

2.4 Continual Learning

The goal of applying CL is to prevent catastrophic forgetting. Proposed methods to address this problem have focused on (i) regularizing intrinsic levels of plasticity to protect acquired knowledge [4,8,12], (ii) allocating new neurons or network layers to accommodate novel knowledge [16,17], and (iii) using complementary learning networks with experience replay for memory consolidation [8,15,19,20]. We used Averaged Gradient Episodic Memory (AGEM) [13], which is a combination of regularization and replay methods. AGEM modifies the gradients for updates and minimizes catastrophic forgetting by storing a subset of the observed examples from previous tasks and constraining the gradient based on those samples. When training for a new task, AGEM ensures that the loss of every episodic memory is non-increase [13]. The loss function for AGEM is calculated as:

$$minimize(\frac{1}{2}||g - \bar{g}||_2^2) \quad s.t \quad \bar{g}^T g_{ref} \geq 0 \tag{4}$$

This constrained optimization problem can now be solved very quickly; when the gradient g violates the constraint, it is projected via:

$$\bar{g} = g - \frac{g^T g_{ref}}{g_{ref}^T g_{ref}} g_{ref} \tag{5}$$

where g_{ref} is a gradient computed using a batch randomly sampled from the episodic memory of all the past tasks. We applied re-sampling to get the samples from the previous task. As the samples are similar for all tasks, we only need memory to store the labels in the sequential learning scenario.

3 Experiments and Results

We first investigated the effectiveness of re-sampling and trimming in the single-task framework. Then we compared the performance of models in the multi-task framework. We trained the ResNet50 using the WSI-level labels for the tiles and obtained the final WSI-level prediction by simply calculating the mean probability over the tiles for each WSI.

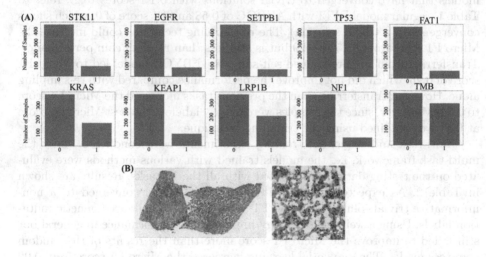

Fig. 2. A) Class distribution for the 10 genetic mutations. B) Examples of a WSI with TMB-H (left) and a patch of 512×512 pixels extracted from the WSI (right).

Single-task training was conducted following the methods introduced in Sect. 2.1. Evaluations were performed on the testing dataset of each task when the training of the model for the current task was finished. The results from various methods are shown in Table 1. For comparing the F1 score to a random solution as a baseline, we calculated the F1 score for a random coin-toss scenario in which we assumed the model randomly assigned positive labels to half of the samples and negative labels to the rest in each task.

Table 1. F1 score/AUROC testing WSI result for single-task training.

Task	Regular	reSample	reSample+BYOL	Transfer	Trim	Coin-toss F1
STK11	0.54/0.16	0.53/0.20	0.60/0.15	-	0.58/0.30	0.24
EGFR	0.50/0.12	0.61/0.41	0.73/0.34	0.75/0.50	0.73/0.34	0.23
SETBP1	0.54/0	0.44/0.16	0.50/0	0.50/0.08	0.48/0.31	0.21
TP53	0.70/0.62	0.68/0.59	0.60/0.59	0.65/0.62	0.69/0.64	0.47
FAT1	0.58/0	0.57/14	0.55/0	0.60/0	0.71/0.24	0.21
KRAS	0.41/0.13	0.46/0.40	0.53/0.37	0.55/0.40	0.48/0.47	0.38
KEAP1	0.51/0	0.41/0.15	0.55/0.21	0.57/0.34	0.52/0.31	0.28
LRP1B	0.52/0.20	0.46/0.32	0.57/0.37	0.54/0.52	0.62/0.58	0.42
NF1	0.54/0	0.50/0	0.41/0.08	0.46/0.09	0.72/0.26	0.23
TMB	0.58/0.31	0.52/0.50	0.50/0.52	0.55/0.55	0.66/0.65	0.47
Micro F1	0.15	0.29	0.26	0.34	0.41	0.31

Our results demonstrate that AUROC may not be an appropriate measurement for comparing different models in this setting as it does not reflect the models that have converged to trivial solutions with 0 F1 scores (e.g., refer to Table 1, regular model FAT1 with AUROC of 0.58 and F1 score of 0, which shows convergence to a trivial solution). The re-sampling technique could increase the Micro F1 score from 0.15 to 0.29 but is still less than random coin performance. Transferring from the pre-trained self-supervised BYOL model led to Micro F1 score of 0.26, which did not improve the performance compared with re-sampling alone. However, transferring from the previous tasks increased the Micro F1 score to 0.34. Moreover, since the samples were weakly labeled, the best Micro F1 score at 0.41 was obtained using the trimming technique.

Multi-task and sequential training experiments were conducted under the multi-task framework, i.e. the models trained with various methods were evaluated on the testing datasets associated with all the 10 tasks. Results are shown in Table 2. As expected, the multi-task baseline model converged to a non-informative trivial solution and had F1 score of 0 for imbalanced genetic mutation labels. Using a weighting strategy improved the performance in general but still failed to improve the Micro F1 score more than the results of the random coin-toss model. The sequential learning increased the Micro F1 score from 0.09 to 0.38, and trimming increased it even further to 0.41, which was the best performance in terms of the Micro F1 score amongst all methods under the multi-task framework.

Results of the AGEM-based CL with re-sampling are shown in Table 3 in comparison with the results of sequential learning with re-sampling. It is observed that CL can not improve its performance in terms of the Micro F1 score.

Table 2. F1 score/AUROC testing WSI-level results for multi-task training.

Task	Multi-task	Multi-task-weighted	pre-trained-BYOL	pre-trained-ImageNet	Sequential-resample	Sequential-trimming
STK11	0/0.50	0.08/0.45	0/0.43	0/0.64	0.30/0.60	0.25/0.51
EGFR	0/0.63	0.25/0.56	0/0.66	0/0.62	0.46/0.68	0.38/0.53
SETBP1	0/0.54	0.14/0.50	0/0.42	0/0.49	0.24/40	0.25/0.37
TP53	0.51/0.66	0.59/0.66	0.10/0.60	0.51/0.63	0.50/0.56	0.59/0.67
FAT1	0/0.59	0.22/0.57	0/0.60	0/0.73	0.16/0.52	0.50/0.56
KRAS	0/0.40	0.33/0.40	0.04/0.45	0/0.43	0.46/0.57	0.25/0.64
KEAP1	0/0.50	0.13/0.43	0.08/0.49	0/0.54	0.37/0.57	0.37/0.52
LRP1B	0.26/0.57	0.45/0.60	0/0.60	0/0.55	0.56/0.52	0.59/0.69
NF1	0/0.51	0.13/0.53	0.06/0.42	0/0.63	0.22/0.54	0.23/0.54
TMB	0.13/0.55	0.49/0.52	0.34/0.65	0.13/0.66	0.55/0.55	0.66/0.67
Micro F1	0.09	0.28	0.06	0.06	0.38	0.41

Table 3. F1 score/AUROC testing WSI-level results comparing sequential learning with re-sampling (sequential-resample) and continual learning with re-sampling (CL-resample).

Task	Sequential-resample	CL-resample
STK11	0.30/0.60	0.05/0.38
EGFR	0.46/0.68	0.29/0.57
SETBP1	0.24/0.40	0/0.43
TP53	0.50/0.56	0.16/0.28
FAT1	0.16/0.52	0.15/0.61
KRAS	0.46/0.57	0.26/0.43
KEAP1	0.37/0.57	0.21/0.0.57
LRP1B	0.56/0.52	0.42/0.68
NF1	0.22/0.54	0.13/0.48
TMB	0.55/0.55	0.49/0.68
Micro F1	0.38	0.22

4   Conclusion and Discussion

We targeted the class imbalance problem in the prediction of genetic mutations using H&E WSI. Experiments are conducted on the TCGA-LUAD dataset for the prediction of 10 genetic mutation labels. Our results demonstrate that AUROC may not be a suitable measurement for prediction accuracy as it does not reflect the models converging to trivial solutions with a 0 F1 score, which is more probable to occur when predicting multiple labels with imbalanced classes. The standard multi-task model obtained a very low F1-score due to the extreme class imbalance in multiple tasks. Starting from a Resnet50 model pre-trained with the self-supervised BYOL approach, combining trimming with sequential multi-task learning was effective in handling the problem, especially for the tasks at the end of the sequence. The Micro F1 scores of our proposed sequential multi-task learning approach were on par with the strong baseline results obtained under the single-task framework, and significantly outperformed the established baseline multi-task solution [3]. To mitigate catastrophic forgetting, we made a limited investigation of continual learning. However, we were not able to obtain improvement in terms of the Micro F1 score using a popular CL method AGEM. It was reported that AGEM might fail in the case of long task sequences [14] due to the difference between new and previous tasks, which could have made a negative impact in our setting with multiple labels. Overall, results show that the prediction of multiple genetic mutations remains a challenging problem. For future research, efforts need to be made on studying the effect of changing the order of sequential learning tasks. More sophisticated CL methods will also need to be investigated.

References

1. Arpit, D., et al.: A closer look at memorization in deep networks. In: International Conference on Machine Learning, pp. 233–242. PMLR (2017)
2. Ciga, O., Xu, T., Martel, A.L.: Self supervised contrastive learning for digital histopathology. Mach. Learn. Appl. **7**, 100198 (2022)
3. Coudray, N., et al.: Classification and mutation prediction from non-small cell lung cancer histopathology images using deep learning. Nat. Med. **24**(10), 1559–1567 (2018)
4. Douillard, A., Chen, Y., Dapogny, A., Cord, M.: PLOP: learning without forgetting for continual semantic segmentation. arXiv preprint arXiv:2011.11390 (2020)
5. Fu, Y., et al.: Pan-cancer computational histopathology reveals mutations, tumor composition and prognosis. Nat. Cancer **1**(8), 800–810 (2020)
6. Graham, S., Vu, Q.D., Jahanifar, M., Minhas, F., Snead, D., Rajpoot, N.: One model is all you need: multi-task learning enables simultaneous histology image segmentation and classification. arXiv preprint arXiv:2203.00077 (2022)
7. Grill, J.B., et al.: Bootstrap your own latent-a new approach to self-supervised learning. In: Advances in Neural Information Processing Systems, vol. 33, pp. 21271–21284 (2020)
8. Jung, H., Ju, J., Jung, M., Kim, J.: Less-forgetting learning in deep neural networks. arXiv preprint arXiv:1607.00122 (2016)
9. Kather, J.N., et al.: Pan-cancer image-based detection of clinically actionable genetic alterations. Nat. Cancer **1**(8), 789–799 (2020)
10. Kim, Y., Kim, J.M., Akata, Z., Lee, J.: Large loss matters in weakly supervised multi-label classification. In: Proceedings of the IEEE/CVF Conference on Computer Vision and Pattern Recognition, pp. 14156–14165 (2022)
11. Li, J., et al.: A multi-resolution model for histopathology image classification and localization with multiple instance learning. Comput. Biol. Med. **131**, 104253 (2021)
12. Li, Z., Hoiem, D.: Learning without forgetting. IEEE Trans. Pattern Anal. Mach. Intell. **40**(12), 2935–2947 (2017)

13. Lopez-Paz, D., Ranzato, M.: Gradient episodic memory for continual learning. arXiv preprint arXiv:1706.08840 (2017)
14. Mai, Z., Li, R., Kim, H., Sanner, S.: Supervised contrastive replay: revisiting the nearest class mean classifier in online class-incremental continual learning. arXiv preprint arXiv:2103.13885 (2021)
15. Parisi, G.I., Kemker, R., Part, J.L., Kanan, C., Wermter, S.: Continual lifelong learning with neural networks: a review. Neural Netw. **113**, 54–71 (2019)
16. Parisi, G.I., Tani, J., Weber, C., Wermter, S.: Lifelong learning of human actions with deep neural network self-organization. Neural Netw. **96**, 137–149 (2017)
17. Rusu, A.A., et al.: Progressive neural networks. arXiv preprint arXiv:1606.04671 (2016)
18. Sener, O., Koltun, V.: Multi-task learning as multi-objective optimization. In: Advances in Neural Information Processing Systems, vol. 31 (2018)
19. Shin, H., Lee, J.K., Kim, J., Kim, J.: Continual learning with deep generative replay. arXiv preprint arXiv:1705.08690 (2017)
20. Soltoggio, A.: Short-term plasticity as cause-effect hypothesis testing in distal reward learning. Biol. Cybern. **109**(1), 75–94 (2015)
21. Wulczyn, E., et al.: Deep learning-based survival prediction for multiple cancer types using histopathology images. PLoS ONE **15**(6) (2020)

Morph-Net: End-to-End Prediction of Nuclear Morphological Features from Histology Images

Gozde N. Gunesli$^{(\boxtimes)}$, Robert Jewsbury, Shan E Ahmed Raza, and Nasir M. Rajpoot

The Tissue Image Analytics Centre, Department of Computer Science, University of Warwick, Coventry, UK
{Gozde.Gunesli,Rob.Jewsbury,Shan.Raza,N.M.Rajpoot}@warwick.ac.uk

Abstract. Analysis using morphological features of different types of nuclei have been shown to be useful for many different tasks in computational pathology. To obtain morphological features of nuclei in an image, a necessary first step in previous studies has been to apply a segmentation (and/or classification) method. The features are then calculated by using the obtained segmentation and classification maps. Although the segmentation and classification models may perform well on pixel-wise segmentation and classification tasks, they are not optimized for obtaining the morphological features. In this paper, we present Morph-Net, an end-to-end model that can directly predict morphological features of different types of nuclei for a given input image. We show that, the morphological features predicted directly by Morph-Net are more accurate compared to calculating them after a segmentation and classification step.

Keywords: Computational pathology · Histology image analysis · Morphometrics

1 Introduction

Automated analysis of tissue morphology in high-resolution histopathology images aims to help relieve the significant clinical burden on pathologists and to improve diagnostic and prognostic patient outcomes [9]. An automated quantification of the underlying tissue and cell morphology in a Whole Slide Image (WSI) could also further enhance our understanding of the tumor micro-environment and lead to the discovery of novel, predictive biomarkers.

WSIs are frequently composed of hundreds of thousands of small components such as cells, nuclei, glands etc. From these small components, many features can be extracted from WSIs related to characteristics of the underlying tissue morphology. For example, by analysis of morphological features at the gland-level, it has been shown that highly accurate grading of colorectal adenocarcinoma is possible [1]. Also, Diao *et al.* [5] were able to predict various molecular

Y. Huo et al. (Eds.): MOVI 2022, LNCS 13578, pp. 136–144, 2022.
https://doi.org/10.1007/978-3-031-16961-8_14

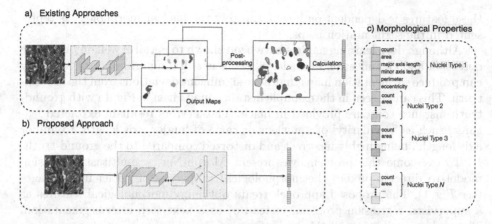

Fig. 1. Overview of existing approaches (a) and the proposed approach (b). For a given input image, the proposed approach directly predicts the morphological properties; while existing approaches apply segmentation/classification, post-processing and feature calculation steps to obtain them. Example morphological properties are presented in (c): six different feature types (i.e., nuclei count, area, major axis length, minor axis length, perimeter, eccentricity) for each nuclei class.

signatures across five different cancer types using cell and tissue level features (e.g. cell-level counts and densities of cell types in different tissue types).

Nuclear features are a subset of WSI features which contain spatial, textural and morphological characteristics of various types of cell nuclei. Cancer pathology has long been associated with alterations in nuclear morphology (e.g., nuclear pleomorphism) [17]. Development of computerized tools to analyze the relationship between different quantitative nuclear morphological features (morphometrics) and clinical outcomes dates back to 1982 [4]. Since then morphological nuclear characteristics relating to the size and shape of the nucleus (e.g., nuclear area, perimeter, major and minor axis lengths, circularity etc.) are considered to be crucial prognostic indicators in many cancer types such as breast cancer [14], renal cell carcinoma [16] and colorectal adenocarcinoma [11]. More recently, analysis using nuclear features has been shown to be useful for various different tasks, such as diagnosis and prognosis of non-small cell lung cancer [21], prediction of estrogen receptor status in breast cancer [18], likelihood of recurrence in early-stage non-small cell lung cancer [3] and diffuse large B-Cell lymphoma (DLBCL) survival outcome [19].

Existing computational methods apply a detection and/or classification method as the first step in their work-flow (see Fig. 1a). For this step, some have used methods like Otsu Thresholding [21] or watershed transform [3,18], while recent studies use more advanced methods. For example, CNNs are trained in [5] for cell and tissue detection and classification, while [19] uses the Hover-Net [8] deep learning model for more accurate nuclei boundary detection and classification. Nuclear features are then calculated by using the obtained nuclei segmentation and classification maps from the first step. Therefore, reliability of these features is dependent on how accurately the nuclear morphology is represented in the segmentation maps.

Although deep learning models have been shown to perform well on pixel-wise detection and classification of nuclei [8] there is still a margin of error and they can produce segmentation maps that have significant deviations from the ground-truth. This can be seen in the example instance map given in Fig. 1a with ground-truth instance contours provided in black. These errors result in extracted features, such as 'circularity' of a nucleus or ratio of 'major axis length' to 'minor axis length', being highly incorrect and distorted compared to the ground-truth.

To overcome this problem, we present Morph-Net, a multitask regression model to directly predict the morphological properties of nuclei from images (see Fig. 1). The proposed approach treats obtaining morphological features as a supervised regression problem, instead of as a next step after segmentation. The main contributions of this paper are as follows:

- A new end-to-end model, Morph-Net, is proposed with the aim of directly obtaining morphological features more accurately by avoiding the intermediate nuclei segmentation and classification steps currently employed;
- We show that the proposed network can outperform the state-of-the-art segmentation and classification network in this task of predicting morphological properties;
- Visual analysis of Morph-Net's saliency maps show the proposed framework focuses on the corresponding regions of a given nuclear class for predicting the relevant features without being given explicit, localised ground truth during training.

2   Methods

2.1   Quantitative Image Features

Nuclear features are obtained using the ground-truth pixel-level instance segmentation masks of nuclear classes for the images in the dataset. The nuclear feature types used in this study are related to size, shape and density of different classes of nuclei in a given image. These target features are obtained to train the model and to test its performance. Six different features for each nuclear class are obtained using the ground-truth pixel-wise instance maps and class maps for all images in the dataset. First feature type 'Nuclei Count' represents number of nuclei belonging to a nuclear class in the image. This feature type can be used to represent the density of a nuclear class in a WSI. The other features which reflect the size and shape of the nuclei (i.e., 'Area', 'Major axis length', 'Minor axis length', 'Perimeter', 'Eccentricity') are calculated for each nucleus belonging to the four nuclei classes. Features are calculated using scikit-image library [20]. Then, for each image, each feature type is aggregated for each nuclei class by taking the sum. If there are no nuclei belonging to a specific class in an image, then features for that class are assigned to zero. Consequently, there are 24 regression target values (6 *feature types* × 4 *classes*) for each image.

Table 1. Comparison metrics of Hover-Net [8] and Morph-Net models. The average results for each feature type across all nuclei classes across three dataset splits are reported here. Standard deviations are reported in parentheses.

	Metrics	Hover-Net [8]	Morph-Net
Count	RMSE	4.643(±0.901)	**3.645(±0.723)**
	R^2	0.796(±0.103)	**0.875(±0.063)**
Area	RMSE	1784.032(±510.594)	**1420.795(±415.291)**
	R^2	0.813(±0.078)	**0.872(±0.081)**
Major axis length	RMSE	118.030(±28.240)	**93.751(±24.352)**
	R^2	0.821(±0.069)	**0.883(±0.059)**
Minor axis length	RMSE	72.660(±15.982)	**57.018(±13.796)**
	R^2	0.810(±0.101)	**0.877(±0.081)**
Perimeter	RMSE	315.952(±78.884)	**245.337(±63.653)**
	R^2	0.816(±0.075)	**0.884(±0.065)**
Eccentricity	RMSE	3.452(±0.702)	**2.748(±0.559)**
	R^2	0.794(±0.086)	**0.871(±0.054)**

2.2 The Morph-Net Model

The proposed Morph-Net model is a multi-task regression model, with a backbone architecture based on the DenseNet121 model [10]. An overview of the proposed Morph-Net model is shown in Fig. 1. Instead of the final fully connected layer in DenseNet121, we have used two fully connected layers, with sizes 256 and 24, the latter being the size of the output per input image.

As we predict all 24 different output regression tasks simultaneously, one challenge is to adjust the contribution weights of different tasks' losses with respect to the total loss. A solution used for similar challenges in the literature [12,15] is modeling loss contribution weights as trainable parameters and based on individual task's uncertainty. While training Morph-Net, we employed the approach of [15], (we call it Adaptive Weighting Losses or AWL). During the network training, while Mean Squared Error (MSE) loss is used to calculate individual losses of each task, AWL is used to adjust the loss contribution weights. Following [15], with output tasks $\tau \epsilon T$, ground-truth values y_τ and predictions y'_τ, the total loss L_T is defined as:

$$L_T = \sum_{\tau \epsilon T} \frac{1}{2c_\tau{}^2} MSE(y_\tau, y'_\tau) + ln(1 + 2c_\tau{}^2), \qquad (1)$$

where all c_τ are added to the learnable network parameters.

3 Experimental Results and Discussion

To compare with the standard approach, using a segmentation and classification model, we have used the state-of-the-art Hover-Net model [8]. Nuclear

Table 2. Comparison of different Morph-Net variations: average RMSE metric values for each feature type (Count, Area (a), Major Axis Length (b), Minor Axis Length (c), Perimeter (d), Eccentricity (e)) across all nuclear classes across three dataset splits

		Count	(a)	(b)	(c)	(d)	(e)
Morph-Net		**3.65 (±0.72)**	**1420.80 (±415.29)**	**93.75 (±24.35)**	**57.02 (±13.80)**	**245.34 (±63.65)**	**2.75 (±0.56)**
Morph-Net - withoutAWL		3.74 (±0.78)	1431.13 (±421.39)	95.04 (±24.17)	57.71 (±13.60)	**248.18 (±62.52)**	2.81 (±0.58)
Morph Net with fewer target featuretypes	Only Count	3.65(±0.80)	-	-	-	-	-
	Count+(a)	3.65(±0.72)	**1415.46**(±406.36)	-	-	-	-
	Count+(b)+(c)	**3.63**(±0.74)	-	**93.08**(±24.69)	**56.80**(±13.72)	-	-
	Count+(d)	3.65(±0.67)	-	-	-	250.51(±63.29)	-
	Count+(e)	3.66(±0.78)	-	-	-	-	**2.77**(±0.64)

properties are calculated using postprocessed segmentation and classification maps predicted by the model, the same way they are calculated from ground-truth maps for Morph-Net model training and testing. Additionally, we trained Morph-Net with fewer types of target features to understand how performance is affected by different feature types. Finally, we also tested the Morph-Net model without using the AWL strategy in training. In this case, the weights of each task is fixed to one.

3.1 The Dataset

We used the PanNuke [6,7] dataset for our experiments. This is a nuclei instance segmentation and classification dataset containing tissue images and corresponding ground-truth instance maps across 19 different tissue types. Four nuclei classes are annotated: Neoplastic cells, Inflammatory, Connective/Soft tissue cells and Epithelial. The PanNuke dataset has three folds of data samples containing 2656, 2523, 2722 256×256 images respectively. All models were trained and tested on three splits. Each training/validation/test set in each split contains one fold of data - same ones used for performance comparison in [7].

3.2 Implementation Details

All backbone models are initialized with ImageNet [13] weights. The Adam optimizer is used with initial learning rate of 0.001 and the learning rate is halved every 25 epochs. Early stopping approach based on validation loss with patience of 100 epochs was taken. Various kinds of input data augmentations were applied in training time randomly (i.e., Vertical Flip, Horizontal Flip, Rotate 90°, Gaussian Noise, Gaussian Blur, Median Blur). At the time of training, the target feature values were scaled to [0,1] based on maximum and minimum values of that feature type for all nuclei classes in the training set. These minimum and maximum values in the training set were saved and used in the testing time, to re-scale predicted values to normal range. Other than re-scaling, no post-processing step was applied to Morph-Net predictions.

Table 3. Exhaustive comparison metrics of Hover-Net and Morph-Net models. The average results for each feature type and for each nuclei class (1: Neoplastic cells, 2: Inflammatory, 3: Connective/Soft tissue cells, 4: Epithelial) across three dataset splits are reported here. Standard deviations are reported in parentheses.

Property name	Nuclei class	RMSE		R^2	
		Hover-Net	Morph-Net	Hover-Net	Morph-Net
Count	Class 1	5.88(±0.41)	**4.59(±0.41)**	0.844(±0.008)	**0.905(±0.010)**
	Class 2	3.64(±0.17)	**3.08(±0.36)**	0.912(±0.011)	**0.936(±0.018)**
	Class 3	5.00(±0.17)	**3.93(±0.19)**	0.635(±0.012)	**0.774(±0.016)**
	Class 4	4.04(±0.06)	**2.97(±0.07)**	0.791(±0.008)	**0.887(±0.006)**
Area	Class 1	2536.46(±128.90)	**1991.04(±77.40)**	0.889(±0.010)	**0.931(±0.004)**
	Class 2	1137.34(±124.40)	**842.11(±35.72)**	0.871(±0.026)	**0.929(±0.005)**
	Class 3	1631.63(±27.07)	**1514.09(±66.22)**	0.695(±0.005)	**0.737(±0.021)**
	Class 4	1830.68(±15.21)	**1335.91(±47.46)**	0.796(±0.004)	**0.892(±0.007)**
Major axis length	Class 1	158.45(±6.76)	**125.15(±7.30)**	0.868(±0.005)	**0.918(±0.006)**
	Class 2	80.01(±4.78)	**61.56(±4.15)**	0.898(±0.010)	**0.939(±0.008)**
	Class 3	120.50(±3.25)	**105.34(±4.51)**	0.722(±0.003)	**0.787(±0.013)**
	Class 4	113.15(±1.44)	**82.93(±2.73)**	0.795(±0.005)	**0.890(±0.007)**
Minor axis length	Class 1	97.13(±5.08)	**77.12(±5.458)**	0.880(±0.006)	**0.924(±0.007)**
	Class 2	53.72(±4.02)	**40.38(±2.86)**	0.908(±0.011)	**0.948(±0.007)**
	Class 3	68.75(±1.75)	**59.01(±2.55)**	0.649(±0.010)	**0.741(±0.019)**
	Class 4	71.02(±1.02)	**51.54(±1.35)**	0.804(±0.008)	**0.897(±0.005)**
Perimeter	Class 1	433.76(±22.29)	**330.71(±19.32)**	0.865(±0.007)	**0.921(±0.006)**
	Class 2	215.88(±15.66)	**161.73(±9.69)**	0.900(±0.012)	**0.944(±0.007)**
	Class 3	310.03(±7.75)	**269.73(±12.22)**	0.705(±0.005)	**0.777(±0.016)**
	Class 4	304.13(±4.32)	**219.17(±5.55)**	0.795(±0.007)	**0.893(±0.005)**
Eccentricity	Class 1	4.35(±0.25)	**3.43(±0.24)**	0.834(±0.006)	**0.897(±0.008)**
	Class 2	2.61(±0.12)	**2.25(±0.22)**	0.897(±0.012)	**0.923(±0.017)**
	Class 3	3.84(±0.12)	**3.08(±0.16)**	0.663(±0.008)	**0.783(±0.018)**
	Class 4	2.99(±0.04)	**2.21(±0.07)**	0.780(±0.006)	**0.879(±0.008)**

3.3   Evaluation Metrics

To evaluate the models' regression performance, R^2 (coefficient of determination) and Root Mean Square Error (RMSE) are used. R^2 is the percentage of the variation in the variables that the model can explain. RMSE is used as a metric for comparing the errors of different models' predictions.

3.4   Performance Comparison

In Table 1, a comparison of the Hover-Net and Morph-Net models is presented. In this table, we report R2 and RMSE metrics for each feature type averaged across all nuclei classes across the three dataset splits. We provide a full, detailed comparison of per-class performance for each feature type in Table 3. They show that Morph-Net is able to outperform the current state-of-the-art Hover-Net model, with a lower RMSE and a higher R^2, for every feature type and for every nuclear class.

In Table 2, comparative results of different variations of Morph-Net model are reported. Here we see that for all of the target feature types, training the model with AWL gives better results. We postulate that adjusting loss contribution weights may have a small effect because models are trained with feature-wise scaled targets as explained. Additionally, comparing the entire Morph-Net with Morph-Net models which are trained to predict fewer target feature types we show that adding multiple types of features does not decrease the performance significantly and it may even be helping learning some tasks better. For example, the entire Morph-Net model is able to achieve lower RMSE when predicting the perimeter of nuclei compared to a model that only predicts the nuclei count and their perimeter. This is also observed for the eccentricity feature.

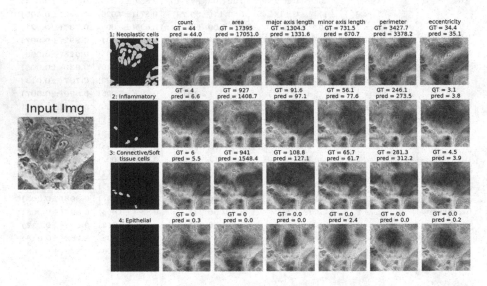

Fig. 2. Saliency maps: leftmost column is ground-truth segmentation maps, other columns are visualizations of the model's focus for a given feature. We also detail the ground-truth (GT) values and the model predictions (pred) above each corresponding saliency map.

3.5   Saliency Maps

We used Grad-cam++ [2] to visualize the significant regions of an image in predicting a given nuclei class' morphological features. Some examples can be seen in Fig. 2. They show that the significant regions for predicting a given nuclei class' properties are localised and correspond to the locations of that nuclear type within the input image. This is observed to be consistent for all nuclei types and for all the features for a given class. Interestingly we also see in Fig. 2 that for the epithelial class, of which there are no nuclei present in this example, that the regions highlighted by Grad-cam are areas often areas in which no nuclei are present.

These activation maps indicate that the model has implicitly learnt the characteristics of the different nuclei in the training data and that the location of these characteristics are important for the given tasks e.g. the count of neoplastic cells is related to locations within the image that have neoplastic cells. It has learnt this without any labels as to where different nuclei are or what class nuclear instances belong to.

4 Conclusion

The proposed Morph-Net model can accurately predict morphological properties of nuclei in histology images, without an explicit segmentation step, as opposed to existing methods in the literature. It has significant benefits in terms of better performance on obtained features and reduced computation time by skipping the segmentation, classification and post-processing steps. In addition, this model can be employed to extract nuclear features, without requiring any domain knowledge on specifics of individual features. This would make analysis straightforward and less tedious. An interesting question arising from the study is how much we can diversify the set of predicted features without performance deteriorating.

We envisage that in future, this framework can be utilized for downstream analysis. It's superior performance and lower resource requirements compared to current methods make it an interesting avenue for exploration at WSI level.

Acknowledgements. This work was partly supported by the Innovate UK grant (18181) for PathLAKE project.

References

1. Awan, R., et al.: Glandular morphometrics for objective grading of colorectal adenocarcinoma histology images. Sci. Rep. **7**(1), 1–12 (2017)
2. Chattopadhay, A., Sarkar, A., Howlader, P., Balasubramanian, V.N.: Grad-CAM++: generalized gradient-based visual explanations for deep convolutional networks. In: 2018 IEEE Winter Conference on Applications of Computer Vision (WACV), pp. 839–847. IEEE (2018)
3. Corredor, G., et al.: Spatial architecture and arrangement of tumor-infiltrating lymphocytes for predicting likelihood of recurrence in early-stage non-small cell lung cancer. Clin. Cancer Res. **25**(5), 1526–1534 (2019)
4. Diamond, D.A., Berry, S.J., Umbricht, C., Jewett, H.J., Coffey, D.S.: Computerized image analysis of nuclear shape as a prognostic factor for prostatic cancer. Prostate **3**(4), 321–332 (1982)
5. Diao, J.A., et al.: Human-interpretable image features derived from densely mapped cancer pathology slides predict diverse molecular phenotypes. Nat. Commun. **12**(1), 1–15 (2021)
6. Gamper, J., Alemi Koohbanani, N., Benet, K., Khuram, A., Rajpoot, N.: Pan-Nuke: an open pan-cancer histology dataset for nuclei instance segmentation and classification. In: Reyes-Aldasoro, C.C., Janowczyk, A., Veta, M., Bankhead, P., Sirinukunwattana, K. (eds.) ECDP 2019. LNCS, vol. 11435, pp. 11–19. Springer, Cham (2019). https://doi.org/10.1007/978-3-030-23937-4_2

7. Gamper, J., et al.: Pannuke dataset extension, insights and baselines. arXiv preprint arXiv:2003.10778 (2020)
8. Graham, S., et al.: Hover-net: simultaneous segmentation and classification of nuclei in multi-tissue histology images. Med. Image Anal. **58**, 101563 (2019)
9. Gurcan, M.N., Boucheron, L.E., Can, A., Madabhushi, A., Rajpoot, N.M., Yener, B.: Histopathological image analysis: a review. IEEE Rev. Biomed. Eng. **2**, 147–171 (2009)
10. Huang, G., Liu, Z., Van Der Maaten, L., Weinberger, K.Q.: Densely connected convolutional networks. In: Proceedings of the IEEE Conference on Computer Vision and Pattern Recognition, pp. 4700–4708 (2017)
11. Ikeguchi, M., Sakatani, T., Endo, K., Makino, M., Kaibara, N.: Computerized nuclear morphometry is a useful technique for evaluating the high metastatic potential of colorectal adenocarcinoma. Cancer **86**(10), 1944–1951 (1999)
12. Kendall, A., Gal, Y., Cipolla, R.: Multi-task learning using uncertainty to weigh losses for scene geometry and semantics. In: Proceedings of the IEEE Conference on Computer Vision and Pattern Recognition, pp. 7482–7491 (2018)
13. Krizhevsky, A., Sutskever, I., Hinton, G.E.: Imagenet classification with deep convolutional neural networks. In: Advances in Neural Information Processing Systems, vol. 25 (2012)
14. Kronqvist, P., Kuopio, T., Jalava, P., Collan, Y.: Morphometrical malignancy grading is a valuable prognostic factor in invasive ductal breast cancer. Br. J. Cancer **87**(11), 1275–1280 (2002)
15. Liebel, L., Körner, M.: Auxiliary tasks in multi-task learning. arXiv preprint arXiv:1805.06334 (2018)
16. Özer, E., et al.: Prognostic significance of nuclear morphometry in renal cell carcinoma. BJU Int. **90**(1), 20–25 (2002)
17. Pienta, K.J., Partin, A.W., Coffey, D.S.: Cancer as a disease of DNA organization and dynamic cell structure. Cancer Res. **49**(10), 2525–2532 (1989)
18. Rawat, R.R., Ruderman, D., Macklin, P., Rimm, D.L., Agus, D.B.: Correlating nuclear morphometric patterns with estrogen receptor status in breast cancer pathologic specimens. NPJ Breast Cancer **4**(1), 1–7 (2018)
19. Vrabac, D., et al.: DLBCL-Morph: morphological features computed using deep learning for an annotated digital DLBCL image set. Sci. Data **8**(1), 1–8 (2021)
20. Van der Walt, S., et al.: scikit-image: image processing in python. PeerJ **2**, e453 (2014)
21. Yu, K.H., et al.: Predicting non-small cell lung cancer prognosis by fully automated microscopic pathology image features. Nat. Commun. **7**(1), 1–10 (2016)

A Light-Weight Interpretable Model
for Nuclei Detection
and Weakly-Supervised Segmentation

Yixiao Zhang[1]($\boxtimes$), Adam Kortylewski[2], Qing Liu[3], Seyoun Park[1],
Benjamin Green[1], Elizabeth Engle[1], Guillermo Almodovar[1], Ryan Walk[1],
Sigfredo Soto-Diaz[1], Janis Taube[1], Alex Szalay[1], and Alan Yuille[1]

[1] Johns Hopkins University, Baltimore, MD 21218, USA
yzhan334@jhu.edu
[2] Max Planck Institute for Informatics, 66123 Saarbrücken, Germany
akortyle@mpi-inf.mpg.de
[3] Adobe Systems, Inc., San Jose, CA 95110, USA

Abstract. The field of computational pathology has witnessed great
advancements since deep neural networks have been widely applied.
These networks usually require large numbers of annotated data to train
vast parameters. However, it takes significant effort to annotate a large
histo-pathology dataset. We introduce a light-weight and interpretable
model for nuclei detection and weakly-supervised segmentation. It only
requires annotations on isolated nucleus, rather than on all nuclei in the
dataset. Besides, it is a generative compositional model that first locates
parts of nucleus, then learns the spatial correlation of the parts to further
locate the nucleus. This process brings interpretability in its prediction.
Empirical results on an in-house dataset show that in detection, the proposed method achieved comparable or better performance than its deep
network counterparts, especially when the annotated data is limited. It
also outperforms popular weakly-supervised segmentation methods. The
proposed method could be an alternative solution for the data-hungry
problem of deep learning methods.

Keywords: Nuclei detection and segmentation · Weakly-supervised

1 Introduction

Histopathology images provide an understanding of the microenvironment of
various diseases. Nuclei detection and segmentation plays an important role for
the analysis of cell morphology and organization. Unfortunately, the non-uniform
chromatin texture, irregularity in size and shape as well as touching cells and
background clutters put a big challenge to automated nuclei detection and segmentation [2,13,24].

Supplementary Information The online version contains supplementary material
available at https://doi.org/10.1007/978-3-031-16961-8_15.

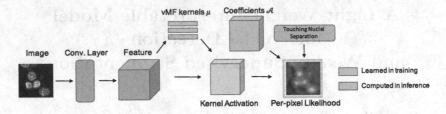

Fig. 1. Flowchart of the proposed method for nuclei detection. A convolution layer is used as feature extractor. For training, we cropped nucleus image patches and learn model parameters (μ and $\mathcal{A}$) in an unsupervised way. In testing, we compute the nucleus existence probability with learned parameters, together with a shape decomposition algorithm to separate touching nuclei, to obtain a per-pixel likelihood prediction.

Recently, deep convolutional neural networks (DNNs) have shown remarkable and reliable performance in histopathology image nuclei detection and segmentation [5,12,16,23,28]. Some works adapt a top-down object detector such as Faster RCNN [18] to histopathology images [3,4]. Others formalize detection as regression to a proximity map, where values on the proximity map represent the proximity to or probability of a nucleus center [8,21,26]. However, the collection of a large number of annotated data is critical and becomes a bottleneck to train conventional DNNs for the analysis of new modalities. To address this issue, there have been interests in nuclei segmentation with weak supervision. Most works in this direction exploited pseudo labels such as progressive model output [14], Voronoi and clustering labels [17], and super-pixel [6]. Nevertheless, a large collection of data is still needed, and most works regard DNNs as a black box without exploring its hidden representations, thus having little interpretability in their decision process. Considering nuclei shapes are invariant to stains, generative models for nuclei detection and segmentation learned from a small dataset are an alternative for efficient and robust analysis of pathology images.

In this study, we propose a light-weight interpretable model for nuclei detection and weakly supervised segmentation. We aim to design a generative model for a single nucleus, therefore only annotations on isolated nucleus are required, which significantly reduces the annotation cost. Inspired by the Compositional Networks [11], we developed a model that do explicit compositional modeling of a nucleus. In this way, the proposed method is able to locate nuclei by finding image regions that it can explain with high probability, and give human interpretable explanations for its prediction. To the best of our knowledge, we are the first to adapt Compositional Networks to nuclei detection and segmentation on histopathology images. To further boost the performance at touching nuclei that are hard to locate and segment precisely, we introduce a non-learning algorithm that requires no annotations to separate touching nuclei. Near-convex shape decomposition has been widely studied in its application to segment binary shapes into parts. However, little has been studied in its effectiveness in separating touch nuclei in histopathology images. We adapted a near-convex shape decomposition algorithm by developing novel ways of defining cuts and assigning pathologically reasonable weights to the cuts, which proved to be well suited for this task. The output of the separation algorithm is integrated into the compositional model. Empirical results on an in-house DAPI (4',6-diamidino-2-phenylindole) stained pathology image dataset demonstrate the effectiveness and data efficiency of the proposed method for nuclei detection and weakly-supervised segmentation.

2 Method

In Sect. 2.1, we discuss Compositional Network [11], which was originally introduced for natural image classification. We discuss its interpretability for nuclei detection in Sect. 2.2. Section 2.3 discusses our extension based on the Compositional Networks to multiple instance detection, where each nucleus is regarded as an object instance. Finally, in Sect. 2.4, we utilize the prior knowledge about the near-convex shape of nuclei, and introduce near-convex shape decomposition into the developed model, which further facilitates the separation of touching nuclei. The whole flowchart is illustrated in Fig. 1.

2.1 Compositional Networks for Nuclei Modeling

Compositional Network [11] explains the feature map from a convolutional layer in a generative view. Denote a feature map as $F \in \mathbb{R}^{H \times W \times D}$, with H and W being the spatial size and D being the channel size. The feature vector f_i at position i are assumed independently generated, and each is modeled as a mixture of von-Mises-Fisher (vMF) distributions:

$$p(F|\mathcal{A}, \Lambda) = \prod_i p(f_i|\mathcal{A}_i, \Lambda), \tag{1}$$

$$p(f_i|\mathcal{A}_i, \Lambda) = \sum_k \alpha_{i,k} p(f_i|\mu_k), \tag{2}$$

$$p(f_i|\mu_k) \propto \exp \{\sigma f_i^T \mu_k\}, \|f_i\| = 1, \|\mu_k\| = 1, \tag{3}$$

where $\Lambda = \{\mu_k\}$ are kernels for vMF distribution, which can be regarded as the "mean" feature vector of each mixture component k, and $\mathcal{A}_i = \{\alpha_{i,k}\}$ are the spatial coefficients, which learn the probability of μ_k being activated at position i. We say that a vMF kernel μ_k is activated at position i if f_i and μ_k have a high cosine similarity. We set the hyperparameter $\sigma = 30$ for tractability. Given a set of feature maps, the mixture coefficients $\{\alpha_{i,k}\}$ and the vMF kernels $\{\mu_k\}$ can be learned via Maximum Likelihood Estimation in an unsupervised way.

2.2 Interpretable Modeling of Nucleus

An important property of convolutional networks is that the spatial information is preserved in the feature maps. To utilize this property, the set of spatial coefficients $\{\alpha_{i,k}\}$ are introduced to describe the expected activation of a kernel μ_k at a position i. Thus, α_k at all positions can be intuitively thought of as a 2D template, which depicts the expected spatial activation pattern of parts of a nucleus – e.g. where the edges are expected to be located in the image. Therefore, the decision process of the proposed model can be interpreted as first detecting parts, then spatially combining them to get a probability about the nucleus' presence. Note that this implements a part-based voting mechanism.

As the spatial pattern varies dramatically with the shape, size and orientation of nuclei, we further represent F as a mixture of compositional models:

$$p(F|\Theta) = \sum_{m=1}^{M} \nu_m p(F|\mathcal{A}^m), \tag{4}$$

with $\mathcal{V}=\{\nu^m \in \{0,1\}, \sum_m \nu_m=1\}$. Here M is the number of compositional models in the mixture distribution and ν_m is a binary assignment variable that indicates which compositional model is active. Intuitively, each mixture component m will represent a different set of nuclei with specific shape and size (see Fig. 3 in Appendix). The parameters of the mixture components $\{\mathcal{A}^m\}$ need to be learned in an EM-style manner by iterating between estimating the assignment variables $\mathcal{V}$ and maximum likelihood estimation of $\{\mathcal{A}^m\}$.

2.3   Adaptation to Nucleus Detection

Previous work has proposed to detect salient object in natural images based on Compositional Network [25]. However, it is limited by the assumption that only one salient object is present in an image. Due to the significant difference between histopathology images and natural images, the adaptation for nucleus detection is non-trivial.

First, the background in DAPI stained histopathology images is cleaner than natural images. However, this encourages the model to rely heavily on the background signals, which is undesirable and results in false positives in background regions. We propose to get rid of the disturbance of background signals by masking. For each mixture component m, we pick a subset from $\mathcal{A}^m$ to obtain a soft foreground mask: $M^m = \sum_{k \in K_f} \alpha_k^m$, where K_f is a subset of vMF kernels which represents foreground parts (interior, edge, etc.). Then, we modify the computation of log-likelihood of $p(F|\mathcal{A}^m)$ as:

$$\log p(F|\mathcal{A}^m) = \frac{\sum_i M_i^m \log p(f_i|\mathcal{A}_i^m, \Lambda)}{\sum_i M_i^m} \tag{5}$$

which gives more weights to vMF kernels activated at foreground.

Second, we extend the model to multiple objects by modifying the likelihood:

$$p(\mathcal{F}) = \prod_i \prod_n p(F_i)^{z_{i,n}} \tag{6}$$

where F_i are patches from a whole feature map $\mathcal{F}$, and $\{z_{i,n} \in \{0,1\}| \sum_n z_{i,n} = 1\}$ are indicators of existence of object n at patch F_i. Note that by the design of the likelihood, only one object model can be active at one position in the feature map. We maximize the likelihood defined in Eq. 6 by applying the model in sliding windows, then selecting the local maxima in the resulted likelihood map after non-maximum suppression.

2.4 Touching Nuclei Separation

Nuclei usually clump and touch with each other, makeing it difficult to recognize single nucleus. The compositional model is able to explain for a single nucleus, but insufficient to separate touching nuclei precisely. We introduce a non-learning algorithm to segment nucleus that requires no annotations. The algorithm is adapted from near-convex shape decomposition [19]. The decomposition output is integrated into the compositional model as a shape prior.

First, we select the vMF kernel μ_0 that respond to the background. Given a feature map F, we compute $1 - \mu_0^T f_i$ at each position i to obtain a nucleus foreground score map. It is further binarized to get foreground connected components. These connected components may consist of a single nucleus or touching nuclei. To distinguish between them, we leverage the following observations: 1) The shapes of nuclei are usually convex. 2) When multiple nuclei cluster together, there are usually concave points along the boundary of the connected component. Based on these observations, we propose to use a near-convex shape decomposition algorithm to process each connected component.

Following [19], a near-convex decomposition of a shape S, $D_\phi(S)$, is defined as a set of non-overlapping parts P_i each with concavity $c(P_i)$:

$$D_\psi(S) = \{P_i | \bigcup_i P_i = S, \forall P_i \cap P_j = \emptyset, c(P_i) \le \psi\} \qquad (7)$$

$$c(P_i) = \max_{v_1,v_2 \in Boundary(P_i)} \{c(v_1,v_2)\} \qquad (8)$$

where P_i denotes the decomposed parts; $\psi = 3$ is a parameter for near-convex tolerance. For any two points v_1, v_2 on the boundary of P_i, $c(v_1,v_2)$ is intuitively defined as the max distance from a boundary point u between v_1, v_2 to the line segment v_1v_2. If $c(v_1,v_2) > \psi$, they are named mutex pairs. A set of potential cuts is needed to split S. We compute the curvature of the boundary of S and locate concave points on it. A potential cut is formed by the line segment between two concave points if the line segment lies inside S. To comply with the near-convex constraint, all mutex pairs must be cut into different parts. Furthermore, a specifically designed weight is assigned to each cut, which encourages the selected cuts to be perpendicular to the local boundary and be short, in accord with human intuition. In Appendix 1, we give detailed illustration, formulation and solution for this algorithm.

Nuclei Candidates as Prior. After decomposing the nuclei foreground connected components, the obtained regions are near convex and are taken as candidates of single nucleus. These candidates serve as a prior guiding where to pay attention to for nucleus detection. We define the prior probability of nucleus existence q as Gaussian distributions centered at each candidate. The final detection probability is obtained by integrating the prior into the compositional model and the final probability map is defined as:

$$p(\mathcal{F}) = \prod_i \prod_n p(F_i)^{z_{i,n}} q(i). \tag{9}$$

2.5 Weakly-Supervised Nuclei Segmentation

The nuclei candidates obtained from Sect. 2.4 can also be used as segmentation masks. Since the algorithm only receives bounding box as supervision which is used to crop nucleus images, it achieves segmentation masks in a weakly-supervised way. The obtained segmentation masks have a property to be near convex. Although rare nuclei can have concave shapes and be wrongly cut, it can be indicative of potential annotation errors (*e.g.* where the annotator mistakenly recognized a pair of touching nuclei as a single one).

3 Experiments and Results

Dataset. Multiplexed immunofluorescence (mIF) and immunohistochemistry (IHC) are emerging technologies with better predictions for immunotherapy [15]. The mIF images were obtained using Vectra-3 and Vectra Polaris microscopes (Akoya BioSciences, MA, USA) from six patients with liver cancer (3), lung adenocarcinoma (1), lung small cell carcinoma (1), and melanoma (1). For the nuclei detection and segmentation, DAPI(4',6-diamidino-2-phenylindole) stained images were used in this study among the multispectral images. The selected images were manually annotated and checked by trained researchers. Totally 18312 nuclei were annotated on 210 images, 186 for training and 24 for testing.

3.1 Nuclei Detection

Baselines & Evaluation Metrics. Our motivation is to develop data-efficient models to save annotation efforts, meanwhile being interpretable. Therefore, we compare our model with a classic baseline patch-CNN [22], and one of the state-of-the-art methods [27], which utilized structured regression with a U-Net-like backbone [20]. For patch-CNN, the model complexity is close to ours and the same patch size was used, which makes the comparison fair. The structured regression (SR) [27] method is trained with full image supervision rather than on isolated nuclei, as it was designed. Therefore, it serves as an upper-bound for comparison. Following [1,7,10,21], we adopt the commonly used precision (P) - recall (R) metrics to evaluate nucleus detection methods.

Implementation Details. The proposed method uses the first layer of a U-Net [20] as a feature extractor, which is pretrained on unsupervised nuclei super-pixel segmentation. It is followed by the generative compositional model defined in Sect. 2. We used 3097 isolated nuclei to learn the model parameters. We empirically found that 12 vMF kernels are sufficient to model different parts of a nucleus (See Fig. 2 in Appendix). The number of compositional models in the

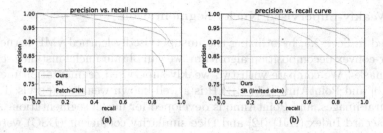

Fig. 2. Evaluation of nucleus detection by Precision-Recall curve. (a) Trained with full data; (b) Trained with 10% data.

mixture is set to $M = 20$, each represents nuclei with a specific size and shape (See Fig. 3 in Appendix). To detect nuclei with various orientations, we rotated input images by every 30°. The hyper-parameters were chosen via evaluation on a validation set.

Results. Figure 2 shows the P-R curve of the baseline Patch-CNN, SR and the proposed method. The proposed method surpasses patch-CNN by a large margin, which shows the effectiveness of the proposed method. We believe this is due to the explicit generative modeling of nuclei features, which boosts performance while keeping the model to be light-weight. Due to extended model complexity and full image supervision training, SR outperforms the proposed method. This is understandable since the SR model is a much deeper network and has a larger field of view with full image supervision. However, deep neural networks like SR are data hungry and require large amounts of data to learn their parameters, while the proposed method only requires the annotations of isolated nuclei, which saves much effort for human experts.

To verify the hypothesis that our method is more data-efficient than deep neural networks, we made a comparison between SR and our method under approximately the same amount of training data in terms of the number of nuclei used. For SR, this was implemented by limiting the number of training images to ensure the total number of nucleus seen in training are about the same. In Fig. 2(b), we can see that when trained with approximately the same amount of data, the performance of SR degrades significantly. This result proves that when large amounts of annotated nuclei samples are not available, our method is able to present superior nuclei detection results than an over-parameterized (in terms of the dataset size) deep neural network.

Table 1. Weakly supervised segmentation performance measured in AJI and DSC on the in-house dataset.

	AJI	DSC
BBTP	0.6765	0.8513
PointAnno	0.5991	0.7805
Ours	**0.7030**	**0.8900**

3.2   Weakly-Supervised Nuclei Segmentation

As stated in Sect. 2.5, by utilizing the unsupervisedly learned vMF kernels and the near-convex decomposition algorithm, we can obtain nuclei instance segmentation masks. We compare with two weakly-supervised segmentation methods, BBTP [9] and PointAnno [17]. BBTP is a well-known weakly-supervised model for natural images, and PointAnno is developed for nuclei segmentation. Aggregated Jaccard Index (AJI) [12] and Dice similarity coefficient (DSC) were used as metrics. AJI focuses more on the correct matching between segmented nuclei instances and ground-truths, while DSC focuses on the foreground/background classification.

Table 1 shows the segmentation performance of the three methods. Our method outperforms BBTP and PointAnno on both AJI and DSC. What's more, our method requires little training (only the clustering of vMF kernels), which is an advantage over deep networks. Qualitative results are shown in Fig. 3. Our method is able to precisely locate the foreground and cut touching nuclei, even for hard cases where more than two nuclei are touching with each other. Compared with BBTP and PointAnno, the segmentation masks obtained by the proposed method aligns better with the ground-truth nuclei contours, thanks to the accurate detection of foreground as well as the cutting at reasonable positions between touching nuclei.

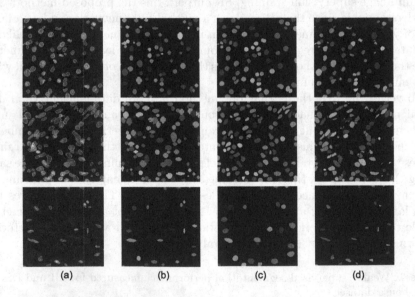

Fig. 3. Qualitative segmentation results. Each line shows one image from the test set and the segmentation masks obtained by three methods on it. (a) is the DAPI stained image with the boundaries of each nucleus annotated. (b) are the predictions of BBTP, (c) are the predictions of PointAnno, and (d) are the predictions of our method.

4   Conclusion

We introduce a light-weight interpretable model for nuclei detection and segmentation. It is data-efficient that ease the data annotation cost for data hungry deep learning methods. In addition, it is interpretable in that it exploits the hidden features and builds probabilistic models for nucleus. We hope our work would contribute to the study of data efficiency and interpretability in the histology image analysis community.

References

1. Alom, M.Z., Yakopcic, C., Taha, T.M., Asari, V.K.: Microscopic nuclei classification, segmentation and detection with improved Deep Convolutional Neural Network (DCNN) approaches (2018)
2. Arteta, C., Lempitsky, V., Noble, J.A., Zisserman, A.: Learning to detect cells using non-overlapping extremal regions. In: Ayache, N., Delingette, H., Golland, P., Mori, K. (eds.) MICCAI 2012. LNCS, vol. 7510, pp. 348–356. Springer, Heidelberg (2012). https://doi.org/10.1007/978-3-642-33415-3_43
3. Baykal, E., Dogan, H., Ercin, M.E., Ersoz, S., Ekinci, M.: Modern convolutional object detectors for nuclei detection on pleural effusion cytology images. Multimed. Tools App. **79**(21-22), 15417–15436 (2020). https://doi.org/10.1007/s11042-019-7461-3
4. Du, J., Li, X., Li, Q.: Detection and classification of cervical exfoliated cells based on faster R-CNN. In: 2019 IEEE 11th International Conference on Advanced Infocomm Technology, ICAIT 2019 (2019). https://doi.org/10.1109/ICAIT.2019.8935931
5. Graham, S., et al.: Hover-Net: simultaneous segmentation and classification of nuclei in multi-tissue histology images. Med. Image Anal. **58**, 101563 (2019)
6. Guo, R., Pagnucco, M., Song, Y.: Learning with noise: mask-guided attention model for weakly supervised nuclei segmentation. In: de Bruijne, M., et al. (eds.) MICCAI 2021. LNCS, vol. 12902, pp. 461–470. Springer, Cham (2021). https://doi.org/10.1007/978-3-030-87196-3_43
7. Hagos, Y.B., Narayanan, P.L., Akarca, A.U., Marafioti, T., Yuan, Y.: ConCORDe-Net: cell count regularized convolutional neural network for cell detection in multiplex immunohistochemistry images. In: Shen, D., et al. (eds.) MICCAI 2019. LNCS, vol. 11764, pp. 667–675. Springer, Cham (2019). https://doi.org/10.1007/978-3-030-32239-7_74
8. Höfener, H., Homeyer, A., Weiss, N., Molin, J., Lundström, C.F., Hahn, H.K.: Deep learning nuclei detection: a simple approach can deliver state-of-the-art results. Computerized Medical Imaging and Graphics **70**, 43–52 (2018). https://www.sciencedirect.com/science/article/pii/S0895611118300806
9. Hsu, C.C., Hsu, K.J., Tsai, C.C., Lin, Y.Y., Chuang, Y.Y.: Weakly supervised instance segmentation using the bounding box tightness prior. In: Advances in Neural Information Processing Systems, vol. 32 (2019)
10. Kashif, M.N., Raza, S.E., Sirinukunwattana, K., Arif, M., Rajpoot, N.: Handcrafted features with convolutional neural networks for detection of tumor cells in histology images. In: Proceedings - International Symposium on Biomedical Imaging. vol. 2016-June (2016)

11. Kortylewski, A., Liu, Q., Wang, A., Sun, Y., Yuille, A.: Compositional convolutional neural networks: a robust and interpretable model for object recognition under occlusion. Int. J. Comput. Vis. **129**(3), 736–760 (2021)
12. Kumar, N., Verma, R., Sharma, S., Bhargava, S., Vahadane, A., Sethi, A.: A dataset and a technique for generalized nuclear segmentation for computational pathology. IEEE Trans. Med. Imaging **36**(7), 1550–1560 (2017)
13. Kuse, M., Wang, Y.F., Kalasannavar, V., Khan, M., Rajpoot, N.: Local isotropic phase symmetry measure for detection of beta cells and lymphocytes. J. Pathol. Inform. **2**, 2 (2011)
14. Lee, H., Jeong, W.-K.: Scribble2Label: scribble-supervised cell segmentation via self-generating pseudo-labels with consistency. In: Martel, A.L., et al. (eds.) MICCAI 2020. LNCS, vol. 12261, pp. 14–23. Springer, Cham (2020). https://doi.org/10.1007/978-3-030-59710-8_2
15. Lu, S., et al.: Comparison of biomarker modalities for predicting response to PD-1/PD-L1 checkpoint blockade: a systematic review and meta-analysis. JAMA Oncol. **5**(8), 1195–1204 (2019)
16. Naylor, P., Lae, M., Reyal, F., Walter, T.: Nuclei segmentation in histopathology images using deep neural networks. In: Proceedings - International Symposium on Biomedical Imaging (2017)
17. Qu, H., et al.: Weakly supervised deep nuclei segmentation using partial points annotation in histopathology images. IEEE Trans. Med. Imaging **39**(11), 3655–3666 (2020)
18. Ren, S., He, K., Girshick, R., Sun, J.: Faster R-CNN: towards real-time object detection with region proposal networks. In: Advances in Neural Information Processing Systems, vol. 28 (2015)
19. Ren, Z., Yuan, J., Li, C., Liu, W.: Minimum near-convex decomposition for robust shape representation. In: Proceedings of the IEEE International Conference on Computer Vision (2011)
20. Ronneberger, O., Fischer, P., Brox, T.: U-net: convolutional networks for biomedical image segmentation. In: Navab, N., Hornegger, J., Wells, W.M., Frangi, A.F. (eds.) MICCAI 2015. LNCS, vol. 9351, pp. 234–241. Springer, Cham (2015). https://doi.org/10.1007/978-3-319-24574-4_28
21. Sirinukunwattana, K., Ahmed Raza, S.E., Tsang, Y.-W., Snead, D., Cree, I., Rajpoot, N.: A spatially constrained deep learning framework for detection of epithelial tumor nuclei in cancer histology images. In: Wu, G., Coupé, P., Zhan, Y., Munsell, B., Rueckert, D. (eds.) Patch-MI 2015. LNCS, vol. 9467, pp. 154–162. Springer, Cham (2015). https://doi.org/10.1007/978-3-319-28194-0_19
22. Sirinukunwattana, K., Raza, S.E., Tsang, Y.W., Snead, D.R., Cree, I.A., Rajpoot, N.M.: Locality sensitive deep learning for detection and classification of nuclei in routine colon cancer histology images. IEEE Trans. Med. Imaging **35**(5), 1196–1206 (2016)
23. Tofighi, M., Guo, T., Vanamala, J.K., Monga, V.: Deep networks with shape priors for nucleus detection. In: Proceedings - International Conference on Image Processing, ICIP (2018)
24. Veta, M., Van Diest, P.J., Kornegoor, R., Huisman, A., Viergever, M.A., Pluim, J.P.: Automatic nuclei segmentation in h&e stained breast cancer histopathology images. PloS ONE **8**(7), e70221 (2013)
25. Wang, A., Sun, Y., Kortylewski, A., Yuille, A.: Robust object detection under occlusion with context-aware compositionalNets. In: Proceedings of the IEEE Computer Society Conference on Computer Vision and Pattern Recognition (2020)

26. Xie, Y., Xing, F., Kong, X., Su, H., Yang, L.: Beyond classification: structured regression for robust cell detection using convolutional neural network. In: Navab, N., Hornegger, J., Wells, W.M., Frangi, A.F. (eds.) MICCAI 2015. LNCS, vol. 9351, pp. 358–365. Springer, Cham (2015). https://doi.org/10.1007/978-3-319-24574-4_43
27. Xie, Y., Xing, F., Shi, X., Kong, X., Su, H., Yang, L.: Efficient and robust cell detection: a structured regression approach. Med. Image Anal. **44**, 245–254 (2018)
28. Xu, J., Xiang, L., Liu, Q., Gilmore, H., Wu, J., Tang, J., Madabhushi, A.: Stacked sparse autoencoder (SSAE) for nuclei detection on breast cancer histopathology images. IEEE Trans. Med. Imaging **35**(1), 119–130 (2016)

A Coarse-to-Fine Segmentation Methodology Based on Deep Networks for Automated Analysis of *Cryptosporidium* Parasite from Fluorescence Microscopic Images

Ziheng Yang[1]([✉]), Halim Benhabiles[1], Feryal Windal[1], Jérôme Follet[1],
Anne-Charlotte Leniere[1], and Dominique Collard[2]

[1] Univ. Lille, CNRS, Centrale Lille, Univ. Polytechnique Hauts-de-France, Junia,
UMR 8520 - IEMN - Institut d'Electronique de Microélectronique et de
Nanotechnologie, 59000 Lille, France
{ziheng.yang,halim.benhabiles,feryal.windal}@junia.com
[2] LIMMS/CNRS-IIS The University of Tokyo, IRL 2820, Lille, France

Abstract. In this paper, we present a deep learning-based framework for automated analysis and diagnosis of *Cryptosporidium parvum* from fluorescence microscopic images. First, a coarse segmentation is applied to roughly delimit the contours either of individual parasites or of grouped ones in the form of a single object from original images. Subsequently, a classifier will be applied to identify grouped parasites which are separated from each other by applying a fine segmentation. Our coarse-to-fine segmentation methodology achieves high accuracy on our generated dataset (over 3,000 parasites) and permit to improve the performance of direct segmentation approaches.

Keywords: *Cryptosporidium parvum* analysis · Fluorescence microscopic image · Coarse-to-fine segmentation

1 Introduction

Cryptosporidiosis is a diarrheal disease caused by the *Cryptosporidium* parasite, which affects a wide range of host in all groups of vertebrate not only in mammals. Among the 40 existing *Cryptosporidium* species, C. parvum is of major concern as it is present in most of the human as well as livestock outbreaks [1,2]. In human, infected persons may have several symptomes notably acute gastroenteritis, abdominal pain and diarrhea [3,4]. One should note that *Cryptosporidium* is the fifth pathogenic agent leading to diarrheal disease in toddler under 5 years old. Moreover, the presence of this parasite was associated with an increase in death rate in young children [5]. In livestocks, cattles (and more

Supported by H4DC (Health for Dairy Cows) project.

particularly calves) are considered as major reservoir for the parasite. Indeed, infected animal can excrete more that 1 million oocysts per gram of stool [6]. The VIDA (Veterinary Investigation Diagnosis Analysis) 2014 report has shown that between 2007 and 2011, *Cryptosporidium* is one out of the 4 major causes of diarrhoea in calves. It is responsible of growth rate decrease and stunting. This parasite is also responsible of young animals death leading to major economic impact by the decrease of rentability in farms [7]. Exclusive of labour costs, the cost of treating each sick calf is at least £34 [8].

In farms, the parasite is excreted into the external environment in a form called Oocyst through the feces of infected cows, directly contaminating water or food and causing more infections [9,10]. Hence, the control of the parasite propagation will obviously bring a real benefit to the economic plan and will help to limit the risk on human health. However, reaching this goal represents a challenge in reason of i) the parasite high resistance to its environmental conditions, ii) the absence of effective drugs to treat infected animals (as well as humans) [11]. In this context, the development of a fully efficient drug against this parasite will permit to stop its propagation notably in farms in case of an infection. The lack of drug is essentially due to a lack of automated and easy to use tool to screen drug library. No highthroutput system are currently available to ease caracterization processes of new antiparasitic compounds.

When researchers want to assess drug efficiency against pathogenic agents, they start their trials in vitro by the use of cell layer infection. Following time of incubation (ranging from 24 h to 72 h in the case of *Cryptosporidium* studies) infected cells are fixed. Then fluorescently tagged antibodies are used to specifically identify parasites on microscopic slides [12]. The microscopic observation will lead to assess the decrease of parasite infection and in some cases to discriminate the different parasite life stages (from asexual life stages to sexual ones). However, counting the number of parasites by the biologist is a fastidious task and prone to error. Therefore, this manual analysis method does not permit transition to large-scale tests where thousands of molecules are experimented to accelerate drug discovery. Moreover, direct exploitation of the existing methods on *Cryptosporidium* images is not sufficient to develop a reliable tool due to the particular visual aspect of this parasite. Indeed, as illustrated in Fig. 1, the parasites have irregular shapes with confused contours notably for stuck parasites and their surfaces as well as their fluorescence are highly varied. All these observations make the characterization of the parasite by existing deep architectures a real challenge.

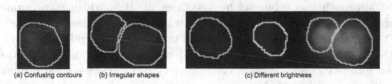

(a) Confusing contours   (b) Irregular shapes   (c) Different brightness

Fig. 1. Example of challenges for detecting parasite contours, observed from the labelings of the biologist expert. Different situation as follows: (a) Confusing contours (b) Irregular shapes (c) Different brightness.

In this context and within the frame of the H4DC (Health for Dairy Cows) interregion european project, we propose an original deep learning-based framework that permits to segment automatically a population of *Cryptosporidium parvum* parasites from microscopic images. The main contributions of our work are summarized as follows: Firstly, we proposed a coarse-to-fine segmentation approach that permits to delineate precisely the contours of parasites whatever their shapes, their sizes and their situations in the image (grouped or isolated). Secondly, we propose a dataset of *Cryptosporidium parvum* parasite. The dataset is composed of 58 microscopic images acquired in our laboratory from infected HCT-8 cell lines (Declinai HCT). The images contain over 3,000 parasites which have been manually segmented by a biologist expert.

2   Related Work

Until now, there is only one study based on microscopic image analysis of *Cryptosporidium parvum*. In [13], artificial neural networks (ANN) were applied to identify *Cryptosporidium parvum* oocysts. A histogram measuring the pixel intensity of the grayscale images was used to convert digital images to the format used by the neural network before training. Subsequently, the network was optimized by employing different number of training images and different number of hidden neurons. The results demonstrated that the correct recognition rates were 81% to 97% for the oocyst images and 78% to 82% for the non-ocyst images in multiple tests.

Although few studies related to the detection of *Cryptosporidium parvum* based on microscopic images are available, an abundance of studies are relevant to the detection of parasites, especially malaria parasites make up the majority. Most malaria diagnosis automation processes include joint image segmentation and classification tasks [14–16]. Unlike other studies, the malaria image analysis in [16] was based entirely on deep learning architectures. Moreover, the approach proposed in the framework relies on the analysis of the parasite itself, rather than the cell. Specifically, the framework implements segmentation of parasites in images and classifies them into four species: *P. falciparum*, *P. malaria*, *P. ovale*, and *P. vivax*. Experimental studies with multiple datasets have proved the high generalization potential of the proposed framework with competitive performance on six data sources. Apart from malaria parasites, we also found some studies related to image analysis on intestinal parasite [17–19]. For instance, a hybrid approach was proposed by Osaku et al. [19], which incorporates the views of two decision systems (support vector machines and deep neural networks Vgg-16) with complementary properties to improve the overall efficiency.

In the field of biomedical images, cell detection or cell nuclei detection has attracted more attention. Indeed, cells (nuclei) and parasites have similar morphology and the subject of the image is a group of small objects. In [20], Kromp et al. compared the segmentation performance of several architectures on fluorescence nuclear images, including 5 deep learning architectures (U-Net [21], U-Net ResNet, Cellpose [22], Mask R-CNN [23], KG instance segmentation [24]) and 2 conventional methods (Iterative h-min based watershed [25], Attributed relational graphs [26]). The experimental results indicated that the deep learning architecture outperformed traditional methods in every metric. Additionally, Prangemeier et al. [27] proposed an attention-based cell detection transformer (Cell-DETR) for instance segmentation. Cell-DETR was much simpler and faster with comparable segmentation performance to state-of-the-art methods.

3   Our Methodology

Figure 2 shows the overview of our proposed framework. Our coarse-to-fine segmentation approach goes through three successive analysis steps using deep learning models namely: 1) a coarse segmentation model that takes in input a microscopic image and outputs a mask containing delineated contours which delimit either individual parasites or grouped ones. 2) a shape classification model that permits to take in input croped images of parasites identified in the previous step and output their categories (grouped or isolated). 3) a fine segmentation model that takes in input only crops that have been identified as grouped parasites in the previous step and separate them individually by delineating their respective contours. In the following, we will present the architectures used for the segmentation and the shape classification tasks.

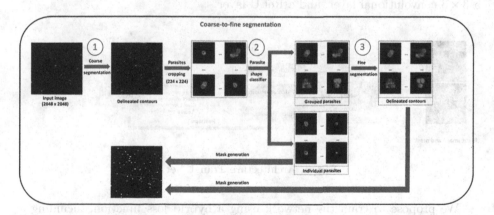

Fig. 2. An overview of our proposed framework, which is a coarse-to-fine segmentation.

3.1   Segmentation Architecture

We trained a variant of the segmentation architecture named TransUNet [28]. It is worth mentioning that the design of the segmentation architecture is the same for both coarse and fine tasks. The main difference relies on the training set of images used by the architectures. More specifically, the coarse segmentation model is learned from a set of images containing a population of segmented parasites (the entire microscopic images), while the fine segmentation model is learned from a set of crops containing a small group of segmented parasites that share common contours (as displayed in Fig. 3).

Fig. 3. Parasite fine segmentation for grouped parasites.

As illustrated in Fig. 4, the architecture consists of two processing modules, the encoder and the decoder. The encoder performs feature extraction by passing the input image to a series of convolutional layer blocks (16, 32, 64, 128, 256, 512), each followed by an intermediate max pooling operation. Subsequently, a linear projection operation transforms the feature maps obtained from the convolution operations into matrices that are used to pass through a sequence of transformer blocks. After reshaping the output of the transformer blocks, we cascade multiple upsampling blocks to decode the hidden features to output the final segmentation mask, where each block contains a 2× upsampling operator, a 3 × 3 convolutional layer, and a ReLU layer.

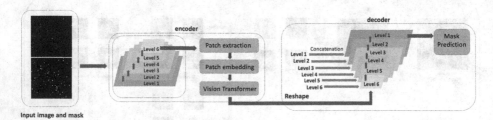

Fig. 4. Architecture TransUNet.

We propose to train the network using a hybrid loss function, including a Jaccard loss and a Cross-Entropy loss, enabling both local and global features to be optimized:

$$Loss_{Jac} = 1 - \frac{\sum y_{ij} t_{ij}}{\sum y_{ij} + \sum t_{ij} - \sum y_{ij} t_{ij}} \tag{1}$$

where $y_{ij} \in [0,1]$ and $t_{ij} \in [0,1]$ denote the output and target for each pixel at position (i, j). We employ the Cross-Entropy loss as an auxiliary loss to be able to optimize the local region of the image. It is formulated as:

$$Loss_{CE} = - \sum_{i}^{C} t_i log(s_i) \tag{2}$$

where t_i and s_i are the groundtruth and the CNN score for each class i in C. Based on the above two losses, our loss function is given as follows:

$$Loss_{our} = \alpha Loss_{Jac} + (1 - \alpha)Loss_{CE} \qquad (3)$$

where $\alpha \in [0, 1]$. To minimize the loss function, the Adam [29] optimizer is applied.

3.2 Shape Classification Architecture

We designed a customized architecture that combines CNN and transformer blocks to build a parasite shape classifier. The architecture is inspired from the encoder module of the segmentation architecture presented in the previous section.

As shown in Fig. 5, the architecture is first composed of 10 blocks (5 consecutive double blocks) of convolutional layers, each followed by a ReLU activation function and a max pooling operation. After converting the feature maps into matrices, the network is then connected to 6 ViT blocks. A flatten operation comes after ViT blocks and is followed by a dense layer of 256 units with a ReLU activation. Finally, a 1-unit output dense layer is used to obtain the predicted probability of the parasite shape by a sigmoid activation function.

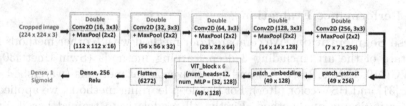

Fig. 5. Our proposed classification architecture TransCNN.

4   Experiments

4.1   Data Preparation

Our dataset for *Cryptosporidium parvum* analysis consists of 58 microscopic images. These images have been acquired in the laboratory by infecting HCT-8 cell lines with Cryptosporidium parvum (24 h of infection) and staining them using specific fluorescent markers. The parasite is visualized in the green channel of the microscope after staining. All images have been manually labelled by a parasitologist to delineate parasites' contours of each identified parasite. Table 1 indicates the size of the training and validation sets, and also image resolutions exploited to train the models of our coarse-to-fine segmentation method (namely coarse segmentation model, shape classification model and fine segmentation model).

Table 1. Detailed information of dataset used in different steps

Steps	Training set	Validation set	Image resolution
Coarse segmentation	51 images (2510 parasites)	7 images (589 parasites)	1024×1024
Shape classification	244 crops (122 per class)	60 crops (30 per class)	224×224
Fine segmentation	122 crops (263 parasites)	30 crops (65 parasites)	224×224

Several data augmentation techniques have been applied only for the coarse segmentation. We followed 3 scenarios for data augmentation. Scenario_1: Data augmentation based on spatial transformations. For this scenario, we applied the rotation, horizontal flip and vertical flip for both original images and associated masks. Scenario_2: Data augmentation based on texture transformations. We applied the contrast enhancement, brightness enhancement and gaussian blur only for original images and kept the associated mask unchanged. Scenario_3: Data augmentation based on both spatial and non-spatial transformations.

4.2   Performance Evaluation

Coarse Segmentation. We compared our method with 5 other methods from the state of the art, including 3 deep learning methods (Swin-Unet [30], U-Net_VGG19, U-Net_ResNet34) and two conventional methods (watershed algorithm [31] and HSV color filter). For the deep learning methods, we applied the same scenarios as our method. Firstly, all models were trained based on the original data without augmentation (without scenario 1, 2, 3 as we presented). Figure 6(a) shows the AP (Average Precision) curves of the six architectures calculated over the validation set of the coarse segmentation (data augmentation under the scenario_3 during the training part, which gave the best performance for all the methods over the other augmentation scenarios and the basic dataset as well). The AP is defined as $AP = TP/(TP + FP + FN)$, where TP is true positive, FP is false positive, FN is false negative in term of parasite objects compared to the ground-truth ones. They are calculated using IoU (Intersection over Union) metric with a threshold ranged from 0.5 to 1. The curves show that our model outperforms the other architectures. Indeed, our coarse model reached an AP of 67% at an IoU threshold of 0.5. One can also notice that the performance of the conventional segmentation methods (watershed and color filter) are very low compared to the CNN ones which clearly indicates that exploiting simple features such as the color is not enough to address the issue of parasite segmentation.

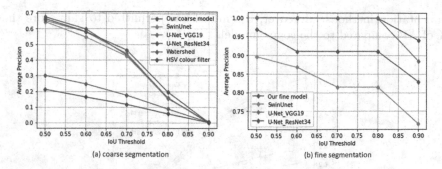

Fig. 6. AP curves over the validation set: (a) coarse segmentation (b) fine segmentation.

Shape Classification. We compared some CNN classifiers from the state of the art with our classification model (CNN combined with ViT blocks). Table 2 shows the performance of different models. Our model succeeds to classify all the validation data, which is the same as VGG16. However, as indicated in the table, the VGG16 model is 19 times larger than our model (134M vs 7M).

Table 2. Comparison of the performance and the number of parameters between our classification architecture and some CNN architectures

Model	Accuracy	Precision	Recall	Parameters number
VGG16	1	1	1	134M
ResNet50	0.98	0.98	0.98	23M
Simple CNN (6 convolution layers)	0.96	0.96	0.96	25M
Our model	1	1	1	7M

Fine Segmentation. Similar to the coarse segmentation experiments, we have also compared our model to the 3 deep learning methods. We also followed the same protocol of training as well as the evaluation metric (Average Precision). Figure 6(b) shows the AP curves of our fine segmentation model calculated over the validation set. The curves show that our model has better performance than others. It is worth mentioning that the AP value of our model remains the best among the other models even at a high level of the IoU threshold which indicates a high accuracy in term of parasite separation.

Direct Segmentation vs Coarse-to-Fine Segmentation. The purpose of this section is to demonstrate the contribution of our coarse-to-fine segmentation approach compared to standard approaches that carry out segmentation directly. It can be observed from the Fig. 7 that our coarse-to-fine model reached an AP of 73.45% at an IoU threshold of 0.5, outperforming all the compared segmentation methods. Moreover, the model has permitted to gain more than 5% of AP compared to the coarse model.

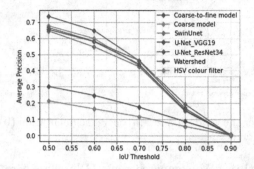

Fig. 7. AP curves over the validation set of coarse-to-fine segmentation.

5   Conclusion

A deep learning-based framework for automated analysis and diagnosis of *Cryptosporidium parvum* has been presented in this paper. The framework permits to segment a population of parasites from microscopic images by adopting a coarse-to-fine approach. Compared with the result of the direct segmentation, our coarse-to-fine segmentation framework has reached an average precision of 73.45% on our validation dataset and permitted to improve the performance of direct segmentation methods by gaining at least 5% more of AP. We believe that our coarse-to-fine segmentation framework can reveal more efficiency on images characterized by a high density of parasites where they will have more chance to be stuck to each other.

Funding Information. This project has received funding from the Interreg 2 Seas programme 2014–2020 co-funded by the European Regional Development Fund under subsidy contract No. 2S05-043 H4DC.

References

1. O'Leary, J.K., Sleator, R.D., Lucey, B.: Cryptosporidium spp. diagnosis and research in the 21st century. Food Waterborne Parasitol. **24**, e00131 (2021)
2. Feng, Y., Ryan, U.M., Xiao, L.: Genetic diversity and population structure of cryptosporidium. Trends Parasitol. **34**(11), 997–1011 (2018)
3. Hatam-Nahavandi, K., Ahmadpour, E., Carmena, D., Spotin, A., Bangoura, B., Xiao, L.: Cryptosporidium infections in terrestrial ungulates with focus on livestock: a systematic review and meta-analysis. Parasit. Vectors **12**(1), 1–23 (2019)
4. Gerace, E., Presti, V.D.M.L., Biondo, C.: Cryptosporidium infection: epidemiology, pathogenesis, and differential diagnosis. Eur. J. Microbiol. Immunol. **9**(4), 119–123 (2019)

5. Kotloff, K.L., et al.: Burden and aetiology of diarrhoeal disease in infants and young children in developing countries (the global enteric multicenter study, GEMs): a prospective, case-control study. The Lancet **382**(9888), 209–222 (2013)
6. Blackburn, B.G., et al.: Cryptosporidiosis associated with ozonated apple cider. Emerg. Infect. Dis. **12**(4), 684 (2006)
7. APHA: Veterinary investigation diagnosis analysis (VIDA) report, 2014 (2014)
8. Thomson, S., et al.: Bovine cryptosporidiosis: impact, host-parasite interaction and control strategies. Vet. Res. **48**(1), 1–16 (2017)
9. Del Coco, V.F., Córdoba, M.A., Basualdo, J.A.: Cryptosporidium infection in calves from a rural area of Buenos Aires, Argentina. Vet. Parasitol. **158**(1–2), 31–35 (2008)
10. Feng, Y., et al.: Prevalence and genotypic identification of cryptosporidium spp., giardia duodenalis and enterocytozoon bieneusi in pre-weaned dairy calves in Guangdong, China. Parasit. Vectors **12**(1), 1–9 (2019)
11. Chellan, P., Sadler, P.J., Land, K.M.: Recent developments in drug discovery against the protozoal parasites cryptosporidium and toxoplasma. Bioorg. Med. Chem. Lett. **27**(7), 1491–1501 (2017)
12. Lichtman, J.W., Conchello, J.-A.: Fluorescence microscopy. Nat. Methods **2**(12), 910–919 (2005)
13. Widmer, K.W., Oshima, K.H., Pillai, S.D.: Identification of cryptosporidium parvum oocysts by an artificial neural network approach. Appl. Environ. Microbiol. **68**(3), 1115–1121 (2002)
14. Madhu, G.: Computer vision and machine learning approach for malaria diagnosis in thin blood smears from microscopic blood images. In: Rout, J.K., Rout, M., Das, H. (eds.) Machine Learning for Intelligent Decision Science. AIS, pp. 191–209. Springer, Singapore (2020). https://doi.org/10.1007/978-981-15-3689-2_8
15. Shi, L., Guan, Z., Liang, C., You, H.: Automatic classification of plasmodium for malaria diagnosis based on ensemble neural network. In: Proceedings of the 2020 2nd International Conference on Intelligent Medicine and Image Processing, pp. 80–85 (2020)
16. Yang, Z., Benhabiles, H., Hammoudi, K., Windal, F., He, R., Collard, D.: A generalized deep learning-based framework for assistance to the human malaria diagnosis from microscopic images. Neural Comput. Appl. **34**, 1–16 (2021)
17. Roder, M., Passos, L.A., Ribeiro, L.C.F., Benato, B.C., Falcão, A.X., Papa, J.P.: Intestinal parasites classification using deep belief networks. In: Rutkowski, L., Scherer, R., Korytkowski, M., Pedrycz, W., Tadeusiewicz, R., Zurada, J.M. (eds.) ICAISC 2020. LNCS (LNAI), vol. 12415, pp. 242–251. Springer, Cham (2020). https://doi.org/10.1007/978-3-030-61401-0_23
18. Machaca, M.Y.P., Rosas, M.L.M., Castro-Gutierrez, E., Dıaz, H.A.T., Huerta, V.L.V.: Data augmentation using generative adversarial network for gastrointestinal parasite microscopy image classification (2020)
19. Osaku, D., Cuba, C.F., Suzuki, C.T., Gomes, J.F., Falcão, A.X.: Automated diagnosis of intestinal parasites: a new hybrid approach and its benefits. Comput. Biol. Med. **123**, 103917 (2020)
20. Kromp, F., et al.: Evaluation of deep learning architectures for complex immunofluorescence nuclear image segmentation. IEEE Trans. Med. Imaging **40**(7), 1934–1949 (2021)
21. Ronneberger, O., Fischer, P., Brox, T.: U-Net: convolutional networks for biomedical image segmentation. In: Navab, N., Hornegger, J., Wells, W.M., Frangi, A.F. (eds.) MICCAI 2015. LNCS, vol. 9351, pp. 234–241. Springer, Cham (2015). https://doi.org/10.1007/978-3-319-24574-4_28

22. Stringer, C., Wang, T., Michaelos, M., Pachitariu, M.: Cellpose: a generalist algorithm for cellular segmentation. Nat. Methods **18**(1), 100–106 (2021)
23. Ren, S., He, K., Girshick, R., Sun, J.: Faster R-CNN: towards real-time object detection with region proposal networks. In: Advances in Neural Information Processing Systems, vol. 28 (2015)
24. Yi, J., et al.: Multi-scale cell instance segmentation with keypoint graph based bounding boxes. In: Shen, D., et al. (eds.) MICCAI 2019. LNCS, vol. 11764, pp. 369–377. Springer, Cham (2019). https://doi.org/10.1007/978-3-030-32239-7_41
25. Koyuncu, C.F., Akhan, E., Ersahin, T., Cetin-Atalay, R., Gunduz-Demir, C.: Iterative h-minima-based marker-controlled watershed for cell nucleus segmentation. Cytometry A **89**(4), 338–349 (2016)
26. Arslan, S., Ersahin, T., Cetin-Atalay, R., Gunduz-Demir, C.: Attributed relational graphs for cell nucleus segmentation in fluorescence microscopy images. IEEE Trans. Med. Imaging **32**(6), 1121–1131 (2013)
27. Prangemeier, T., Reich, C., Koeppl, H.: Attention-based transformers for instance segmentation of cells in microstructures. In: 2020 IEEE International Conference on Bioinformatics and Biomedicine (BIBM), pp. 700–707. IEEE (2020)
28. Chen, J., et al.: TransUNet: transformers make strong encoders for medical image segmentation, arXiv preprint arXiv:2102.04306 (2021)
29. Kingma, D.P., Ba, J.: Adam: a method for stochastic optimization, arXiv preprint arXiv:1412.6980 (2014)
30. Cao, H., et al.: Swin-Unet: Unet-like pure transformer for medical image segmentation, arXiv preprint arXiv:2105.05537 (2021)
31. Najman, L., Schmitt, M.: Watershed of a continuous function. Signal Process. **38**(1), 99–112 (1994)

Swin Faster R-CNN for Senescence Detection of Mesenchymal Stem Cells in Bright-Field Images

Chunlun Xiao[1], Mingzhu Li[1], Liangge He[2], Xuegang Song[1], Tianfu Wang[1], and Baiying Lei[1(✉)]

[1] School of Biomedical Engineering, National-Regional Key Technology Engineering Laboratory for Medical Ultrasound, Guangdong Key Laboratory for Biomedical Measurements and Ultrasound Imaging, Shenzhen University, Shenzhen, China
leiby@szu.edu.cn
[2] Department of Medical Cell Biology and Genetics, Guangdong Key Laboratory of Genomic Stability and Disease Prevention, Shenzhen Key Laboratory of Anti-Aging and Regenerative Medicine, Shenzhen University, Shenzhen, China

Abstract. iPSC-derived mesenchymal stem cells (iMSCs) can differentiate into a wide range of mesodermal cell types for tissue repair, and play an important role in cell therapy in regenerative medicine. The therapeutic effect of mesenchymal stem cells (MSCs) is largely affected by their differentiation ability and cell activity, and the therapeutic effect of senescent cells is often worse than that of young cells. Biologically senescent detection of iMSCs can only be performed by vital staining, which is time-consuming, labor-intensive, and financial-intensive. To solve this problem, we apply a deep learning method to the senescence identification research of iMSCs to achieve the purpose of rapid and accurate detection without vital staining. We propose a Swin Transformer-based Faster R-CNN network for senescence identification of MSCs in bright-field images. In particular, we exploit the self-attention mechanism of the Swin Transformer to extract features of dense cell regions in the picture, enabling the network to learn the strong discriminative properties of different classes of cells. In addition, we perform multi-scale fusion on the features extracted by the backbone network to address the problem of inconsistent cell sizes in the data. Experiments on self-collected datasets show that our method achieves good performance on each generation of datasets and achieves the highest detection precision (mAP) of 0.816 on our collected mixed datasets.

Keywords: Mesenchymal stem cells · Cell senescent detection · Bright-field microscopy image · Swin transformer · Faster R-CNN

1 Introduction

Mesenchymal stem cells (MSCs) are currently regarded as one of the key therapeutic tools in regenerative medicine [1, 2]. MSCs can be derived from a variety of neonatal and adult tissues and can also differentiate into different mesodermal cell lines, such as osteocytes and adipocytes, in vitro and in vivo. Induced pluripotent stem cells (iPSCs) can differentiate into different mesodermal cell lineages, such as osteocytes, muscle cells, etc. [3]. Due to the multi-directional differentiation, self-renewal and immunomodulatory properties, MSCs have an ideal therapeutic effect on injured or lost cells and tissue sites in vivo. These characteristics make iMSCs a possible drug for treating biological injury [4]. MSCs derived from induced pluripotent stem cells (iPSCs) possess complete genetic information of donor and have great potential of proliferation and differentiation, which can be applied to personalized cell therapy.

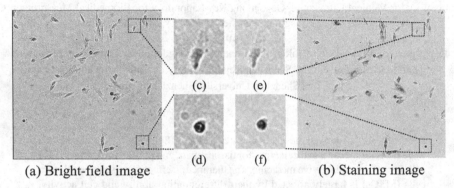

(a) Bright-field image   (b) Staining image

Fig. 1. Visualization of iMSCs dataset. (a) A 640 × 640 pixels bright-field image; (b) A staining image corresponding to bright-field image; (c) and (d) are aging and young cells in bright-field image, (e) and (f) are the corresponding staining cells.

However, the lifespan of iMSCs in vitro is quite limited similar as other normal stem cells. After a certain number of cell divisions, iMSCs enter senescence, have morphological characteristics of enlarged and irregular cell shapes, flattened cells, etc., and eventually stop proliferating [5]. The tissues of any organism will be constantly renewed and metabolized by living stem cells. Senescent MSCs usually show weakened abilities in proliferation, differentiation and immunomodulatory, and often fail to obtain the expected treatment results after transplantation, or even accelerate the aging of surrounding normal tissues, and limited their clinical application [6]. Therefore, iMSCs senescence recognition in vitro is crucial for quality control in cell therapy.

In order to examine the degree of cellular senescence, it usually uses SA-β-gal to stain cells [7]. This process is time-consuming and labor-intensive. The morphological differences between young and senescent cells make it realizable to use artificial intelligence methods for classification. As shown in Fig. 1, there are differences between young cells and senescent cells, but it is difficult to distinguish morphology and color. Besides, there are also some external factors that can deteriorate the cell detection task, such as insufficient quality and quantity in annotation labels, class imbalance, etc. The work in [8] used unlabeled light-sheet microfluidic cytometry for cellular senescence detection, but this method requires high cost and is unsuitable for our work. In the study of using deep learning approaches for this task, methods based on convolutional neural network (CNN) have been developed to address the task of cell detection with excellent performance. For example, the work [9] successfully applied the framework of Faster R-CNN to detect adherent cells in phase-contrast microscopy images. The work [10] tackled the task of precise neural cell detection by adapting the original single shot multibox detector (SSD) [11] into a lightweight model. These methods are limited in specific cases. The works in [12, 13] used a morphology-based CNN system to identify senescent cells and assess the probability of cell senescence. However, the current studies mainly used single-cell data for training and realize classification rather than pinpointing the cells in the data. A deep learning-based method [14] uses cell similarity to construct a region-generating network to detect cells and nuclei in histological images, but this method is not suitable for bright-field images of MSCs, because young and senescent cells have very high large similarities, the boundaries of the two types of cells are not clearly defined. In this paper, we use Faster R-CNN [15] to detect young and senescent cells in iMSCs in a dataset of self-acquired bright-field images. Since the cell concentration in the image is large and the boundaries between the two types of cells are not clear, we add the Swin Transformer module [16] to the backbone network to improve feature extraction performance of the model. To extract multi-scale features, we use feature pyramid network (FPN) [17] to improve the detection performance of small cells in bright-field images.

Our main contributions are as follows: 1) We use multi-cellular data for training, and utilize the Swin Transformer network to learn strong discriminative features in the data, which can identify and precisely localize cells in each image. 2) We perform ablation experiment to verify the effectiveness of the Swin Transformer and FPN networks, and compare the proposed method with state-of-the-art methods on mixed datasets, which demonstrates the effectiveness of our proposed method. 3) We evaluate each generation of iMSCs and compare each generation of cells based on the evaluation results.

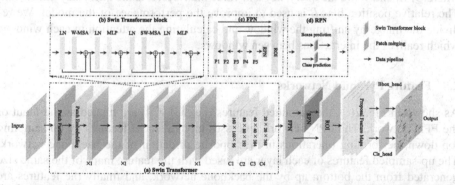

Fig. 2. The architecture of Swin Faster R-CNN network. (a) The architecture of a Swin Transformer, C1–C4 are the feature layers generated by the backbone network; (b) Swin Transformer blocks, W-MSA is multi-head self-attention module with regular window and SW-MSA is self-attention module window with shifted window; (c) A feature pyramid network (FPN) for fusing multi-scale features, it fuses C1–C4 multi-scale into P1–P5; (d) A region proposal network (RPN) that computes the proposals (bounding boxes) of the feature maps.

2   Methodology

2.1   Network Architecture

Figure 2 shows an overview of the proposed framework, which is designed on traditional Faster R-CNN framework. First, we use the Swin Transformer backbone network to extract feature maps from input images. Second, we use the FPN module to process the feature maps, fuse them based on the proposals generated by the region proposal network (RPN) module, and obtain the proposal feature maps after region of interest (ROI) pooling. Third, we calculate the category of each proposal through the subsequent classification and regression head, and obtain the precise position of each cell by performing regression for each bounding box.

2.2   Backbone Network

In this part, we use the Swin Transformer architecture to extract feature maps from input images, which consists of four parts. The numbers are 1, 1, 3, and 1, and the output features are C1–C4. The specific architecture of the block is shown in Fig. 2(b). W-MSA is the window attention, and SW-MSA is the shifted window attention. W-MSA computes the attention of each token within a window and limits the computation of attention to each window. The equation of calculating the attention in each window is defined as:

$$Z = softmax\left(\frac{QK^T}{\sqrt{d_k}} + B\right)V, \tag{1}$$

where Q, K, and V are the query, key and value matrices; d is the query/key dimension. The relative position bias B is used to improve the performance of the model. We re-divide the image by shifting the window and calculating the attention in each window, which realizes the interactions between windows.

2.3   Feature Pyramid Networks

As shown in Fig. 2(c), the outputted features (i.e., C1–C4) are treated as the input of the FPN network. The FPN network processes more abstract features by up-sampling top-down, performing operations in the opposite direction of the backbone network. The up-sampled features of each layer are fused with the feature maps of the same size generated from the bottom up by the backbone network, and finally the features are mapped into four scales P1–P4. This module solves the multi-scale problem in bright-field images, and improves the model's ability to detect small cells. The down-sampling operation on P4 obtains higher-level semantic information P5, which is used as the input of the RPN network to generate bounding boxes to distinguish foreground and background. P1–P4 are processed together with the output of the RPN network as the input of the ROI layer.

2.4 Region Proposal Network

In Fig. 2(d), Faster R-CNN directly uses the RPN network to generate bounding boxes, which greatly improves the generation speed of bounding boxes. First, the image is divided into grids of the same size, each grid point is an anchor point, and a large number of anchor points generate bounding boxes covering every possible position of the input image. The network optimizes each bounding box, adjusts the detector's parameters, and assigns a label to each candidate bounding box during training. Considering the differences in cell size and shape, we assign multiple anchor boxes of different scales and aspect ratios to the locations.

$$L(\{p_i\}, \{t_i\}) = \frac{1}{N_{cls}} \sum\nolimits_i L_{cls}(p_i, p_i^*) + \lambda \frac{1}{N_{reg}} \sum\nolimits_i p_i^* L_{reg}(t_i, t_i^*), \qquad (2)$$

where p and t represent the predicted values of the classification and regression. p^* and t^* represent the ground truth. The cross-entropy loss is used in the classification branch, and L1 loss is applied in the regression branch.

3 Experiment

3.1 Experimental Details

We stain the iMSCs with senescence-specific β–galactose, crop the original images into 640×640 slices, and label cells as young and senescent cells in the bright-field images. During the experiment, we use the part bright-field images as the original dataset that includes the fifth, sixth, seventh, eighth, ninth, and tenth generations of the replicative senescent iMSCs (hereafter referred to as P5, P6, P7, P8, P9, and P10), and use three generations of sub-datasets (i.e., P5, P8 and P10) to form a mixed dataset (hereinafter referred to as P5810). The reasons for choosing P5, P8, and P10 as a mixed dataset are as follows: 1) We can preserve the differences between each generation of cells, 2) We consider that the cell concentration is uncontrollable. The growth concentration of these three generations of cells is better than other generations of cells, which is also reflected in the subsequent experiments, as shown in Table 3. During training, we perform data augmentation operations through random horizontal flipping, random horizontal scaling, and random scale cropping to generate more training samples. In the FPN module, we use three scales and aspect ratios, which results in 9 anchor boxes per location. We set the IOU threshold for positive samples to 0.7, and the IOU threshold for negative samples to 0.3.

3.2 Ablation Experiment

We conduct ablation experiments on mixed datasets, as shown in Table 1, and all variants are designed using the Faster R-CNN network framework. We use the ResNet network to compare with the Swin Transformer network, comparing the model performance with and without FPN, to verify the effectiveness of the Swin Transformer and FPN modules on the bright-field dataset. Our purpose is ultimately to calculate the senescence rate of each generation of cells, and we need to detect young cells and aging cells in cells more accurately. mAP, as an indicator for evaluating the accuracy of the detection boxes in the detection results, can better reflect the performance of various detection methods. Therefore, we use this indicator (mAP) as the main indicator for evaluating various methods, a relatively low mAR value is not a big problem. Where mAP represents the average precision when the IOU threshold is 0.5, and mAR represents the average recall when the IOU threshold is 0.5. Compare with ResNet50, the Faster R-CNN model with Swin Transformer backbone network (Faster Swin) has a higher mAP value of 0.031 than Faster R-CNN ResNet50. Comparing the Faster R-CNN ResNet50 fpn and Faster R-CNN ResNet50, we found that the Faster R-CNN model after adding the FPN module has worse performance. But after using the Swin Transformer backbone network and FPN together, the performance of our model is improved by 0.024 compared to Faster Swin, which proves that the two modules of Swin Transformer and FPN are indeed effective.

Table 1. Ablation experiment results on mixed datasets (P5810).

Method	mAP	mAR
Faster R-CNN ResNet34 FPN	0.737	0.885
Faster R-CNN ResNet50 FPN	0.737	0.883
Faster R-CNN ResNet101 FPN	0.766	0.901
Faster R-CNN ResNet50	0.761	0.896
Faster Swin	0.792	**0.904**
Ours (Swin + FPN)	**0.816**	0.859

3.3 Comparative Experiment

We use P5810 for comparative experiments, and the ratio of the training set, validation set, and test set is 4:1:1. The network models participating in the experiment include Cascade R-CNN [18], Faster R-CNN [15], TOOD [19], YOLOv3 [20] and PPyolo [21]. The methods we compare include a one-stage detector and a two-stage detector. The experimental results are shown in Table 2.

It can be found that although our method achieves quite poor performance on AR, its value is also higher than 0.85, and our method achieves the highest AP value of 0.816. At the same time, in order to facilitate researchers to observe the growth of each type of cells in the data in more detail, and determine whether the batch of cells can be put into the next cell experiment, we conduct detailed evaluation on each category of cells and the evaluation results are shown in Table 3.

We measure various parameters of various methods on young cells and aging cells. Among them, AP represents the average precision calculated at 101 points when the IOU threshold is 0.5. AR is similar to AP, and the precision, recall and F1_score is calculated by taking one of the points under the condition when the IOU threshold is 0.5.

Table 2. Comparisons with other methods on the mixed datasets (P5810), which measures the overall parameters of the dataset.

Method	mAP	mAR
Cascade R-CNN	0.778	0.892
Faster R-CNN	0.761	0.896
TOOD	0.779	**0.924**
YOLOv3	0.725	0.923
Ppyolo	0.770	0.923
Ours	**0.816**	0.859

Table 3. Comparing experiments with other methods on mixed datasets (P5810), which are measured by various indicators of different categories, separately.

Method	Aging cells				Young cells			
	Precision	F1_score	Recall	AP	Precision	F1_score	Recall	AP
Cascade R-CNN	0.800	0.845	0.896	0.788	0.721	0.796	0.888	0.769
Faster R-CNN	0.784	0.852	0.932	0.805	0.606	0.711	0.861	0.716
TOOD	0.781	0.860	**0.956**	0.813	0.652	0.754	0.893	0.744
YOLOv3	0.706	0.804	0.932	0.737	0.608	0.730	0.914	0.713
Ppyolo	0.758	0.852	0.931	0.799	0.668	0.772	**0.914**	0.741
Ours	**0.916**	**0.917**	0.917	**0.860**	**0.895**	**0.845**	0.800	**0.772**

It can be seen that our method achieves the best performance among several network models, with AP reaching the highest 0.860. Compared with the methods in Table 3, our method achieves the best performance on all metrics except recall, and its precision. F1 scores are higher than 0.9 on the senescent cell class, which is better than other methods (Faster R-CNN FPN) with a maximum difference of 0.162. Note that our method outperforms the original Faster R-CNN model by 5.5 percentage points in AP (Table 3).

Table 4 shows the experimental results of our method on the P5, P6, P7, P8, P9 and P10 six-generation sub-datasets. We also visualize the detection results of the iMSCs, as shown in Fig. 3. It can be seen that there are missed detections in Fig. 3, and the experimental results of the P5, P8, and P10 data are better than the experimental results of the other three generations. This is because the cell density of the other three-generation data is relatively large, and there are many overlapping areas of cells.

Table 4. Experimental results of ours on each generation dataset.

iMSC	Aging cells				Young cells			
	Precision	F1_score	Recall	AP	Precision	F1_score	Recall	AP
P5	0.734	0.807	0.895	0.782	0.754	0.822	0.903	0.776
P6	0.618	0.720	0.862	0.703	0.710	0.790	0.890	0.755
P7	0.676	0.761	0.870	0.724	0.479	0.592	0.773	0.581
P8	0.815	0.841	0.868	0.773	0.749	0.801	0.860	0.759
P9	0.627	0.723	0.853	0.842	0.842	0.853	0.863	0.785
P10	0.649	0.729	0.831	0.706	0.816	0.850	0.887	0.793

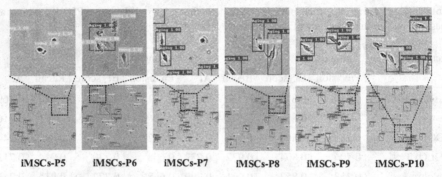

iMSCs-P5   iMSCs-P6   iMSCs-P7   iMSCs-P8   iMSCs-P9   iMSCs-P10

Fig. 3. Visualization of detection results of iMSCs sub-datasets. First row: a partially enlarged view of the bright-field image detection results of the six-generation sub-dataset; Second row: visualization of bright-field image detection results for six generations of sub-datasets. Aging cells are depicted in purple bounding boxes and young cells in yellow bounding boxes. (Color figure online)

4   Conclusion

In this paper, we conduct experiments using 6 datasets with different time periods and a mixed dataset. In the biological field, the overall senescence degree of iMSCs can only be known by in vivo staining. SA-β-gal needs to avoid light treatment during the addition process, and it is easy to cause cell contamination during the medium change and staining process. This paper uses the attention mechanism in the Swin Transformer, and applies the Faster R-CNN detector framework to detect and recognize MSC bright-field images. At the same time, we compare the detection performance of the popular one-stage detector and two-stage detector. iMSCs can be stained to verify whether the cells are senescent, which provides a new idea and preliminary exploration. During the experiment, it was also found that deep learning has deficiencies, such as inaccurate identification of cells at the critical point of aging and young, and false detection and missed detection in overlapping cells. In addition, the density of cell growth in each generation dataset was different, leading to differences between datasets. In future work, we need to consider the influence of the distribution between cells of different generations on the experimental results, and use this distribution difference to improve the performance of the detector.

References

1. Horwitz, E., et al.: Clarification of the nomenclature for MSC: the international society for cellular therapy position statement. Cytotherapy **7**(5), 393–395 (2005)
2. Piñeiro-Ramil, M., et al.: Usefulness of mesenchymal cell lines for bone and cartilage regeneration research. Int. J. Mol. Sci. **20**(24), 6286 (2019)
3. Jiang, Y., et al.: Pluripotency of mesenchymal stem cells derived from adult marrow. Nature **418**(6893), 41–49 (2002)
4. Zhao, C., Ikeya, M.: Generation and applications of induced pluripotent stem cell-derived mesenchymal stem cells. Stem Cells Int. **2018**, 9601623 (2018)
5. Wagner, W., et al.: Replicative senescence of mesenchymal stem cells: a continuous and organized process. PLoS ONE **3**(5), e2213 (2008)
6. Ho, A.D., Wagner, W., Mahlknecht, U.: Stem cells and ageing: the potential of stem cells to overcome age-related deteriorations of the body in regenerative medicine. EMBO Rep. **6**(S1), S35–S38 (2005)
7. Evangelou, K., et al.: Robust, universal biomarker assay to detect senescent cells in biological specimens. Aging Cell **16**(1), 192–197 (2017)
8. Lin, M., et al.: Label-free light-sheet microfluidic cytometry for the automatic identification of senescent cells. Biomed. Opt. Express **9**(4), 1692–1703 (2018)
9. Zhang, J., Hu, H., Chen, S., Huang, Y., Guan, Q.: Cancer cells detection in phase-contrast microscopy images based on faster R-CNN. In: 2016 9th international symposium on computational intelligence and design (ISCID), vol. 1, pp. 363–367. IEEE, Hangzhou, China (2016)
10. Yi, J., Wu, P., Hoeppner, D.J., Metaxas, D.: Fast neural cell detection using light-weight SSD neural network. In: Proceedings of the IEEE Conference on Computer Vision and Pattern Recognition Workshops, pp. 108–112. Hawaii, USA (2017)
11. Liu, W., et al.: SSD: single shot multiBox detector. In: Leibe, B., Matas, J., Sebe, N., Welling, M. (eds.) ECCV 2016. LNIP, vol. 9905, pp. 21–37. Springer, Cham (2016). https://doi.org/10.1007/978-3-319-46448-0_2
12. Kusumoto, D., et al.: Anti-senescent drug screening by deep learning-based morphology senescence scoring. Circulation **142**(Suppl_3), A13576–A13576 (2020)
13. Kusumoto, D., et al.: Anti-senescent drug screening by deep learning-based morphology senescence scoring. Nat. Commun. **12**(1), 257 (2021)
14. Sun, Y., Huang, X., Zhou, H., Zhang, Q.: SRPN: similarity-based region proposal networks for nuclei and cells detection in histology images. Med. Image Anal. **72**, 102142 (2021)
15. Ren, S., He, K., Girshick, R., Sun, J.: Faster R-CNN: towards real-time object detection with region proposal networks. Adv. Neural Inf. Process. Syst. **28** (2015)
16. Liu, Z., et al.: Swin transformer: Hierarchical vision transformer using shifted windows. In: Proceedings of the IEEE/CVF International Conference on Computer Vision, pp. 10012–10022. Montreal, Canada (2021)
17. Lin, T.-Y., et al.: Feature pyramid networks for object detection. In: Proceedings of the IEEE Conference on Computer Vision and Pattern Recognition, pp. 2117–2125. Hawaii, USA (2017)
18. Cai, Z., Vasconcelos, N.: Cascade R-CNN: delving into high quality object detection. In: Proceedings of the IEEE Conference on Computer Vision and Pattern Recognition, pp. 6154–6162. Salt Lake City, USA (2018)

19. Feng, C., Zhong, Y., Gao, Y., Scott, M.R., Huang, W.: Tood: task-aligned one-stage object detection. In: 2021 IEEE/CVF International Conference on Computer Vision (ICCV). IEEE Computer Society, pp. 3490–3499. Montreal, Canada (2021)
20. Redmon, J., Farhadi, A.: Yolov3: An incremental improvement, arXiv preprint arXiv:1804. 02767 (2018)
21. Long, X., et al.: PP-YOLO: An effective and efficient implementation of object detector, arXiv preprint arXiv:2007.12099 (2020)

Characterizing Continual Learning Scenarios for Tumor Classification in Histopathology Images

Veena Kaustaban, Qinle Ba[✉], Ipshita Bhattacharya, Nahil Sobh,
Satarupa Mukherjee, Jim Martin, Mohammad Saleh Miri, Christoph Guetter,
and Amal Chaturvedi

Roche Sequencing Solutions, Santa Clara, CA, USA
qinle.ba@roche.com

Abstract. Recent years have seen great advancements in the development of deep-learning models for histopathology image analysis in digital pathology (DP) applications, evidenced by the increasingly common deployment of these models in both research and clinical settings. Although such models have shown unprecedented performance in solving fundamental computational tasks in DP applications, they suffer from catastrophic forgetting when adapted to unseen data with transfer learning. With an increasing need for deep-learning models to handle ever-changing data distributions, including evolving patient population and new diagnosis assays, continual learning (CL) models that alleviate model forgetting need to be introduced in DP-based analysis. However, to our best knowledge, there's no systematic study of such models for DP-specific applications. Here, we propose CL scenarios in DP settings, where histopathology image data from different sources/distributions arrive sequentially, the knowledge of which is integrated into a single model without training all the data from scratch. We then established an augmented dataset for colorectal cancer H&E classification to simulate shifts of image appearance and evaluated CL model performance in the proposed CL scenarios. We leveraged a breast tumor H&E dataset along with the colorectal cancer to evaluate CL from different tumor types. In addition, we evaluated CL methods in an online few-shot setting under the constraints of annotation and computational resources. We revealed promising results of CL in DP applications, potentially paving the way for application of these methods in clinical practice.

Keywords: Digital pathology · Continual learning · Tumor tissue classification

---

I. Bhattacharya—Work done at Roche.

Supplementary Information The online version contains supplementary material available at https://doi.org/10.1007/978-3-031-16961-8_18.

Y. Huo et al. (Eds.): MOVI 2022, LNCS 13578, pp. 177–187, 2022.
https://doi.org/10.1007/978-3-031-16961-8_18

1   Introduction

Deep learning has achieved unprecedented performance in solving complex problems in digital pathology (DP) based analysis [5,9,12,26]. There are, however, two challenges in model development for DP applications. Firstly, the increasing volume of data waiting to be analyzed. The increasingly wide adoption of DP along with development of new assays with, for example, the emerging multiplexing technologies, produce a near continuous stream of data to analyze [2,7]. Secondly, evolving data distributions for modeling, such as varying image digitization conditions, diverse patient populations, onset of new diseases and so on. For example, it is commonly observed that the use of different staining chromogens, changes in stainers, digital scanners and vendor platforms all result in a shift in appearance of the digitized images. Such ever-evoling image data call for iterative model development and model update even after model deployment.

A general strategy to learn from multiple datasets considers training all the existing and newly arrived data from scratch. Such an approach in general ensures performance, but requires storage of all the data and an increasing amount of computing resources each time a model is updated, which is not only inefficient, but also increases development cost and delays algorithm deployment/update. On the other hand, updating a model with transfer learning, albeit with no extra cost of data storage and computing resources, is known to suffer from catastrophic forgetting [14]. To efficiently and effectively adapt a model to new data streams without forgetting of learned knowledge, continual learning (CL) algorithms have been proposed and investigated in the machine learning community [8,14,17,20]. However, these CL algorithms have largely been tested on relatively less complex datasets from non-DP domains, including MNIST [1,8,17] and CIFAR [1,8,17,20], the insights from which thus cannot be directly transferred to DP data. In the biomedical imaging field, despite a number of studies for medical imaging [3,4,15,19,29,31], to our best knowledge, there is no systematic study so far on CL performance on deep learning/machine learning models designed for histopathology images, and consequently, no appropriate CL baselines for DP. In this study, we compare different CL methods with a sequential stream of DP images. New streams of data were designed to simulate real world scenarios where shifts in distribution, class labels or data volume can occur and thus the need to update an existing model.

Our contributions are three-fold: (1) we identify continual learning scenarios practical for DP-based analysis and systematically characterized the performance of recent CL methods in these scenarios (Sect. 2); (2) we establish a dataset with augmented H&E images, simulating data streams from multiple data sources (Fig. 1), including different scanners, stainers and reagents, to evaluate CL methods (Fig. 1 and Fig. 2); (3) we have explored the feasibility and provided insights into performance of both learning continuously from more than one type of tumor (Fig. 4) and applying online CL methods (Fig. 3).

2   Continual Learning Scenarios in DP

We identify four learning scenarios [8,10,27] for DP-based analysis in the continual learning (CL) framework. **Data Incremental Scenario (Data-IL)** Continuously learn from new streams of data from an identical underlying distribution during model development or update. Data-IL does not consider new classes or considerable shifts of data distribution and is thus expected to be the easiest among all CL scenarios. In DP, it is common for expert pathologists to generate annotations for a dataset in multiple batches and thus each batch can be considered as a sample of the same data distribution. **Domain Incremental Scenario (Domain-IL)** Continuously update a model with new streams of data from shifted distributions. Examples in clinical settings include variations of tissue processing/staining reagents, patient populations, scanning instruments and so on. Note that in practice the extent of domain shift is a continuum and challenging to predict beforehand, and thus the categorization of a scenario into Data-IL or Domain-IL is a design choice and/or empirical decision. As an extreme example, multiple tissue types can be sequentially included into the same class label, where there are domain shifts within the same class. **Class Incremental Scenario (Class-IL)** Continuously extend an existing model to unseen classes with new streams of data. Since the knowledge to learn from each batch of unseen classes is largely non-overlapping, this scenario is expected to be the hardest among CL scenarios. For example, adding new tissue types in a tumor classification model or adding new cell types into a cell detection model for AI-assisted diagnosis. **Task Incremental Scenario (Task-IL)** any of the above scenarios can be considered as Task-IL if each data stream is defined as a new task and during inference prior knowledge is always given as to which task (task identity, i.e. task ID) the test data should be predicted with. In this study, we tested the task IL scenario with new classes introduced at each task. For example, a clinical-grade model incorporates patient data from different populations and uses patient meta-data as prior (i.e. task ID) for generating prediction.

3   Materials and Methods

3.1   Datasets

CRC: We characterized CL model performance with a colorectal cancer (CRC) dataset from [13], whose training and test set are composed of stain-normalized [18] 224×224 patches at $20\times$ from hematoxylin and eosin (H&E) stained whole-slide images (136 patients) with tile-wise class labels for 9 tissue types - tumor, stroma, normal, lymphocyte-rich, mucin, muscle, adipose, debris, background. To establish a class-balanced dataset, we randomly selected 8700 images from each class for training (7000 train; 2700 validation) and the entire test set (7150 images) for testing. All the selected images were used for stain augmentation (see Sect. 3.2). **PatchCam:** To characterize the effectiveness of CL methods on learning from multiple tissue types, PatchCam from [5] was used for breast cancer classification, which comprises 96×96 patches with class labels of "normal" and

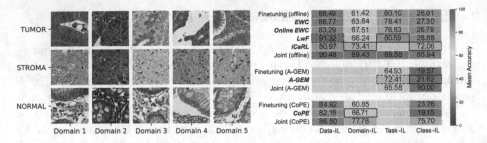

Fig. 1. Left: example augmented CRC images from 5 domains (3 of 9 classes are shown). Right: test accuracy of offline and online methods on augmented CRC. Online methods were compared to online baselines. Black outline: best performing method in the particular scenario exceeding finetuning (lower bound). Dashed outline: best performing method in the particular scenario exceeding joint training (upper bound).

"tumor" from 400 breast cancer H&E whole-slide images at 20× resolution. We stain-normalized [18] the patches to be consist with colorectal cancer dataset.

3.2   Methods

Simulating Domain Shifted Data Streams. To systematically evaluate the CL algorithms in DP settings, we need a sequence of data to simulate CL scenarios. To the best of our knowledge, no such benchmark has been proposed for DP-based analysis. We thus generated an augmented CRC dataset comprised of multiple subsets, each with distinct colors and stain intensities, simulating the commonly observed variations of stain appearance (i.e. domain shifts) from multiple data sources. Except for the images provided by CRC (Domain 1), we simulated 4 additional data sources (Domain 2–5) (Fig. 1 Left). For each data split, We first randomly divided images in each of the 9 classes into 5 splits, kept 1 split unchanged for Domain 1 and performed stain unmixing [21] for the remaining splits. We further applied the following augmentation to remix the stain-unmixed intensity images into augmented H&E and refer to this augmented dataset as **augmented CRC**. Pseudocode for creating this augmented dataset is at https://github.com/kaustabanv/miccai2022-cl-in-dp.

– Domain 2 (increased stain intensity, simulating, for example, concentration increase of the eosin and/or hematoxylin solutions, each with a different extent of change): eosin intensity was randomly increased with a scaling factor sampled from [1.75, 2.75], hematoxylin from [1.5, 2.0].
– Domain 3 (decreased eosin stain intensity, simulating, for example, slides prepared from many years ago with fading stain): eosin intensity scaling factor sampled from [0.4, 2.75].
– Domain 4 (change of hue, simulating, for example, change of reagent manufacturer, scanner or stainer): eosin hue changed by a scaling factor sampled from [−0.05, −0.03], hematoxylin from [0.05, 0.08].

- Domain 5 (change of hue and saturation, simulating, for example, change of reagent manufacturer, scanner or stainer): eosin hue changed by [0.03, 0.05]; saturation increased for eosin by [1.2, 1.4] and hematoxylin by [1.1, 1.3].

Qualitative Assessment of Augmented CRC. We presented four randomly selected images from each domain to two pathologists. Both of them confirmed that images of Domain 1–4 look realistic and one pathologist thought the Domain 5 is slightly deviating from majority of DP images from our organization.

CL Setup with Augmented CRC. For *Domain-IL*, the 5 domains were used as individual batches of data with domain shifts, where each domain contains examples from all 9 classes (e.g. for training, $8700/5 = 1740$ examples per class per domain). In *Class-IL*, each data batch contains all examples from the new classes and thus the same number of examples from each domain for each class. In *Data-IL*, each data batch was randomly selected and roughly contained the same number of examples from each domain.

CL Methods: Recent proposed CL methods can be largely classified into three categories: replay, regularization and parameter isolation [28]. With replay methods, original images [20], deep representations [27] or model-generated pseudo samples [25] are selected via various heuristics, stored in memory and replayed at later learning stages to overcome forgetting. Regularization-based methods [14,23,30] avoid storing examples and instead include a regularization term in the loss function to penalize model updates that could lead to large deviation from an existing model, thus avoiding forgetting of learned knowledge. Parameter isolation methods assign different model parameters to each task. Note that while replay and regularization apply to all scenarios, parameter isolation only applies to Task-IL, because such methods are designed to either pre-allocate different parts of the network for different tasks [24], or freezing previous model parameters [22]: both require multi-headed designs and use task IDs to select a task-specific head during inference. Here we evaluate the following CL methods.

- *EWC/Online EWC:* Regularization-based methods that use model parameters as prior [14] to learn new data. The loss function includes a regularization term, which penalizes large changes to network weights that are important for previous tasks (knowledge from previous data) and is controlled by a weighting hyperparameter. The magnitude of penalty for each model weight is proportional to its importance for previous tasks. In EWC, the number of quadratic penalty terms grows linearly with the number of tasks. Online EWC [23] uses a single quadratic penalty term on parameters whose strength is determined by a running sum of parameter importance from previous tasks. Online EWC includes an additional hyperparameter to determine the magnitude of decay of each previous task's contribution.
- *LwF:* Data-focused regularization method [16] which distills knowledge from a previous model to an updated model trained on new data. The loss function has an additional distillation loss for replayed data. Each input is replayed with a soft target obtained using a copy of the model stored after finishing training on the most recent task.

- *iCaRL:* Replay-based method using stored original images from previous
  data streams [20]. This method stores a subset of most representative examples per class in memory (GPU, CPU, disk, etc.), which are chosen according
  to approximate class means in the learned feature space. The memory size
  can be determined by grid search and/or availability of computing resources.
- *A-GEM:* In this online constrained replay-based method [8], model updates
  are constrained to prevent forgetting by projecting the estimated gradient on
  the direction determined by randomly selected samples from a replay buffer.
  Buffer size and sampling size from the buffer are both tunable hyperparameters. In the literature, A-GEM was tested only in Class-IL and Task-IL
  scenarios as reported in [8].
- *CoPE:* An online rehearsal based approach [10], which enables rapidly evolving prototypes with balanced memory and a loss function that updates the
  representations or pseudo prototypes (i.e. from model-generated pseudo samples), thus alleviating catastrophic forgetting. We tested CoPE in Data-IL,
  Domain-IL and Class-IL scenarios.

Model Evaluation Strategies. We refer to learning from a batch of data for
CL as an experience. Within each experience, we split data into train, validation,
test (see Sect. 3.1; e.g. images from the training set of augmented CRC were
kept as training). We report (1) accuracy averaged over test sets at the end
of training the last experience from multiple repeats (Fig. 1 Right, Table S1)
and (2) accuracy over multiple repeats at each experience (Fig. 2, 3 and 4).
(3) While evaluation on test sets from past experiences indicates how well the
model retains past knowledge without forgetting (backward transfer), accuracy
on current/future test sets reflects new knowledge assimilation (forward transfer)
(Fig. S1–S4).

Baselines. All the methods were compared against two baselines: 1) joint training (upper bound), where a model was trained on all the data available so far;
2) finetuning (i.e. transfer learning; lower bound), where a model was trained
sequentially with exposure to only the data from the current experience. For
A-GEM and CoPE we also compared the online versions of baselines for fair
comparison: the A-GEM baselines were trained in an online setup for 1 epoch
and for the CoPE baselines, the experiences were divided into mini experiences
(128 samples each) in a data incremental fashion and trained for 1 epoch per mini
experience, similar to its set-up in Data-IL, Domain-IL and Class-IL scenarios.

4   Experiments

4.1   Implementation and Results

We used a ResNet-18 [11] feature extraction layers followed by a single-layer
nearest mean classifier [20], where the feature vectors generated from the feature
extractor were used to assign the class label with the nearest prototype vector.
Training was conducted with 15 epochs and a batch size of 16 on 1 NVIDIA V100

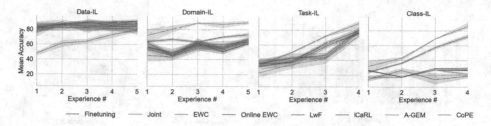

Fig. 2. Results from online and offline CL methods at each experience across scenarios with offline baselines.

or A100 GPU for 3–5 repeats. For Task-IL, in the multi-headed designs, each head was trained for a different task. Models were optimized with Stochastic Gradient Descent starting with a learning rate of 0.1 and momentum of 0.9 and a weight decay of 0.00001 applied after epochs 10 and 13. In all scenarios we ran grid search for best hyperparameters (See details at https://github.com/kaustabanv/miccai2022-cl-in-dp).

Comparison of Offline CL Methods on Augmented CRC. Overall, the accuracy of joint baseline was comparable across scenarios, while the performance of finetuning varies among scenarios with best performance on Data-IL and worst on Class-IL (Fig. 1 Right and Table S1). Of the offline CL methods tested, LwF and iCaRL performed much better than finetuning in all scenarios except for Data-IL. Accuracy of EWC/online EWC was comparable to finetuning in all scenarios except for Domain-IL, where online EWC was 6.09% higher than EWC. It should be noted that the computation time for joint baseline was much longer (250 ± 18 min) compared to that of for CL methods across scenarios (70 ± 8 min). In **Data-IL**, though CL methods were expected to outperform finetuning, we found that only LwF (accuracy: 91.32%) outperformed finetuning and even 2.87% higher than the upper bound joint training. While iCaRL was the best method for other scenarios, it was 7.52% lower than finetuning. iCaRL was designed and tested for Class-IL in [20] and the replay memory was divided equally to store examples from each class. In our Data-IL setting, the allocated memory for each class was split further for each of the five domains. We hypothesized a bigger memory with more examples for each class per domain could have produced better results. In **Domain-IL**, iCaRL achieved the best accuracy of 73.41%. An interesting observation is that while other methods show a reduction in performance after learning Domain 2 and 4, the performance of iCaRL continued to improve (Fig. 2). Domain 1 (original stain-normalized images) and Domain 4 (change of hue and saturation) showed minimal forgetting (Fig. S2), while Domains 2 and 3 with eosin intensity changes were much harder for CL, suggesting that intensity changes in practice due to, for example, scanner differences, may lead to larger challenges for CL than hue/saturation changes due to, for example, changes in staining reagent/condition. These 2 domains were the farthest from baseline DP settings in appearance. Note that here the 5 domains were designed to have relatively large domain gaps with

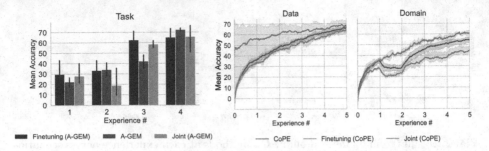

Fig. 3. Left: A-GEM Task-IL accuracy at the end of each experience. Right: CoPE accuracy at each mini experience in Data- and Domain-IL with respective baselines.

non-overlapping augmentation settings and in practice by performing stain normalization during model training or for datasets with smaller domain shifts, the domain gaps would be reduced and thus potentially improving CL performance. In **Task-IL**, finetuning accuracy was much higher than that of Class-IL, likely due to the presence of task-specific network modules and additional information leveraged (taks IDs) during inference. However, unlike [19,27,28] have reported, LwF was the only method that performed better than finetuning (Fig. 1 Right and S3). This could be because in our network design task identities were only used in the output layer, while it was reported to be more effective to embed task identities in hidden layers [10]. **Class-IL** is the most difficult learning scenario and as expected most methods suffered from severe forgetting of previous knowledge. iCaRL had the best overall accuracy of 72.06% when tested with a random ordering of classes (Fig. S4). This is consistent with [27] that replay methods are more effective in Class-IL than regularization methods. We also studied the impact of class order, class grouping and number of classes with iCaRL. The results (Table S2) were consistent with the hypothesis of curriculum learning that knowledge is better captured if harder tasks follow easier tasks [6].

Comparison of Online CL Methods on Augmented CRC. A-GEM outperformed the online joint baseline for A-GEM (Fig. 3 Left) in Task-IL by 6%, but suffered from catastrophic forgetting without task identity. CoPE was worse than finetuning in Data-IL and Class-IL, but was 6% better in Domain-IL (Fig. 3 Right), demonstrating that online CL poses challenges, which calls for more attention in research. Despite lower performance compared to offline methods, knowledge retention (backward transfer) with CoPE was much better in Data-IL and Domain-IL (Fig. S1 and S2). We note that CoPE was sensitive to softmax temperature and further finetuning could help improve forward transfer.

Continually Learning from Multiple Tumor Types. We tested a dramatic domain shift in data streams by training a model with the original CRC images in one experience and PatchCam dataset in another experience. We experimented with LwF for continually learning the two datasets in a Domain-IL setting, where each tumor type is considered as one domain. We experimented with ordering of the domains as well as the volume of PatchCam data used in training.

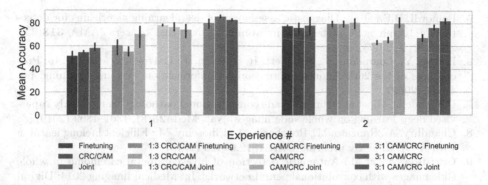

Fig. 4. Continual learning with CRC and PatchCam in Domain-IL

As shown in Fig. 4, joint baseline accuracy was around 80%. Interestingly, LwF performed better than finetuning when PatchCam was introduced first during training followed by CRC in the subsequent experience. As expected, including 3 times more data in training improved accuracy by over 11% (Table S2).

4.2 Discussion

We present a systematic study that characterizes the performance of recently proposed CL methods for different scenarios using augmented DP images with domain shifts. We found that though regularization-based methods performed well in Data-IL and Domain-IL, only iCaRL, a rehearsal method, is effective in the most challenging Class-IL. Surprisingly, Task-IL scenarios may not be as easy to learn for DP as for other domains. CL methods were also computationally efficient, taking only about 28% of the runtime as joint training. Though patient data evolve quickly nowadays, FDA has not approved algorithms based on CL [28] and extensive research is needed to establish regulations for safely incorporating CL in clinical settings. Our evaluation approaches and proposed method to generate domain-shifted datasets can potentially serve as the first step towards this goal.

References

1. Aljundi, R., Rohrbach, M., Tuytelaars, T.: Selfless sequential learning. arXiv preprint arXiv:1806.05421 (2018)
2. Ardon, O., et al.: Digital pathology operations at an NYC Tertiary Cancer Center during the first 4 months of COVID-19 pandemic response. Acad. Pathol. **8**, 23742895211010276 (2021)
3. Baweja, C., Glocker, B., Kamnitsas, K.: Towards continual learning in medical imaging. arXiv preprint arXiv:1811.02496 (2018)
4. Bayasi, N., Hamarneh, G., Garbi, R.: Culprit-Prune-Net: efficient continual sequential multi-domain learning with application to skin lesion classification. In: de Bruijne, M., et al. (eds.) MICCAI 2021. LNCS, vol. 12907, pp. 165–175. Springer, Cham (2021). https://doi.org/10.1007/978-3-030-87234-2_16

5. Bejnordi, B.E., et al.: Diagnostic assessment of deep learning algorithms for detection of lymph node metastases in women with breast cancer. JAMA **318**(22), 2199–2210 (2017)
6. Bengio, Y., Louradour, J., Collobert, R., Weston, J.: Curriculum learning. In: Proceedings of the 26th Annual International Conference on Machine Learning, pp. 41–48 (2009)
7. Campanella, G., et al.: Clinical-grade computational pathology using weakly supervised deep learning on whole slide images. Nat. Med. **25**(8), 1301–1309 (2019)
8. Chaudhry, A., Ranzato, M., Rohrbach, M., Elhoseiny, M.: Efficient lifelong learning with A-GEM. arXiv preprint arXiv:1812.00420 (2018)
9. Cruz-Roa, A., et al.: Automatic detection of invasive ductal carcinoma in whole slide images with convolutional neural networks. In: Medical Imaging 2014: Digital Pathology, vol. 9041, p. 904103. SPIE (2014)
10. De Lange, M., Tuytelaars, T.: Continual prototype evolution: learning online from non-stationary data streams. In: Proceedings of the IEEE/CVF International Conference on Computer Vision, pp. 8250–8259 (2021)
11. He, K., Zhang, X., Ren, S., Sun, J.: Deep residual learning for image recognition. In: Proceedings of the IEEE Conference on Computer Vision and Pattern Recognition, pp. 770–778 (2016)
12. Janowczyk, A., Madabhushi, A.: Deep learning for digital pathology image analysis: a comprehensive tutorial with selected use cases. J. Pathol. Inform. **7**(1), 29 (2016)
13. Kather, J.N., et al.: Predicting survival from colorectal cancer histology slides using deep learning: a retrospective multicenter study. PLoS Med. **16**(1), e1002730 (2019)
14. Kirkpatrick, J., et al.: Overcoming catastrophic forgetting in neural networks. Proc. Natl. Acad. Sci. **114**(13), 3521–3526 (2017)
15. Lenga, M., Schulz, H., Saalbach, A.: Continual learning for domain adaptation in chest X-ray classification. In: Medical Imaging with Deep Learning, pp. 413–423. PMLR (2020)
16. Li, Z., Hoiem, D.: Learning without forgetting. IEEE Trans. Pattern Anal. Mach. Intell. **40**(12), 2935–2947 (2017)
17. Lopez-Paz, D., Ranzato, M.: Gradient episodic memory for continual learning. In: Advances in Neural Information Processing Systems, vol. 30 (2017)
18. Macenko, M., et al.: A method for normalizing histology slides for quantitative analysis. In: 2009 IEEE International Symposium on Biomedical Imaging: From Nano to Macro, pp. 1107–1110. IEEE (2009)
19. Perkonigg, M., et al.: Dynamic memory to alleviate catastrophic forgetting in continual learning with medical imaging. Nat. Commun. **12**(1), 1–12 (2021)
20. Rebuffi, S.A., Kolesnikov, A., Sperl, G., Lampert, C.H.: iCaRL: incremental classifier and representation learning. In: Proceedings of the IEEE Conference on Computer Vision and Pattern Recognition, pp. 2001–2010 (2017)
21. Ruifrok, C., Johnston, A.: Quantification of histochemical staining by color deconvolution. Anal. Quant. Cytol. Histol. **23**(4), 291–299 (2001)
22. Rusu, A.A., et al.: Progressive neural networks. arXiv preprint arXiv:1606.04671 (2016)
23. Schwarz, J., et al.: Progress & compress: a scalable framework for continual learning. In: International Conference on Machine Learning, pp. 4528–4537. PMLR (2018)
24. Serra, J., Suris, D., Miron, M., Karatzoglou, A.: Overcoming catastrophic forgetting with hard attention to the task. In: International Conference on Machine Learning, pp. 4548–4557. PMLR (2018)

25. Shin, H., Lee, J.K., Kim, J., Kim, J.: Continual learning with deep generative replay. In: Advances in Neural Information Processing Systems, vol. 30 (2017)
26. Sornapudi, S., et al.: Deep learning nuclei detection in digitized histology images by superpixels. J. Pathol. Inform. **9**(1), 5 (2018)
27. Van de Ven, G.M., Tolias, A.S.: Three scenarios for continual learning. arXiv preprint arXiv:1904.07734 (2019)
28. Vokinger, K.N., Feuerriegel, S., Kesselheim, A.S.: Continual learning in medical devices: FDA's action plan and beyond. The Lancet Digit. Health **3**(6), e337–e338 (2021)
29. Yang, Y., Cui, Z., Xu, J., Zhong, C., Wang, R., Zheng, W.-S.: Continual learning with Bayesian model based on a fixed pre-trained feature extractor. In: de Bruijne, M., et al. (eds.) MICCAI 2021. LNCS, vol. 12905, pp. 397–406. Springer, Cham (2021). https://doi.org/10.1007/978-3-030-87240-3_38
30. Zenke, F., Poole, B., Ganguli, S.: Continual learning through synaptic intelligence. In: International Conference on Machine Learning, pp. 3987–3995. PMLR (2017)
31. Zhang, J., Gu, R., Wang, G., Gu, L.: Comprehensive importance-based selective regularization for continual segmentation across multiple sites. In: de Bruijne, M., et al. (eds.) MICCAI 2021. LNCS, vol. 12901, pp. 389–399. Springer, Cham (2021). https://doi.org/10.1007/978-3-030-87193-2_37

Author Index

Printed in the United States
by Baker & Taylor Publisher Services